In pu
VISION

The Story of the
Church of Scotland's
developing relationship
with the Churches emerging
from the missionary movement
in the twenty-five years
from 1947 to 1972

DAVID H. S. LYON

EDINBURGH

First published in 1998 by
SAINT ANDREW PRESS
BOARD of COMMUNICATION
CHURCH of SCOTLAND
121 George Street, Edinburgh EH2 4YN

on behalf of
BOARD of WORLD MISSION
CHURCH of SCOTLAND

ISBN 0 86153 265 1

British Library Cataloguing in Publication Data
A catalogue record for this book
is available from the British Library.

ISBN 0861532651

The author and publisher acknowledge with gratitude the financial assistance of the Pollock Missionary Trust.

Cover design by Mark Blackadder.
Background photograph by Paul Turner; **insert photographs** by David H. S. Lyon.
Typeset in 11/12.5 pt Bembo by Neil Gowans and Lesley A Taylor.
Printed and **bound** in Great Britain by Redwood Books, Trowbridge, Wiltshire.

Contents

✳

✳

Preface
and Acknowledgements

*

THE original intention of this book was to follow up Elizabeth Hewat's history, *Vision and Achievement*, taking up where her book ended. The Rev. John Langdon, who had taught history at Wilson College, Bombay, where Dr Hewat served and was at the time convener of one of the committees of the Board of World Mission, had been invited to undertake this work. Sadly, however, John Langdon died before he could start to write.

John Langdon and I were friends and colleagues for many years, both in India and on the Board. We shared an enthusiasm and had talked on what lies behind this book many times. When he died the task came to me.

In our discussions about the book we agreed that it might be wiser to begin afresh and not to attempt to add further chapters to Elizabeth Hewat's book. Not only did she have her own inimitable style, but the stance from which she wrote, appropriate at the time, was not entirely so any longer. There had been many changes which imperceptibly altered how we look at what had been spoken of as the 'foreign missionary movement'. It was not a history of foreign missions that was now required, but rather an account of the developing relationship between the Church of Scotland and the Churches that had emerged, or were emerging from that movement, and were now being called to serve together in mission in what was being seen to be one world.

Instead, also, of beginning in 1956 where her book ended, it seemed more relevant to start at 1947 when the Foreign Mission Committee (FMC) of the Church of Scotland had begun a determinative reappraisal of its work after the end of the War, and which in so many ways was such a decisive year in the mission of the Church.

The book as it now stands reflects our discussions and has turned out to be different in many ways from the original plan.

The changing perspective has resulted in more emphasis being given to the involvement of the Church of Scotland as a whole in the work of mission abroad and not just of its Foreign Mission Committee. What had been to some extent an operation expressing a special concern of interested groups within the Church, had begun to be understood more generally as the responsibility of the Church as Church. Although other committees of the Church had their own priorities and their own claims to make, both for the interest of the Church and for resources, those could often overlap with the concerns of the FMC. Many practical questions, for instance, in connection with budgets and the recruitment of staff affecting mission overseas, were matters also of priority affecting the Church as a whole, and in the long run clearly the business of the General Assembly. Like many other issues they were matters of policy, raising important theological questions. That this was so meant that questions about the very nature of mission worldwide and the place of the Church within it had to be given more prominence. At the same time partnership in mission between the Church of Scotland and Churches in former 'mission fields', now increasingly a reality, was bringing new and creative relationships. And to that had to be added the growing influence of ecumenical conferences.

The book deals with the Church of Scotland's involvement in world mission over a critical 25 year period of great change from 1947 to 1972. After a personal introductory chapter it starts with a description of the situation immediately after the War, and follows with four chapters, covering periods of five to seven years each, in which the developing relationship is traced between the Church of Scotland and the Churches in Asia, Africa, and the Caribbean that have had a connection with the FMC. Each of those chapters begins by giving a background of international affairs, and by outlining major ecumenical and missiological themes dominant at the time. The division of chapters chronologically, and in short sections, should make it easier to see at any one time what was happening from the standpoint of the Church of Scotland, and in an international and ecumenical setting. Readers who would prefer to have had the material set out by countries or areas should find it easy to follow through their particular interest from one chapter to another.

It is recognised that there is an argument for not including in the text the names of living missionaries. There is always a danger of invidious distinctions. In choosing to include certain names, there is no suggestion that those not mentioned have been less influential. The rule we have followed, as far as it goes, has been to use names only to illustrate and give flesh to aspects of the story we are trying to tell. We hope that this will be understood, and that we may be forgiven by colleagues and friends where names do not appear.

★ ★ ★

Without the generous help of many friends who patiently gave of their time to fill out for me the background to reports and minutes, this book would never have reached the stage it has. I am enormously grateful to them. The anonymous writers of this material, upon which it is so largely dependent, will know how much is owed to their careful work. I owe a debt of gratitude to the clerical staff in the Church offices.

I wish especially to thank the Rev. Stanley Wilton, formerly Principal of St Andrews College, Selly Oak, with whom I discussed the manuscript, who read it, and who made constructive comments. To his friendship I owe much. My thanks are due also to Liz Hendry for her invaluable help in searching out relevant archival material, and for her constant enthusiastic support. We would also wish to thank the staffs of New College Library, and the National Library of Scotland for the cordial and willing assistance received from them. I am also grateful to Dr Chris Wigglesworth, who succeeded me as General Secretary, for his many thoughtful courtesies. And finally, may I thank Lesley Taylor, the publisher, for her quiet but decisive encouragement.

DAVID H. S. LYON 1998

★ ★ ★

To Alison
with love

Abbreviations used in Text

✳

AACC	All Africa Council of Churches
AFPRO	Action for Food Production
BCC	British Council of Churches
BOSS	Bureau of State Security
BPC	Bantu Presbyterian Church
CBMS	Conference of British Missionary Societies
CCAP	Church of Central Africa Presbyterian
CCAR	Church of Central Africa in Rhodesia
CLF	Christian Literature Fund
CLSA	Christian Literature Service Association
CPC	Conference Protestante du Congo
CSI	Church of South India
CSIS	Christian Service to Industrial Society
DMS	Danish Missionary Society
DRC	Dutch Reformed Church
DWME	Division of World Mission and Evangelism
EPC	Evangelical Presbyterian Church
EWE	Ewe Presbyterian Church
FLOSY	Front for the Liberation of South Yemen
FMC	Foreign Mission Committee
GA	General Assembly
GAC	General Administration Committee
ICRC	Inter-Church Relations Committee
IMC	International Missonary Council
JAM	Joint Action for Mission
LMMRS	Lay Mission Medical Recruitment Scheme
LMS	London Missionary Society
MCC	Malaysian Christian Council
MMS	Methodist Missionary Society

NAM	Non-Alignment Movement
NATO	North Atlantic Treaty Organisation
NCC	National Christian Council
NCCI	National Christian Council of India
OC	Overseas Council
PCEA	Presbyterian Church of East Africa
PCC	Presbyterian Church of China
PCR	Programme to Combat Racism
PHAM	Private Hospital Association of Malawi
SCAQ	Scottish Council for African Questions
SCM	Student Christian Movement
SIM	Sudan Inland Mission
SPCK	Society for Promoting Christian Knowledge
TEF	Theological Education Fund
UCNI	United Church of Northern India
UCCAR	United Church of Central Africa in Rhodesia
UDI	Unilateral Declaration of Independence
UCZ	United Church of Zambia
UMCA	Universities Mission to Central Africa
UNIP	United National Independence Party
USSR	Union of Soviet Socialist Republics
USPG	United Society for the Propagation of the Gospel
WCC	World Council of Churches
WFM	Women's Foreign Mission
YAR	Yemen Arab Republic
YMCA	Young Men's Christian Association

CHAPTER 1

A Personal Viewpoint

THIS book deals with the Church of Scotland's developing relation in mission with churches across the world. Based largely on official documents, it is a formal record of the Church's participation in the mission of God in a world context and in a period of revolutionary change. At the same time it is a personal story of the gradual unfolding of what it means to share in the mission of God in days like these.

The story began for me in an army camp in Yorkshire during the Second World War. I was an infantry soldier, a young subaltern, in a battalion that was training for the Second Front in Europe. I was in a company made up of men from different parts of the country, though mostly from Glasgow, and from every walk of life: craftsmen, navvies, clerks in offices, bus conductors, shopkeepers, one or two students like myself, some Roman Catholic, some Protestant, some nothing, one Jew. It was in this setting that I was brought to faith in Christ and to baptism.

I have often tried to see what led me to this point. My parents were good and loving, and I was brought up to understand the meaning of duty and honest service, seeing it in them – but Church was not part of life. I am sure that there were many indirect influences that led me to faith, but there is one that sticks in my mind. The Company runner, Private Jock Wallace, a chimney sweep from the Gallowgate in Glasgow, was older than most of us, and wasn't afraid to tease his 'betters'. As a good Roman Catholic, he regarded the young officers who met him in the Company office as a group of heathens, and one day, beyond the teasing, he asked me what I believed, how I felt about going into war, spoke simply about his own faith, and gave me a copy of the *Missal*. That was one step along the way.

A short time later the battalion was stationed in Otley, Yorkshire. I was walking alone on a wet Sunday evening, past a Methodist church. The door was open and there was loud and cheerful singing. Someone standing inside the door saw me and said, 'come in'. Nobody preached at me, and no pressure was put on me, but the warmth of the welcome came home.

It was not long after this I was baptised. On Christmas Day 1943, I was baptised by the Church of Scotland chaplain, and took communion. For me the Gospel was freedom. It brought me great joy. I had lived, as I see it now, in the confines of a kind of secular and much distorted puritanism which laid down in unwritten rules what should and should not be done. A wonderful sense of liberation was given to me, and anxieties fell away.

I had received a copy of the New Testament soon after coming into the army, contributed as a gift from the Church of Scotland. I had not properly read it before. Now I was gripped by what I read. I began to read avidly, and to learn to pray.

Some time after D-Day, when for month after month we had experienced the ugly reality of bloody war in northern France, I made up my mind that when this thing was over I would give my time to the Christian cause. It was suggested to me that I should think of becoming a minister of the Church, and I was put in touch with Professor D. M. Baillie. Donald Baillie had been given responsibility for communicating with ordinands in the forces. His letters characteristically were straightforward and sensitive, and I was encouraged by them to go ahead with plans to study for the ministry.

In November 1945, released from the army, I went to St Mary's College, St Andrews University. It meant turning aside from the law course I had been following in Edinburgh when I left school, but it was clear to me that I was right to do so, and as it has turned out the discipline of law study was not wasted.

At St Andrews I gulped down what I had missed of youth, and in St Mary's revelled in seminars and lectures. I had so much time to make up and so much to learn. One of the first people I met was George More, who was studying in the College before setting out for India. We did not know it at the time, but he and I were to work together for years as friends and colleagues, along with our wives, Mary and Alison.

George and I had met by chance in the army three years before. He was a gunner stationed in the Orkney Islands, not far from the Argylls with whom I served. I had been sent with a football team to his camp, and he entertained me in the mess. We spoke about what we had been doing in civilian life, and what we thought we would be doing after the War. At that time George was an ordinand, and I had no interest at all in the Church, and little knowledge of it. We may have talked about the Church, I cannot remember, but at any rate our short meeting stuck in my mind. It all came back again when we met in the very different circumstances of St Andrews.

Through George, I became involved in the Student Christian Movement and the Iona Community. The first contact I had with the Community was at a conference organised jointly with the Foreign Mission Committee (FMC) in Iona, at which Dr J. W. C. Dougall, the FMC General Secretary, and Bishop Lesslie Newbigin of the Church of South India, were among the speakers (who also included Hendrik Kraemer and Canon Raven).

While I was there, I got to know John Fleming who had recently returned from China. Meeting him and the others, in the context of the Iona Community, with George MacLeod as its leader, made a huge impact. The world Church was opened up to me for the first time, and I was seized by the conviction, which has never left me, that God wills unity, reconciliation, justice and peace, and that those things are at the heart of the Gospel.

The thought of becoming a missionary had not occurred to me until then. It was something I now had to think about. I listened to John Fleming, who put the thought to me; and Katharine Ramsay, at that time a Candidates Secretary, put the claim of the FMC before me and kept me in touch. From the beginning I wanted others to have the joy of faith with me, to share what I had been given. The next stage was to see this impulse as a central part of Christian faith – to see it in relation to the mission of the Church. I was not at all sure that being a missionary was for me, but I became more and more interested nonetheless in the world mission of the Church, and regularly attended a 'World-Church Group' run by Mrs Isobel Forrester, wife of Professor W. R. Forrester, at their home in St Andrews. The group was enormously influential, in terms of theological thinking about world mission, and through it we met people working in different parts of the world. I met Lewis Davidson, for example, and heard the remarkable story of the educational and service community of Knox College, at Spaldings, Jamaica. At this same time I became involved in the Student Christian Movement (SCM).

The SCM led me to the conviction that the unity of the Church and its mission belong inseparably together, and that it is within the world community, and through commitment to serve there, that Faith has to be expressed.

The SCM was an open, lively community which attracted students from many different backgrounds who wanted to face with others the issues of the day, and to look with an enquiring mind at the claims of the Christian Faith. The Movement in St Andrews, as elsewhere, was organised in small groups for study, with joint meetings at regular intervals to hear an outside speaker and to have discussion together. Emil Brunner came as one of those visitors when at the University delivering his Gifford Lectures, while Prof. Donald Baillie was always ready to help and was often called upon. We had much for which to thank Donald Baillie, not least for widening out for us the life of devotion. For me, prayer at this time mattered more and more. That, and the desire I had to share the Faith, led to my room in the residence during those days being tagged 'holy corner' as a motley crew of sceptical fellow students were drawn in to pray. I was the president of the SCM branch, and Alison, my wife to be, was secretary.

After leaving St Andrews I spent two semesters at Union Theological Seminary, New York, where Reinhold Niebuhr taught. As one of the speakers at the SCM Triennial Conference, at Westminster in 1948, Niebuhr made a deep impression on me. Soon after I was given the opportunity to study under him. Although I was not ready at that stage to benefit fully from his teaching, some important things did rub off. From his consistent questioning of 'certainties', for instance, and his focus on the idolatries that make false claims, the importance of doubting for faith that I had glimpsed was developed and strengthened. Despite too his sophisticated dialectic, where the 'no' could often seem to predominate, he expressed beyond the contradictions a profound assurance of God's presence and love that rang true.

Alison and I married after I came back from New York, and quite soon I was offered the job of Scottish Secretary of the SCM. It was a three year appointment, and was to be based in Glasgow, with direct responsibilities for the work in Aberdeen as well.

It was a good time to take up work with the SCM. There had been a surge of new life, as staff and students returned to the universities after the War, and the Movement began to look afresh at what it was trying to do. In January 1950, with representatives of the Churches, it held what was to be a formative conference, in order to review its policy. A major concern was the gulf between the community of those who call Christ Lord, the One Church of the Creed set in the world to serve God, and the Christian organisations and institutions divided from one another. The picture was clear. In the University setting, recognised more and more as virtually a mission field, the divisions of the Church were a serious hindrance.

It was in the Movement – in its study groups, groups for prayer, worship together, and above all in its conferences, where, at least for a period of days there could be experienced life together in the Community of the One Church – that many of us began to see the inadequacy of the separate Churches in stark contrast, and wanted with passion to pursue the unity belonging to the Gospel and to seek for change.

During this period the SCM, in its search for the renewal of the Church in mission, stressed the role of the laity, and the concept of the One Church, as the whole People of God called to serve world-wide. That major thrust, and indeed its whole theological approach, Biblically grounded and related to the issues of the day, were formative influences which led me to missionary service, and to India.

We sailed for India after spending three months in St Colm's Missionary Training College in Edinburgh. At the beginning of February 1953, we arrived in Bombay where we were received by Katherine Ramsay, given hospitality at Wilson College by the Principal and his wife, and met Lesslie Newbigin, whom we had got to know at a Scottish Council Conference held at the close of my time on SCM staff.

An overnight train took us to Nagpur. Missionary colleagues and Indian Church leaders, with whom we were to work closely, were at the station to welcome us. From the train the city spread out in front of us. With the memory of Edinburgh fresh in our minds, where everywhere you see spires or towers of churches, we looked and could see none. There seemed to be no Church, and it was a shock to us. This was another world. The impression when we clambered down onto the platform was of people and more people, and all of them shouting at once, and in unintelligible languages. It was a repeat of what we experienced when we arrived in Bombay. This was India, and we were keyed up to move into it. We were glad to be there.

Our immediate predecessors as missionaries in Nagpur were Dr

William Stewart and his wife Wilma, who would leave for Seram-pore later in the year. We had met in Scotland, where they had taken time to brief us and help us to prepare. Bill also had taken part with me in the Scottish Conference at Wiston and we had become friends. We overlapped with them in Nagpur for three weeks, which was an immensely helpful introduction. From Nagpur we went on to Mahabaleshwar, a hill station in the Western Ghats, to study Marathi at the Language School. By that time it was the beginning of the Hot Weather, and it was a relief to escape the heat, now over 100° fahrenheit and getting hotter.

For the next two years, with many interruptions, we studied the language, either in the School or with pandits outside. In June each year, because of the heavy monsoon which closed everything down in the hills, we had to move out. In the first year we went to Poona, and in the second to Bombay. By August each year we returned to Nagpur, theoretically for the next seven months to study Marathi half-time, before going back again to the Language School. In practice language study was given short shrift as I allowed my enthusiasm to draw me into a great many activities which at that stage I would have been wiser to avoid.

The Nagpur Church Council, the equivalent of a presbytery, had two main jobs in mind for me. The first was to be Youth Worker for the Council, and the second to be in charge of evening services in Nagpur, run interdenominationally with the Methodists, for people who wished to worship in English. Many in Nagpur spoke English, although it was the first language for only a very few. It was widely used, and was the main language medium in the central committees of the Church and in Hislop College, the University College run by the Church. Marathi was the language of the bulk of the population, but it was a Marathi strongly influenced by Hindi which many spoke, and it differed from the pure Marathi of Poona which we were learning. The fact that there was so much to learn and to do, which could be effectively achieved in English, made learning to communicate in Marathi seem less important. I wished later that I had resisted the pressure to become involved in so many activities so early on, for as a result I never became confident in the spoken language. I passed exams, could read simple Marathi, and with much preparation could preach in it – painfully, it should be said for me, and undoubtedly for others – but that was not good enough. Alison did well in Marathi, and her strength in the language paid off in open and loving relationships with children and families.

Taking the English services brought me quickly into contact with the Christian staff of the hospital, the schools and the college, and with educated lay people, many of them from Tamilnadu who found it easier to worship in English. It brought me into touch too with students, and with the Young Men's Christian Association (YMCA) and the Young Women's Christian Association (YWCA). I was drawn into the YMCA quite soon after arriving, and was invited to serve on its Council. The SCM also invited me to help, and I became one of its secretaries, assisting the Mid-India Secretary, who was from Kerala.

Over Christmas and New Year 1954-55, I was privileged to take part in the Triennial Conference of the Indian SCM, held at Peradeniya University, Ceylon. I met several old colleagues and friends with whom I had worked in the British SCM, including Harry Daniel, now back home, who had become the Indian General Secretary. I also got to know several others with whom I was to work in the future. Among those was Lucy Burt from whom I was to learn so much. Meeting Lucy Burt was just one of the extra-ordinary coincidences that were to happen along the way. She had been a missionary in China and a colleague of Langdon Gilkey, who was a fellow student of mine in New York. Langdon Gilkey and she had been prisoners of the Japanese together, and had shared the experiences he describes in his remarkable book, *Shantung Compound*. That book became a kind of text book for me of what living in community is all about, and greatly influenced my thinking. Later she and I were to be colleagues in Selly Oak, where both Langdon Gilkey's and Lucy's insights were to be fed in once more.

Back in Nagpur, with the help of many in the institutions and in the Church who offered their friendship with wonderful generosity, I was able to play a part in encouraging youth fellowships. These began to grow across the denominations, and it was not long before groups of young people were meeting regularly. New impetus was given when young people from the United Church of Northern India, the Methodists and others, joined to help with a programme of flood relief. Working with one another to raise money, and to collect blankets and clothing for the homeless, brought them together in the first place. That quickly led on to the first of many conferences, and to the first work-camp, in which they became involved with village people, almost none of whom were Christian. These

were joyous days for me as friendships grew, and as I felt, along with
Alison, that India was home.

Among the most influential relationships that grew up, helping
us to cross the cultural divide, and to enter the world of India, was
our friendship with K. David and his family. K. David was a Muslim
from the South who had been converted, and who been baptised by
Bishop Lesslie Newbigin. His relatives were incensed by his decision to become a Christian, and he had to leave. Lesslie Newbigin,
having helped to arrange Mr David's marriage to a Christian girl
in Kodaikanal, sent them up to Nagpur, where he was given the job
of Secretary in the Mure Memorial Hospital. K. David and I
shared many interests. We both took for granted the responsibility
of the Church for those outside, and particularly for the poor and
disadvantaged, and we spoke about this very often. In the frequent
discussions we had about the Church, he helped me to see the
Church in its Indian setting, while I was able to raise with him
theological and Biblical issues.

Where previously the missionary movement was simply a theo-
retical topic to be happily pontificated about, now it was real. Already
we had seen much that was good. The friendship we experienced
was a promise of the partnership we spoke about, and we had seen
among young people something of the outreach of the Church.
But that was one side only. The entanglement of the missionary
movement with colonialism was there also, involving attitudes of
superiority and condescension. I could see only too well why many
would write off the missionary enterprise as dated and destructive,
and in response to suggestions about missionary service would say
they wouldn't touch it with a barge pole – a reply that I could have
made myself in the past. It was all very foreign. It is true that there
were not many missionaries at this stage, but they were very visible.
They lived in bungalows built for Europeans, in the style of Empire,
and their presence was felt. The days of the British Raj were over,
but not all that was the Raj had disappeared. 'Tennis teas', at which
the missionaries met once a week in 'the mission compound' as they
had always done, with a close group of Indian colleagues, were a
strange hangover from those days; as were the occasional meetings
of missionaries with a few selected others in the Bishop's house for
social chat. The foreign mission was still an entity in itself, and still
predominant.

We were uneasy about relationships within the Christian community. At first when members of the community welcomed us and made friends, we accepted their approaches with pleasure. That was before we came to realise the influence of divisions and rivalries, and the desire prompting many who came to us that we would join their group and share their suspicion and dislike of others. There were many rival groups and their membership often overlapped, shifting according to the interests the group served at any one time. We soon realised that we had to be extremely careful not to become entrenched in any one group. Some of the rival loyalties had a caste origin. Most of the Christian community were Mahars in background, while others were Mangs, both outcaste Hindu groups. There were also a number of Brahman families. There were caste differences too among those who came from outside, from the South, from Tamilnadu and Kerala, and from the Hindi areas. It was not long before we saw that the missionaries were not outside this complexity of rival groupings. Positively, they helped to hold the community together, but there was a potent negative aspect also. As the various groups learned to manipulate the missionaries for their own advantage, the very presence of the missionaries tended to encourage the rivalries and even to outweigh the good their presence brought, because of the power, financially and in terms of status, which they represented.

In Poona and Bombay the dominance of the Mission was even more obvious, mainly because there were more missionaries in positions of explicit leadership, and many more of missionaries altogether. Besides missionaries from Scotland there were missionaries from England, the USA, and Scandinavia, belonging to different missionary societies, some with little or no relation to any traditional Church. To add to the complexity of the scene there were a number of active undenominational organisations, such as Youth for Christ. The foreignness of the Christian presence was obtrusive, as was the contrast in economic terms between this Christian body and the vast majority of the local population.

There were at that time 23 missionaries of the FMC in Western India. In Poona we had the privilege and good fortune of staying with Elizabeth and Duncan Fraser. No one could have been kinder and more welcoming. Duncan was on the staff of Wilson College, Bombay as Professor of Chemistry, and before their marriage Elizabeth had been a missionary nurse in Western India. Without their seeming to teach, we learned a great deal from them. They had many friends and those friendships were opened up to us. We met their colleagues, missionary and Indian, who served in the institutions, the College, the schools, and the hospital, and were able to see the work being done there.

Dr Victor Das of the Leprosy Mission was one of their friends, and Dr Fraser used to go with him frequently to the Leprosarium at Poladhpur, down the steep Ghat road, where together they were busy altering and improving the facilities for the patients. One day he asked me to go with him and, if I would, conduct a service of Holy Communion for the community. It was an opportunity I could not miss, though it meant taking a service of Communion for the first time in Marathi, and in a very strange setting. It was a service I shall never forget as, within this community of sufferers from leprosy, we shared in faith for our healing the Bread and the Wine, and together gave God glory.

Not long after that Sister Edith Barbour, with whom we were to serve in Nagpur, happened to be at the hospital in Poona at the same time as I, when an urgent message arrived for help to be sent to Jalna, where there was an epidemic of cholera. Edith was invited to go, and I was asked to go with her. I had not met leprosy before and now it was cholera. When we arrived we were met by a great crowd of the very poor, women and children, who were being lined up to receive injections. My job, I soon found, was to dab antiseptic on to one brown arm – one after another, score upon score – while Edith prepared the syringe and stuck it in. If I had had time to think, it would have been very difficult. As it was, looking back, it was an important experience.

We had been critical of the missionary movement, its foreignness, and the contrast between the relative affluence of the missionary lifestyle and the poverty of the people. Since then we had met the missionary enterprise in action, were deeply moved by what we saw, and enormously impressed by our missionary colleagues. The commitment, love and professionalism of our friends did not make us change our minds, however, about the need for radical change. At St Colms we used to discuss the problem of partnership in the missionary movement, and the need for a closer form of identification on the part of missionaries with colleagues in the Third World. It was a topic we discussed also at some length in Mahabaleshwar where so much that we saw sharpened the issue in the most glaringly obvious way. All the worst forms of cultural imperialism, not least among the Americans, seemed to be present. It shamed us and made us want to examine our own ways of life, so that we might begin in practice to remove some at least of the major obstacles that get in the way of effective working together across the cultural and racial divide.

I found myself re-reading Roland Allen's two books: *Missionary Methods: St Paul's or Ours?* (published in 1912), and powerful still; and *The Spontaneous Expansion of the Church* (published in 1927) – both of which sharply challenged the foreign missionary practice of setting up dependent missionary organisations in contrast to independent Churches. A formative work also for me was David Paton's *Christian Missions and the Judgement of God,* in which he discusses, it seemed to me, factors leading to the missionary debacle in China that were closely parallel and relevant to the situation of Church and Mission in India. At the same time I began to read the writings of Mahatma Gandhi and to come under his spell.

I used the Gandhian library in Wardha and quite often visited his Ashram at Sevagram. I met members of the community, and several close followers of Gandhi who were there at that time, including Asha Devi and E. W. Aryanayakam. It was there also that I met Marjorie Sykes for the first time, whom we were to get to know as a friend over the years. I learned much from her friendship, as from her writings on Gandhi, whom she had followed during the last ten years of his life. Her book on C. F. Andrews, one of Gandhi's close disciples, was an inspiration also. It was at this time too that I met Murray Rogers whose life of prayer and disciplined simplicity was such a constant challenge to many of us in India.

Those influences make a strange mixture. I am not sure why they all came together just then, except perhaps for the obvious reason that they all pointed to the importance of people and the primacy of the human over all else, which the cumbersome complexity of the missionary movement so often concealed and hindered ...

After three years and some months in India, we had a happy family holiday. There were four of us by this time. Judy had been born in Glasgow before we left for India, and Catriona, born in Nagpur, was just over two years old. It had become very hot in Nagpur – 116° F – and we were desperate to get away. It had been arranged for us to to go to Kashmir, but the permit to enter had not arrived. As we were to find many times over, Indian colleagues came to the rescue. As if by magic the papers came just in time, and off we went.

Soon after we returned I was invited by Harry Daniel to take part in an All-India SCM Conference to be held at the University College in Alwaye, Kerala, and to prepare material for it. It was another opportunity to widen my experience of India, and to meet friends from whom I could learn.

Later that year we left for our first leave. I had just completed a handbook for youth groups, published by the National Christian Council of India (NCCI), and as a happy gesture from friends it was waiting for us in our cabin – well ahead of the time expected. In India it was well received, and I was glad to hear that it was being used by some people in Scotland as well.

Many times we had discussed the missionary movement and the role of the missionary with George and Mary More, and before going on leave had talked about our own future. We wanted to come back to India. We were happy there and liked the people, but we were uneasy about the role that was being pressed upon us. We felt that we were being asked to do things better done by the people of the place and that we were getting in the way of the Church's independent development. In the discussions held over the years the idea had grown that the Mores and ourselves, with an Indian family, form a community, something in the style of an *ashram,* in the village where the Mores had begun to run a clinic. By the time we left India on leave, plans for this to happen were well advanced.

George raised the matter with a number of senior people in Nagpur – including Dr David Moses, Principal of Hislop College, and Dr Charles Bhatty of the National Christian Council – and found agreement. Meanwhile I was asked to deal with this proposal on my return to Edinburgh. Dr Dougall, General Secretary of the FMC was in sympathy as was Ian Paterson, who had served in India and was now on the FMC staff. They had received a letter, however, from Dr Frank Ryrie, who had been commissioned to advise on policy matters, raising difficulties and advising caution, and asked me to look at his objections and speak to him. Frank Ryrie was afraid that the Allipur Community might bring division between the Church and the missionaries, if missionaries were to withdraw from Nagpur. We had not, it seemed, made clear enough, that it was a pivotal part of the proposal that the Community would provide a centre for the training of the Church. It was fully recognised that without the closest connection between it and the Church based in Nagpur, nothing could be done.

I took pains to put down in writing my response to Frank Ryrie's objections and was pleased to find that he in turn was now ready to go along with the proposal. At that stage Jim Dougall gave me the opportunity to speak to the project at committees of the FMC. The Allipur scheme was enthusiastically received, as now set out with all its various ingredients – concern for the poor, preventative medicine, child care, agriculture, and at its heart training of the laity, Bible study and prayer.

A hurdle, however, remained. It had been decided for some time that new work of any kind would have to be financed without extra money being budgeted by the FMC. The FMC stood firmly by that agreement and we wholly concurred with their position. That could have been a serious difficulty, but it was immediately overcome as Hislop College agreed to contribute through the sale of one of its bungalows. With those various difficulties behind us, we thought all was well. But that was not the end. The proposal now was to postpone the purchase of land and the construction of the build-ings required until we returned after our leave. I resisted that firmly. The decision to go ahead with the project had to be implemented, on the ground, or we would reconsider an offer made to me by the SCM of India to serve on its central staff. I had turned down that offer because I wanted to stay in the Nagpur area, but if that now meant I would be going back to what I had been doing before, then that was not on. When we made plain that we were insistent on action being taken, land was purchased and the buildings that would make possible the running of training courses were built. We breathed a sigh of relief and planned our return.

The third edition of the Plan of Church Union in North India and Pakistan appeared in print soon after we arrived in Scotland, and I found myself being drawn into the controversy over the so-called Bishop's Report, as the anti-ecumenical lobby vehemently opposed proposals for union with the Anglican Church. At the invitation of *The Scotsman,* I wrote an article on the Plan which the paper published on the day of the General Assembly debate. In hindsight it was a mistake to draw attention to Indian Church union at that time. I should have realised that in the highly charged atmos-phere nobody would want to know: 'What happens in India has nothing to do with us.' I found the attitude to Church Union in

Scotland at that time extremely disappointing and was saddened that Church people in Scotland should be so uninterested in their 'partners' enthusiasm for Church union.

Just before Christmas that year Andrew, our third child, was born. We rejoiced.

By the time we arrived back in India, the field in Allipur had been bought, the training centre buildings completed, and two of the three houses. The well had been constructed; and the overhead tank to provide gravity feed for irrigation, and for the buildings. Within a few months the training centre was inaugurated by a youth conference, led by the Rev. Shahu Nawagiri, pastor of the Nagpur Church, United Church of North India (UCNI). It was the first of many and a promising beginning to the close connection hoped for between the new community and the members of the Church in Nagpur. Before developing this side of the work, we had to continue the building programme George More began so successfully during our leave. We had to build a third house, and design and construct a chapel. The learning process was going ahead rapidly. I had always like working with my hands, but I had never had to build a house before or buy the building materials. I learned a great deal during the next months, working with the local craftsman.

We continued to have a bungalow in Nagpur and were there for at least a few days every month keeping in regular touch with the Church. The bungalow, frequently used by missionaries from outside, meant that when we were in Nagpur we often found ourselves unexpectedly sharing our home with others, who were often more frequently there than ourselves. Although we maintained a link with the city, we thought of Allipur as our home.

When the Mores returned from leave we became part with them of the Community, and with the Londhes, the Maharashtrian family who came to join us. We had houses side by side, and we had meals together, morning and evening. At the beginning of each day we had prayers in the chapel, and once a week we celebrated communion. We sang Marathi hymns, very often written by the Maharashtrian poet, Narayan Vaman Tilak, and in Marathi prayed for the Church and the village, and for people by name. That, along with a discipline of economic sharing, which helped to overcome the barrier that money inevitably brought, was at the heart of our life in community. Individually we had different responsibilities: the running of the child welfare clinic and later the leprosy clinic; relations with the village council, involving close collaboration in everything to do with the development of the village; the building of trust and friendship with people in the village individually, and with families; the running of the field and the orange orchard; domestic arrangements, and the conducting of services. My responsibility was chiefly for the leadership of courses, but I worked from time to time in other ways.

Although several large youth conferences were held – in a tent, rather like the kind used for weddings – the preference was for smaller groups that could be accommodated within the Community, and be more fully integrated into its life. In addition to youth groups, mixed groups of lay people came together for short weekend courses – old and young, men and women, to look at the role of the Church, for instance, or attitudes to other religions. On occasions also we ran special programmes for people of different professions or interests: medics, teachers, journalists, clergy, university teachers or students. We got help for all this from friends in Nagpur, particularly from teachers in the College and the schools, and owed much to the enthusiasm and energetic support of K. David. It was the realisation of the partnership for which we had longed.

I served briefly in Hislop College as a tutor in English, which I enjoyed not least because it brought me into touch with young people outside the Church, most of whom were Hindus. They were open and friendly and it was a pleasure when a group of social study students, some of whom I had met, came to Allipur as part of their course and chose to join us in the chapel. Quite often individuals came to visit us from Nagpur or to stay with us for a few days. To a considerable extent the effectiveness of the collaboration between the Community and Nagpur depended upon the friendships that were being built up in those ways.

We got a great deal of support during those days, and were touched by the friendship offered to us. It was moving to have the understanding of so many Indian friends. We were grateful, for instance, when Vinayak Masoji, the distinguished Indian artist, agreed to paint two large works for us – 'The Washing of the Disciples' Feet' and 'The Feeding of the Five Thousand'. They hung in the Community meeting rooms, and attracted many of the village people who used to come up and wonder at them. I often spoke from them at meetings, and often referred to them.

During the time I was involved in lay training, I was invited to give talks outside to clergy groups and others, mainly on the Mission and Unity of the Church, and incidentally on the Plan of Union. This gave me an opportunity to speak from the experience we were being given in the Community of the holistic nature of the Gospel and the Church's task.

A few months before the Third Assembly of the World Council of Churches (WCC) in 1961, I was asked to take over as Editor of the *United Church Review,* the official magazine of the United Church of Northern India, which involved being present at the Assembly as a member of the Press. I was grateful for the opportunity to serve the UCNI as Editor, and felt extremely fortunate to have a place at the World Council of Churches Assembly.

The Editor's job brought me into Nagpur more frequently, and while I was there I worked closely with Ted Wilkinson, Professor of Social Work in Hislop College, on an Economic Survey of Christians in Nagpur, the result of which we fed into group discussions, and published monthly in the *Review.* At the end of 1962 I took part in the Fourteenth General Assembly of the UCNI at Kolhapur, when Bill Stewart was Moderator. I had the privilege of leading the Bible studies, which were always a regular part of Assembly Sessions.

We went on leave from India in July 1963 and looked forward to returning. While I was on leave, the National Christian Council of India (NCCI) asked me to consider the possibility of my joining their staff as Secretary for Christian Literature, and proposed to the FMC that I be permitted to attend the Literature Board meeting in January 1964, on the understanding that the NCCI would underwrite the cost of my return fare. Having discussed this offer with colleagues in India and Scotland, I agreed, and was seconded by the FMC and the UCNI Church Council to the NCCI for a period of three years from July 1964.

Latterly I had been spending more and more time outside the village, lecturing, and dealing with the survey, which involved teaching, so that it was easier than it might have been to move away. We were reluctant to go because we had enjoyed our life in Allipur – a crucial stage in our own journeying. Earlier on, although we had been received with much kindness, and patience, we did not feel that we really belonged. Now we did. I suppose that we understood a little more; perhaps we had even begun to move into the world of India and to feel the pain of the poor.

To be asked to serve on the NCCI staff was not something I

could refuse. I realised that I was being accepted by Indian colleagues and that they were putting their trust in me. They regarded the appointment of Literature Secretary as important for the mission of the Church in India, for the nurture of its members and for its outreach, and they knew it had to be an appointment that would be welcomed by the Churches, and by supporting bodies abroad. The job of Literature was not going to be easy, but it was a challenge to which I looked forward, and it was one that interested me very much.

Christian literature had seldom been given the place it deserved in the list of missionary priorities, but following an All India Conference on Christian Literature, held at Panchmahri in August/ September 1963, there seemed a real possibility of a new start. Joint Action for Christian Literature had caught the imagination, and the promise of a large sum of money for Christian literature similar to that raised for theological education helped to get things moving.

The Panchmahri Conference produced a flood of ideas and by the time I was appointed expectations were high. The picture I got from the Conference Report was of a vast development, requiring a huge expenditure of capital and many new appointments. The Report entitled From 'Dialogue to Deeds' left no doubt that its recommendations demanded major changes. There was a yawning gulf between where we were in India and what the Conference looked to achieve. If the enthusiasm the conference generated was to be effectively harnessed, active co-operation on the part of the Churches and the literature agencies would be required, and detailed and co-ordinated planning stage by stage.

It was a daunting prospect, one that I could not have begun to tackle without the friendship and support of a large number of colleagues, and above all without the tireless patience of Charles Richards, Director of the Christian Literature Fund (CLF), who spent time in India with us.

Initially I visited with him some of the main publishing centres of Christian literature in the country, meeting secretaries of Regional Christian Councils and officers of Printing Presses and Bookshops with whom we discussed plans for future developments. He was a good teacher. I learned the importance of ensuring that projects and schemes for financial support were responsibly thought through, and that rigorous judgements were made about their viability – their clarity of purpose, their importance for the Church, and the practical stages that would have to be followed for their effective completion. It was a good apprenticeship.

I had been concerned for some time that so much material produced in India was designed for the Christian community, and for a small circle within that community. Few books were written by Indian writers. The vast majority were either translations, adaptations, or reprints of books written abroad, or they were the work of missionaries. I was glad to find that there was a ready response to my constant plea for more Indian writers, and for more Indian women and men to be recruited for the literature enterprise.

The move away from reprints and translations to original Indian writing was by far the most difficult undertaking, but it was this that we saw to be the pivot of any true development. Emphasis was given to the running of writers' workshops, and to training centres. Encouragement was given both to creative writing and also to apologetics.

To produce books that could be read by people of all faiths or none and sold in railway or bus station bookstalls required a new category of writing. A series was commissioned on 'Life Issues', dealing with Money, Health, Ambition, Patriotism, and Personal Relationships, and written from the perspective of the Faith. A consultation was held in Ooty, and a report dealing with the subject published, containing the suggested outline of books on those five issues prepared by the participants. A number of manuscripts were produced, and the Report itself was used as a study book and discussion starter in several institutions, both in India and abroad.

I was responsible also at this time along with the Rev. A. D. Manuel, a friend and colleague on the staff of the NCCI, for the editing of *Renewal for Mission*, a series of influential papers given at a consultation held at Nasrapur.

An International Seminar on Literacy and Literature held in Jerusalem, during the Jordanian occupation before the Six Day War, brought together writers, publishers, printers and literature secretaries from all over the Middle East, and was a major source of encouragement and stimulus. I travelled from India with Ezekiel Makunike, a journalist student from what was Southern Rhodesia at that time. He was studying in Hislop College, Nagpur, and had become a close friend. He had understandably strong feelings about colonialism which drew him to identify with the Arab people. He made friends with those he met, and I met Arabs through him. These were difficult times in Jerusalem. Often we would hear firing across the dividing lines. It was my introduction to the Conflict, about which I was to learn more in the years ahead.

September 1967 saw the beginning of a new stage. I had been approached more than once to consider serving in the Selly Oak Colleges in Birmingham, where new developments for training in mission were being planned. That change began to seem possible, and it seemed right for a number of reasons, including the needs of our family. To explore the possibility I accepted the invitation to go to Birmingham for discussion on the proposal. In April 1967 I was formally invited by the Selly Oak Colleges to serve as Dean under a newly formed Council for Training in Christian Mission, representing major missionary bodies in the United Kingdom and a number of associated bodies in Europe. My appointment with the NCCI, being for three years, could be ended. As for the Nagpur Church Council and the FMC, they both agreed to my secondment to the Selly Oak Colleges, the understanding being that I would return to India. I left India in September 1967, having helped with preparations for the NCCI Triennial to be held in Shillong, and having completed the publication of the Council's Report.

Although I was sorry to leave India – it was like leaving home – I looked forward to sharing what I had learned there, or begun to learn there. I knew enough now to know that preparation for mission was all important, and sensed that it would be less than responsible for me not to accept Selly Oak's invitation.

To move from India, and particularly from life in the village, to England and to Birmingham, was a considerable culture shock. There was much to adjust to. It was strange too to be working in a missionary setting, western and missionary society led, and with the presence of the separate denominations – Anglican, Baptist, Congregational, Methodist, et al – never far away. I was received with kindness, and was assured of every support.

From the beginning I made it known that I was interested primarily in training rather than in what was often referred to as 'mission studies'. The priority, as I saw it, was to equip those called to service in mission with basic skills, which would enable them to relate effectively across barriers that divide people from one another, and to communicate the 'challenging relevance of the Gospel'. Courses had to provide as much opportunity as possible for practice in the crossing of frontiers of class, culture, nationality, denomination, and faith, and for entering into situations difficult for mission.

We learn mission by doing mission. Selly Oak's part was to provide a creative setting of community, and a framework of training, which would encourage the toughness of mind that mission demands, and the necessary attitudes of openness and flexibility.

While I was in Selly Oak I visited Churches in Africa and Asia, where member bodies were involved. As a representative from Selly Oak, I was privileged to be received by all the Churches irrespective of denomination and to be taken into their confidence.

The first visit, in 1968, was to six countries in Africa – Ghana, Zaire, Uganda, Kenya, Zambia and Malawi. The Rev. Stanley Wilton, Principal of St Andrews College, Selly Oak, was with me for part of the time, which was a bonus. The purpose was to discuss with Church leaders the role of Western missionaries and to hear what missionaries themselves thought. We met a great many people, individually or in groups. I interviewed either in their homes or in their offices more than 70 Church leaders individually – sometimes with Stanley, sometimes on my own – and had more than a hundred shorter conversations, mostly with Africans. I also met groups of missionaries and Church leaders together – about two dozen meetings, sometimes with Stanley, sometimes alone. In these meetings we asked the same questions: Do the Churches want/need missionaries? What is the place of the missionary? Will there be a place in the future for the missionary? What kind of missionaries are wanted?

The first stop was the Ghana Christian Council where Jean Forrester-Paton, the wife of one of our missionaries, was involved in the Christian Home Movement. Rosina Konuah, at one time on the staff at Selly Oak as the Dorothy Cadbury Fellow, was working on parallel lines to Jean Forrester-Paton, but outside the Church. In Ghana, education on the family and on sex was being seen as an urgent priority. There was a great deal of promiscuity among the young and incidence of venereal disease was high.

A visit to one of the flats built in Nkrumah's time for senior civil servants was an introduction to the cultural mix that was Ghana. It was beautifully furnished, carpeted wall-to-wall, with wide floor-to-ceiling windows. I was startled by the European style luxury. I was made welcome in immaculate English and very soon drawn into relaxed conversation on the preparations being made for Ghana's new constitution.

At Trinity College, built with the help of the Theological Education Fund of the WCC, but also with substantial local funds, the students were encouraged to serve in the northern territory among the very poor and underprivileged. In the University, in Accra, Dr Christian Baeta had been a member of the WCC's Commission on International Affairs, and was a member of the Legislative Assembly. He later gave a distinguished year to the Selly Oak Colleges as the visiting William Paton Lecturer. At the Sunday service in the Church of the Resurrection in Accra, at which I had been invited to preach, there was a congregation of about a thousand. The readings and the hymns were in three languages – Ga, Twee and Ewe.

The Rev. T. A. Kumi, who had been in Scotland with the Church for nine months, served in the new town of Tema in a resettlement project. When the Volta Dam was built, the whole valley was flooded and about 80,000 people had to be moved into resettlement areas. These were organised in such a way that new social groupings were produced that broke up traditional tribal relations – in effect a process of social engineering. We saw some of the new houses, and we heard of the difficulties faced over sanitation and water supplies. There were health problems, and the problem of unemployment. Many of the hundreds of applicants who went to the Labour Exchange in Tema, and were turned away for months on end, came from the resettlement sites.

The next stop on the six country marathon was Zaire. On the way in from the airport to the city we travelled along a great double-laned highway, where we were greeted by portraits of President Mobutu displayed on hundreds of flag poles, one after the other, in three or four different likenesses. The huge portraits were printed on transparent plastic and lit at night.

In an assured and intelligent group of about 20 Congolese pastors, belonging to the Council of Pastors in Kinshasa, the topic of mission and unity was raised. The discussion was in French – happily with available translation. There was a consensus that missionaries were wanted, but for specialist jobs: *eg* as teachers or doctors. They should be part of the Church and work *with* the Congolese. Strong feeling was expressed against the separation of Church and Mission.

Later the General Secretary of the Conference Protestante du Congo (CPC), the Rev. Jean Bokeleale, stated the position of his Church:

There is a need for missionaries, and we want them. We want the best you can send us. We want missionaries who love men and women, who will try to understand us, and will walk with us. We want specialists, including theologians who will train theologians at university level, to provide leadership for strategic planning. We also need missionaries to train pastors to organize their churches properly – we need order in the churches. The Gospel's message of unity, peace, and justice is very important. Unity is a prior necessity in Congo, where the disunity of the Church is a serious hindrance to the country's well-being.

Jean Bokeleale invited us to do some sight-seeing with one of his colleagues in the CPC. On the way home along the boulevard, we met President Mobutu's cavalcade. It took up the whole breadth of the road, and was travelling at 50 miles an hour, sirens blaring. A troupe of motorcyclists came first, then a spearhead of volkswagens – one, then three abreast, then five – followed by two jeeps with machine guns at the ready, and finally a long, black American limousine with the President, and two cars following. We pulled off the road very quickly as soon as this massive parade of power appeared – there was little time to spare.

Stanley Wilton stayed on in Zaire to see more of the work of the Baptist Missionary Society, one of the sponsors of his college in Selly Oak, while I went on to Uganda. I was met at the airport by the Rev. Janana Luwun, Provincial Secretary, and Bishop Designate of the new Diocese of West Nile and Madi, of the Church of Uganda, Rwandi and Burundi, and was taken to the house of the Rev. Misaeri and Geraldine Kauma where I was to stay. I was delighted that arrangements had been made for me to stay with an African family. I was welcomed by the Archbishop, Eric Sabiti. In the course of an interview with him, I raised the question of the place of the foreign missionary. He said that there was a need for missionaries in Uganda, and added, without emphasis, 'in the meantime'.

I was invited that evening to a weekly prayer meeting held in the house of one of the missionaries. I found it surprising that out of a dozen or so people present, all were missionaries except two – an African Bishop and my host. The impression grew on me that there was an awkward and uneasy relationship between the missionaries and the Africans.

In conversation with Dr Roy Billington, whom I met at Mengo

Hospital, we discussed some of the issues raised in the Tübingen Consultation promoted by the Christian Medical Commission. He stressed how concerned he was to ensure that there was outreach from the hospital into the places from which people came and to which they would return, so that a real preventative job might be done affecting whole communities. I went with Roy to a slum area in Kampala. He spoke of the high level of unemployment, and the poverty of the people, the evidence of which was there to see. He said that there was much heavy drinking, and that prostitution was prevalent – the average age of girls involved was 13. I might have expected some political comment to be made, but as in Zaire it was not made. The general understanding in the West was that Obote was weak and administratively incompetent, and moreover was playing into the monstrous hands of Idi Amin. This was not spoken of in my hearing, but I had more than a suspicion that it was widely shared and that people were most uneasy about what was not happening that ought to happen, and what might too easily happen.

The following day at the Grail House in the Roman Catholic Compound at Rubaga, I met Miss Dilworth of the Grail, and her Ugandan colleagues. I knew something of the Grail in Edinburgh. I was glad to be there and was made welcome. I was pressed to speak about the Selly Oak Colleges of which they had heard. Two White Sisters were present, and there was interest in the possibility of sending recruits to the Training in Mission Semester. One of them was to be in Rome shortly and would speak of it. I also met a Roman Catholic Father serving with the Pastoral Institute for East Africa, who wanted me to visit if there had been time.

On Sunday I preached by translation at the morning service in Kampala Cathedral. I preached to a full congregation on the opening words of the Lord's Prayer, which had become increasingly meaningful to me – not least the word 'our' – as I had travelled and met so many people across the frontiers. I had lunch after the service with the Ugandan Dean and his wife. I gathered early on in our conversation that he shared with other colleagues a disquiet about the relationship between the Church and the Missionary Society, similar to that which I knew in India and had noted in other places. I had come to see that there was general feeling that Church/Mission structures were hindering the development of mature human relationships between missionaries and their colleagues. Ugandans wanted men and women who would identify themselves with them, and who would be willing to serve within a diocese as servants of the Church. There was a feeling that missionary salaries should be paid out of grants. Missionaries should become wholly part of the Church. The continuing tie-up between missionaries and missionary societies prolonged the love-hate relations of 'gratitude and resentment'. There was strong feeling about the missionary society style which kept missionaries in a special relationship with one another from which Ugandans were excluded.

On the Sunday after the service I was taken to a Revival Fellowship meeting held out of doors in the garden of one of the leaders. Between 3-400 people were present. Buses and cars brought people in from a radius of 15 miles. After a two month period of mission, this was a special session of thanksgiving and reporting. Those who had 'been saved' were asked to stand up. There was constant hymn singing, with the verse: 'We praise you, Jesus Christ, Lamb of God', sung again and again …

Misaeri Kauma, with whom we had been staying, and whom we knew to be a person with wide sympathies, had been influenced by the revivalist movement. He told us something of his own story. Like so many Christian families, paganism operated in his own family home, superstitious rules and rituals continued in the midst of Christian profession. During the visit of one of the revival leaders – to use his own words – he had been brought from fear and darkness. The revivalist had spoken with his father for almost two hours, seeking to convert him, and Misaeri had listened in. He had seen in these people a freedom and joy he did not see in his own family. He had been helped also by a prefect in his school who was converted at a revival meeting.

I enjoyed my stay with Misaeri and Geraldine Kauma very much, and had learned from them. Before leaving their house for the airport on the Monday morning, we said the Lord's Prayer together.

I left by plane for Nairobi, and was met by the Rev. Oswald Welsh, and his driver, Stephen. I was amazed by the long stretch of open skies, and the long views on the road in from the airport. We went straight to Kikuyu where I was to stay. Oswald Welsh shared his house, which lay just above the Church of the Torch, with the Moderator of the Presbyterian Church of East Africa (PCEA), the Rev. Crispus Kiongo. He and Kiongo were responsible for bringing the need for mission before congregations. They ran courses for elders, and every weekend conducted meetings in churches. Oswald

Welsh shared meals with his cook and his driver, and they had prayers together. Stephen Kariuki, his driver, was later ordained after studying for the ministry in Scotland.

That evening Oswald Welsh and I spoke on Mission to a class at St Paul's United Theological College. The following morning we met the staff of the College, and I had conversation with the African Vice-Principal, who expressed an obviously strongly-held view that missionary societies were outmoded. What was needed was a real partnership of equals between Churches.

I had a useful meeting with the Rev. Douglas Aitken, Minister of St Andrews, Nairobi. He spoke about the broadcast series he was running on current affairs, which had as its theme 'The Word of God for Today'. His opinion was that now, after Independence, it was easier, paradoxically, for foreigners to get a response than for nationals — a reversal of what it had been. He said, for example, that he was able to get through to cabinet ministers direct on the phone.

Travelling with Oswald Welsh, north to Meru, we crossed the line of the equator at Nanyuki. It had been raining heavily and for the last 17 miles the road was very bad. The Rev. Lawe Imathiu, Chairman of Meru District of the Methodist Church of Kenya, and Secretary of the Methodist Synod, met us with Florence, his wife, at their house. We arrived there at seven to be told that we would be addressing a meeting in the church at eight. We got to the church, through pouring rain, mud everywhere. I spoke first, through translation, and Oswald followed. There were about 60 people there. Looking back I remembered the marvellous singing. I talked to Lawe Imathiu the following morning: 'The Church is growing,' he said, 'and there is a great shortage of ministers. We need missionaries to help, and mainly in circuit work. We are satisfied with the young missionaries who are coming out. They work well and under the discipline of the Church.' Imathiu obviously inspired great loyalty and affection.

After further discussion with a group of Methodist pastors, we returned to Nairobi and I had the opportunity to meet the Rev. John Gatu. I was aware of his strongly-held views about the need for the Church to shed its dependence on foreign personnel and funds. I was very much in sympathy with his position and enjoyed meeting him. Although, he said, at this stage missionaries are wanted for work at points of growth, he wished Churches abroad would help by meeting salaries of nationals – for limited periods in connection with agreed projects.

In Kikuyu preparations were being made at the Church of the Torch for a visit from the President who was to be present at the dedication of new windows and doors. We were actually away when he came, but we will not forget his visit. The water pipes into the house in which we were staying ran under the road up to the church, and the badly needed repair of the road was part of the grand preparations. The result was that, for at least the week I was there, our total water supply came in buckets one at a time. It was good to be there at that time, even if it only to catch some of the excitement, and the flourish of Kenyan flags.

One of the people we met spoke about the visit of the President. Although Kenyatta was now a world figure, he was proud of having been to school in Kikuyu and loved coming there. He liked to come back to the place where he was born, and where he ran about as a child. In his address at the service, he said that he and his ministers owed everything to mission schools, and added that if they wanted anything at Kikuyu they must come and see him at his home.

A visit to the Kenya Christian Council included an interview with its General Secretary, John Kamau, who had recently returned from Uppsala. Missionaries, he said, were wanted who would become involved with the Church and the community, but not the kind who would live in the civil lines and go down to the natives and know them only on religious occasions. There was a need for missionaries to work in areas of outreach: in industrial areas, in the slums of Nairobi and in the northern regions where the Government was encouraging the Churches to serve. He wished that the Churches in the West would finance the salaries of Africans on a project basis for work in outreach areas.

In Zambia I was met by Michael Scott, the courageous friend of the African people, whom I remembered meeting through the Iona Community some years before in connection with Central African Federation. At Ndola I met up again with Stanley Wilton.

In the Ecumenical Foundation at Mindolo, a course for women was in its last week of four. We met a member of the Anglican Church who was in charge of the Literature Clearing House where books were recorded and assessed, and from which selected book lists were sent out. At the Africa Literature Centre we had an interview with a journalist who had edited *New Day* in Uganda. We

learned that the Centre was running courses on 'Church Publishing', 'Article Writing' and 'Fiction'. At Mindolo, the next day, we
had some time with Mr Jason Mfula, who was in charge of the
National Development Programme. He outlined for us the plans for
the coming year – a Consultation of newly appointed Members of
Parliament.

Travelling by plane to Lusaka, we met and stayed with the Rev.
Fergus and Maira Macpherson. On Sunday we were with the Rev.
Philip Khazila, Secretary of the Zambia Christian Council, who
was preaching that morning in St Paul's Church. The Rev. Wilmot
Muyimba, who was to be the new minister, was at the service. We
had met him at Selly Oak. On Monday, before flying on to Malawi,
we had an interview with the Rev. Doyce Msunsa, Synod Clerk of
the United Church of Zambia (UCZ).

The Rev. Tom Colvin met us in Blantyre, Malawi, and the Rev.
Alastair Rennie and his wife took us to Mlanje through the tea
estates, and the most beautiful country we had yet seen in Africa,
with a magnificent view of the mountains most of the way. At the
hospital in Mlanje, we met Dr Gwen Dabb and her colleagues.

The following morning in Blantyre we were with the Rev.
Jonathan Sangaya, General Secretary of the Blantyre Synod, of the
Church of Central Africa Presbyterian (CCAP), whom I was to get
to know in the coming years. We talked at length with Tom Colvin,
and his colleague, the Rev. Jim Mein, an Anglican, about the work
of the Christian Service Committee, an extensive and influential
operation handling a major part of community services in Malawi.
Helen, Jim Mein's wife, was the daughter of the Forrester-Patons
in Ghana. Later we had a session with the Secretary of the Private
Hospitals Association of Malawi, representing both Roman Catholic
and Protestant hospitals in the country.

At the Lay Training Centre at Chilema, the Rev. Richard Baxter
was co-director with an Anglican colleague, a missionary of the
United Society for the Propagation of the Gospel (USPG). While we
were there, the Rev. Lindsay Robertson and his wife, whom I had
known in the Iona Community, came over to meet us. He had been
an engineer in the army and his skills were being used by the
Malawian Government to construct a system that would provide a
clean water supply over a large area. His wife, a doctor, was running
a practice in collaboration with him.

We left early on Sunday morning for Zomba, where Richard

Baxter conducted an English service in the CCAP Church. Tom Colvin met us there and took us back to Blantyre. We left by plane for home that afternoon.

Two years later, in November and December 1970, in the course of a visit to churches in South East Asia on behalf of the Selly Oak Colleges, I visited Bombay, Madras, and Nagpur. In Nagpur I was present at the inauguration of the Church of North India, and shared in the opening service of the new Diocese of Nagpur, where I became a Presbyter of the CNI. From India I went to Singapore, to Kuala Lumpur, and then on to Lahore, Sialkot and Karachi. On returning to Birmingham I preached in the Cathedral at a United Service under the auspices of the Birmingham Council of Churches, which gave me the opportunity to speak from experience of the movements for unity in India and Pakistan.

During the years I served in Selly Oak, relations with Missionary Councils and Societies in Europe developed rapidly as more and more students came to the colleges, and I often had the opportunity to visit. My own contact began at a Consultation of Representatives of the Missionary Councils of Denmark, Finland, Germany, Sweden and Switzerland, held in Copenhagen on 5 February 1968.

From Copenhagen I went to Hamburg, where I was warmly received by members of the German Missionary Council. I had not been to Germany since the War and many memories were brought to the surface. Ahrensburg, on the road north from Hamburg, was where the War ended for me. The fact that one of the German Mission Secretaries whom I got to know had been brought up in Ahrensburg, once an enemy now a friend and colleague, helped to make it for me a symbolic place of ending and beginning. It had been a long road from violence to reconciliation.

At the end of my term in Selly Oak, I was invited to serve the Overseas Council of my own home Church as General Secretary Depute, and took up appointment in 1972.

CHAPTER 2

Into the Future

(1947)

I

FROM the wider standpoint of the Church of Scotland and its Foreign Mission Committee (FMC), our story begins in 1947. It was a decisive year. Critical events took place that were to have far-reaching consequences. Drained by the War, which ended just a year and a half before, and virtually bankrupt, the United Kingdom came to the end of its time as the great world power. Early in 1947 it made known its intention to withdraw from its commitments in the Middle East, and by the autumn stepped out of India. The central place in international politics had fallen to the Soviet Union and to the United States of America, who now dangerously confronted one another. By setting up the Cominform, Stalin consolidated the Soviet bloc, and a corresponding consolidation took place on the other side by the introduction of the Truman Doctrine. The iron curtain of which Churchill had spoken the previous year at the University of Fulton descended, and the Cold War began.

People were afraid. There was a real possibility of a Third World War, involving the unimaginable horror of atomic weapons. Many feared the worst.[1]

The dropping of an atomic bomb on Hiroshima was seen to mark a turning point in history, and there was a growing consensus that this was the end of an age.[2] In 1947 Emil Brunner had chosen for his Gifford Lectures, delivered at St Andrews University, the subject 'Christianity and Civilisation', and had assumed throughout – an assumption many shared – that 'western civilisation' faced a 'fundamental crisis'.[3] The War, with its aftermath of confusion and disillusionment, had shaken civilisation as shaped in Europe to its foundations, and there was general recognition that something was desperately wrong.

The year 1947 was one of turmoil. In Palestine, the Irgun and the Stem Gang were waging their struggle against the British forces of the Mandate, and the previous year had seen the blowing up of the King David Hotel in Jerusalem. Jewish immigration was being forcibly suppressed, and the Foreign Office was being accused of anti-Semitism. In the summer of that year, British soldiers were ordered to turn back at gunpoint a ship full of Jewish refugees from Germany; and Exodus '47, called after the name of the ship, became a symbol of the failure of the British Government of the time to deal with the Palestinian problem.

Meantime in Asia, China had been enduring convulsions of violence and war. No sooner had the Japanese invaders left in 1946, than it was in the midst of civil war between the Kuomintang and the Communists. By 1947 there was fighting around both Ichang and Moukden.

India was suffering violence also. Although 1947 was her year of triumph as she gained her independence, it was at the same time one of tragedy as numberless thousands of Hindus, Muslims and Sikhs died in the massacres accompanying the mass transmigrations resulting from partition.

As far as the Church was concerned, 1947 was marked by a further coincidence of remarkable events. 1947 was the year when the Church of South India (CSI) came into being – a landmark in the long haul toward Christian unity, which has been an inspiration for ecumenicity ever since. It was the year too when major steps were taken toward the formation of a sister Church in the north of India. Less dramatic, but no less important, were the decisive moves in 1947 to develop the independence, and strengthen the integrity of Churches born of the missionary movement through schemes of Church and Mission integration.

Finally, in 1947 there were the two great ecumenical meetings – the ecumenical youth conference in Oslo, and the meeting of the International Missionary Council in Whitby, Ontario – which helped to encourage partnership in mission of Churches across the world.

The tragic years of War had affected the work of the Church of Scotland abroad in many ways. Communication with 'the fields', as they were still called at that time, had been impaired. Costs spiralled – in some places astronomically – and finances at home were in serious difficulties. Staffing too was much reduced, mostly by retirement, with 140 vacancies remaining unfilled. Happily there were few actual casualties of war.

It was a time to take stock. By 1946 the committees of the Church responsible for work abroad had started the reassessment of their work that the new situation demanded. The FMC sent commissions to China and West Africa, and the process was well advanced, analysing the picture of needs and opportunities that could begin to be seen after the long disruption of communications. There had been basic theological reflection too on the very nature of the enterprise in which the FMC was engaged: its purpose, motives and methods. The Rev. J. W. C. Dougall, who took over as General Secretary, had a distinctive contribution to make to that study.

The mood of the Church at the time is well summed up in the FMC's Report to the General Assembly of 1947. It was a realistic report, making no attempt to evade the enormous problems facing the Church in its mission to the world – a world entering, it says, 'a prolonged period of insecurity, when the very survival of pity, and decency and faith is threatened' – and yet for all its rigorous realism it was a report full of confident hope. Anticipating what was to be said two months later in Whitby about partnership, the Report underlined the importance of the 'worldwide fellowship of giving and receiving' to which we belong, as 'both the mirror and the means of [God's] healing, forgiving, and transforming love'.[4]

The Whitby Meeting of the International Missionary Council had spoken of 'the terror and the splendour of the present age'. There were many examples of the former, but there were hopeful signs also. One of those signs was India's independence, despite the suffering through which so many of her people had to pass. India became an independent nation on 14 August 1947. Nehru's words on that decisive day will not be forgotten. They have echoed down the years not just as an extraordinarily moving summation of India's feelings, but as the proleptic birth-cry of a whole host of new nations that were soon to be born:

> A moment comes which comes but rarely in history, when we step out from the old to the new, when an age ends, and when the soul of a nation, long suppressed, finds utterance.[5]

The FMC, in its Report, spoke in hope of the role of the Church worldwide in the international scene. It referred to the emerging partnership within the Churches, reflecting God's purpose of love, and being the means of its furtherance. It was those things that became clearest in the two world Church conferences. Ecumenical co-operation was high on the agenda of both. There was widespread recognition that the demand upon the Church in a divided world was to demonstrate the unity that is possible and that God desires. The importance of the conferences lay not just in what was said or written, but in the fact that they took place, bringing together representatives of Churches around the world to meet in ways that promoted reconciliation across the divisions. In Oslo[6], for example, 12,000 young men and women met from over 70 different countries, including those lately at war with one another, and with representatives from Indonesia and the Netherlands, even at that time in conflict. M. M. Thomas, who was present at the conference from India, stressed its significance for the healing of divisions, not just of the Church but of the nations:

> ... yesterday at the Indian delegation meeting when we had to confess that we failed to meet the British delegation as belonging to Christ ... I was overwhelmed by a burden of my own guilt in the matter .... The knowledge of common guilt and divine forgiveness as the basis of common life – this is the political message of Oslo.[7]

In the midst of a world in such patent need of unity, those two international meetings in 1947 were important signs of obedience to the purpose of God. It is, however, the coming into being of the Church of South India (CSI) in 1947 that will be remembered as the ecumenical event surpassing all others.

The inauguration of the CSI took place on 27 September, in St George's Cathedral, Madras – six weeks after the day of India's independence. It was the first time that episcopal and non-episcopal Churches had come together in one body. The Churches involved were these: the South India United Church, with which the Church of Scotland was associated and which was the result of a Presbyterian/Congregational union in 1908; the Methodist Church of South India; and the Church of India, Burma and Ceylon (Anglican). The union was the culmination of 27 years of effort in prayer and discussion, during which many obstacles had to be overcome which at the time seemed insurmountable.

The movement for union had begun at a conference in Tranquebar in 1919, behind which lay years of evangelistic effort carried out by the Churches together. The CSI came into being as the fruit of a commitment to mission. Azariah and the other Indian leaders who worked for it, believed that the Gospel took precedence over Church orders and other traditions, however hallowed, imported from the West. For them the priority was the Church of Christ's calling to mission; mission and unity, they were convinced, belonged together.

Many Church of Scotland missionaries played their part along with colleagues in the other negotiating Churches in the work immediately leading up to union, and were dedicated to the task of making the union work. One of the bishops of the new Church was Lesslie Newbigin, who had been ordained as a missionary of the Church of Scotland in 1936.

The General Assembly of the Church of Scotland, in welcoming the new Church, sent Dr Neville Davidson to represent it at the inauguration. In an article written about the inauguration on his return he wrote:

> A new fact has come into existence. A closed circle has at last been broken through. And members of Churches which are still weakened by the old unhappy divisions, will surely be driven at least to ask themselves some disturbing questions, to re-examine their own consciences, to try and discover whether the Holy Spirit is not pointing them also along some new road.[8]

In a Deliverance of the following year, the General Assembly gave thanks for the CSI, 'realising the significance of this great achievement for the whole cause of Church union'.[9]

The inauguration of the Church of South India was an encouragement to those engaged in negotiations in the North where discussions had been going on since 1924. At the meeting in Allahabad in November 1947 of the General Assembly of the United Church of Northern India (a union of Presbyterian and Congregational Churches with which the Church of Scotland was associated), its union committee reported that a Round Table Conference – consisting of the Church of India, Burma and Ceylon, the Methodist Church and the United Church of North India (UCNI) – had drawn up for consideration a draft Basis of Union. The General Assembly, after full discussion, sent this document down to Church Councils – the equivalent of presbyteries. This was the first major stage in the movement for union in the North, which was to come to fruition in 1970.[10]

II

We turn now to partnership in mission, and to the question associated with it: the freedom and integrity of the indigenous Church. This had dominated the Whitby Conference, in which the theme of one of the main sections was the calling of the whole Church – younger and older alike – to worldwide evangelism as partners together in obedience.

The FMC at this time was preoccupied with the meaning in practice of that partnership, and for a generation and more to come would struggle along with its 'partners' to make partnership ever more real and effective.

The Church of Scotland had always regarded its enterprise of mission overseas as an integral component of its obedience as part of the Church universal called to mission worldwide. In that enterprise its central concern was to bring into being Churches which would take freely upon themselves the same obligation of mission. Those Churches, it is to be noted, were ecclesiastically not to be part of the Church of Scotland,[11] although it was hoped that they would nonetheless continue to be bound to it by ties of fellowship. In carrying out its policy of encouraging free and indigenous growth on the part of the Churches which had emerged from its work, the Church of Scotland intentionally developed missionary organisations in the 'fields' which in the main were independent of the Churches. That had resulted in the strange paradox of a Church whose own commitment to mission was expressed through one of its Church committees – a committee of the General Assembly – setting up separate and parallel structures of Church and Mission abroad.[12]

At this stage it soon became obvious that the state of affairs in which Church and Mission worked in separation was not something that could continue. As it was, Mission Councils controlled the institutions of mission; and those institutions were increasingly dominant, with missionaries very much in charge. There was mounting frustration that freedom and proper dignity were being impaired by the continuance of this foreign management.

The task[13] now was to find the most effective way of integrating the institutions of mission into the structures of the Churches. In doing so the intention was to ensure a continuing involvement of the Church of Scotland, while at the same time recognising that the prime responsibility for mission in any area lay with the Church of that place. It was not devolution that was in mind, whereby a Church of the West would hand over its responsibilities and would cease to share in the life and work of a Church abroad. The intention rather was to promote an integration that would enable an active partnership between two Churches in freedom – the whole work being integrated under the control of the younger Church so-called. It was beginning to be realised that the old era of foreign missions was over, when the control in 'mission fields' had been exercised by missionaries, Mission Councils, and Mission Boards. The era of world mission had begun in which 'older' and 'younger' Churches would share in the privilege of responding to God in his mission to the world together. Reaffirming its solidarity with fellow Christians in the Church world wide, the FMC had this to say in its Report to the General Assembly of 1947:

> … we Christians of the Older Churches can no more stand alone in this post-Christian era without the fellowship of the Indian, Chinese and African Churches than they without us, can be perfected in their mission. We need each other as we need Him who is able to make Home and Overseas one.[14]

A new stage had been reached, and policies had to be examined afresh. It was appropriate that the start should be made in the setting of India, where independence in State and Church had become a vital factor, and where the new Church of South India had come into being. A Special Committee was appointed in 1945 to look at the Relationship between the Older and Younger Churches in India.

The setting up of the committee did not come a moment too soon. Pressure was mounting in the Christian community in India against foreign domination of every kind. At its meeting in 1944 the National Christian Council of India (NCCI) had urged the hastening of the process of bringing all missionary activities within the sphere of the Church's life and witness. 'The time has now come,' the NCCI said, 'when the missions from the West should carry on their activities in and through the organisations of the Church, wherever these have been developed, and cease to function through Mission Councils or other organisations which are not an integral part of the life and work of the indigenous Church.'[15]

Two years later, when the mood in India had become increasingly bitter toward foreign missions, the NCCI made a further statement:

> The Council is of the opinion that Foreign Missions in India should take immediate steps to achieve integration with the Church which they, under God, have helped to bring into being. The situation in the country makes it a matter of extreme urgency that the integration of the Mission with Church should be accomplished in the immediate future.[16]

It was the long-stated policy of the FMC, as we have noted above, to encourage the development of indigenous Churches, so there was no opposition on its part to the demand for change. In fact it welcomed the impetus coming from the NCCI. The FMC had for some years indicated its willingness to move toward integration, and indeed in some places had gone some distance toward it. For example, by 1922 in Nagpur, India a Board of the Church Council was formed which took over the running of primary schools and the work of evangelism, which had up till then been the responsibility of the Mission Council of what was at that time the United Free Church of Scotland. Then five years later in Manchuria, the Synod of the Church of Christ in China assumed responsibility from the Mission Council for allocating funds received from the FMC and for locating missionaries sent from Scotland. Most recently, in Nagpur, there were discussions which had been going on over the previous seven years, with the aim of bringing about a full integration of Church and Mission, and even while the work of the Special Committee was in progress the final stages of the discussion were being reached. In 1946, a few months before the NCCI's meeting of that year, the constitution of a new Mission Board of the Nagpur Church Council of the UCNI with much wider powers than the one of 1922, was completed, and was approved by the FMC. The actual inauguration of the new Board took place in November 1947.[17]

The new Nagpur Board paved the way and provided a practical model for change. In April the following year the FMC, having received the Report of its Special Committee, which had given careful consideration to the resolutions of the NCCI, and having consulted Mission Councils in the 'fields', agreed to a policy statement that represented a decisive shift from control exercised by Mission Councils to control by the indigenous Church, and resolved to make 'a much more general and thorough attempt to apply to its work in India the fundamental principle that the missionary task is the responsibility of the Church in India'.[18]

To carry out the Special Committee's recommendations for integration in all its 'fields' in India, the FMC appointed the Rev. Frank Ryrie, one of its missionaries in Bengal, as its Commissioner in India. It gave him authority to discuss its views with the appropriate people in India, and to convene a conference of representatives of Mission Councils, which would make recommendations to the FMC on the best way of putting its policy into effect. This Conference met in Nagpur in December 1947, under the chairmanship of the Rev. William Stewart, who was chiefly instrumental in bringing the Mission Board of the Nagpur Church Council into being, and who had been appointed its first secretary.

Prior to the Conference, Frank Ryrie reported to the FMC that all Mission Councils, with the exception of Rajputana, had given their unqualified approval to the policy outlined in the Report of the Special Committee. In expressing its own approval of the FMC's policy of Church Mission integration, the Conference declared:

> The Conference ... believes that by this unification members of the Church in India will share increasingly in the concern and responsibility for the work which Christ has laid on the heart of His Church in Scotland and in India ... the Conference rejoices to know that the leaders of the Churches associated with the Church of Scotland's Mission work have warmly welcomed the proposals as expressing the unity of the older and younger Churches in the Universal Church of Christ and as holding out a hope of a new kind of partnership expressing that unity.[19]

Before that 'new kind of partnership' could become a reality, many stages of development had to be patiently worked through, and many years of growing together had to pass. As we shall see as we go along, it was not to be an easy journey. At the time of writing it is not yet completed. It has to be remembered too that there had been a long journey leading up to the events of 1947. The discussions that took place nearly twenty years before, at the meeting of the International Missionary Council in Jerusalem on the same topic, are a reminder of just how slowly change can come. Sometimes almost word for word the same things were being said then, in 1928, as were being said at Whitby in 1947. Indeed a paper by P. O. Philip, Secretary of the NCCI, and an address in 1926 by S. C. Leung and quoted in the third volume of the Jerusalem Report, could well have been given in 1947.[20] In some respects the Philip's paper goes in fact beyond what was implemented or even seriously suggested in that year. And of course 1928 or 1926 were not the beginning of the story. For that we have to go back at least to the 1850s, to the Anglican, Henry Venn, and the American Congregationalist, Rufus Anderson, for the 'three-self' programme with its aim of a self-governing, self-supporting and self-propagating Church.

Although we would not wish in any way to diminish the achievement which the new Board in Nagpur represented – it was a major step forward – it left a number of serious difficulties, in terms of full and responsible partnership, unresolved.

As we have seen, the Special Committee, and those who planned the new Board, were anxious to find a structure for mission that would encourage in every possible way the freedom of the indigenous Christian community to be itself, and to serve the purpose of God in mission as a truly Indian Church. They were concerned too to find a way in which the Church of Scotland might continue to work with the Indian Church as an active partner in the Church universal.

What was achieved in the event was a considerable transference of authority, while allowing at the same time for a continuing involvement. The desire of the Church of Scotland not to sever its long connection with the Indian Church, but to continue to play its part with it in the immense task of mission in India, was not easy to put into effect, without detracting from the freedom and integrity of the indigenous Church. It was difficult, for to participate in the unfinished task of evangelism in India seemed to the FMC an obligation and a privilege from 'which it would not desire the Church of Scotland to be now or at any time excluded'. It was in this context, and despite the threat to freedom it might cause, it pressed on. In strong words the FMC affirmed that it wished to have a share in the development of Policy, which meant in practice continuing to exercise the Control from which it had seemed to be saying it wanted to withdraw.

The difficulty remained and there was a failure to set the indigenous Church free from outside interference. If we look at the Nagpur model, for instance, we see that the missionaries were included in the membership of the new Board, which, though formally under the Church Council, was in fact the place where power was exercised. Foreign missionaries, that is to say, were given a position of influence, regardless of how they might compare in seniority, experience, character or intellect, with Indian colleagues serving in congregations or institutions who were not given that privilege. Even more damaging, from the point of view of the freedom of the indigenous Church, was the section in the constitution dealing with grants, property and the location of missionaries, which made the approval of the FMC a requirement.[21]

The theory of partnership at this stage outran what it was felt possible to implement. Although the new structure now allowed for more free and responsible relationships between Churches in Scotland and India, the imbalance between the strong and the weak – as far as wealth and resources were concerned – continued to be a massive obstacle. No rhetoric of partnership could conceal the reality that the Church of Scotland, through its missionaries and its grants of money, still exercised an inappropriate control.

We are reminded of a point Stephen Neill makes in one of his books on mission. Just as we have learned in politics to look behind appearances to identify the real power structures and in particular those that exercise financial control, he says, so we must do also in our thinking about partnership: 'It is possible to change the entire outward appearance of the fabric, and yet to leave the essential structures untouched.'[22] We would not want at all to suggest that no real change had taken place, but Neill's warning remains.

Before we move on to the reports of the Commissions sent to China and Africa, which were part of the FMC's appraisal of its work after the War, let us continue a little longer with what was happening in the Indian subcontinent.

III

The Indian subcontinent was going through a period of political unrest, and it was a difficult period for the Church. Reports from Mission Councils gave a picture of the situation. First, following partition or in the period before it, there was communal violence in some Council areas, and the effect was felt in others. There was violence in Rajputana and, until the very inauguration of independence, in Calcutta also. In Murray College, Sialkot – by this time in Pakistan – the Hindu and Sikh members of staff had fled for their lives, and less than half the students returned when the College opened for the new session. Then in Jalalpur-Jatan, where Theo Skinner was working under extreme pressure as a missionary doctor, the hospital was swamped by Muslim refugees from India.

Second, from area after area, letters came to the FMC telling of rising costs. The cost of living was two and a half to three times what it was before the War, and prices were continuing to rise. Although efforts were made at local level to soften the effect on the national staff by giving and increasing living allowances, many 'mission workers' suffered badly. One report spoke of staff having to sell clothes to buy food. Rising costs had a serious effect directly not only on individuals but also on institutions. Repeatedly in the minutes of committees we find references like this: 'In view of the present financial position it is not possible to … ', and then comes a decision either to close a school or hospital, or not to develop some institution or other regarded as important for the sake of local people and for mission. A cable which the FMC received from the secretary of the Rajputana Mission Council in March 1947 indicates the scale of the problem in that particular area. The failure to increase grants, it said, would lead to serious retrenchment, involving the immediate closure of nine primary schools, and the dismissal of 21 agents. The closure of other institutions would inevitably follow with more staff having to go.[23]

The contrast between the poverty of the Indian subcontinent and the relative wealth of the West was a major factor in the attitude of local Christians to the 'Mission' (as it continued to be called), and to the missionaries. Most regarded the 'Foreign Mission' as a source of unbounded wealth and power, and deeply resented the kind of influence that foreigners exercised which could lead to their schools being closed or their relatives being deprived of jobs.

Further details of what was happening in India were given by an Indian delegation (led by Dr Rallia Ram, the chairman of the NCCI) who were on a goodwill mission to the UK and the USA, and who were present at the Asia Committee, when the Interim Report of the Special Committee on Relations between the Older and Younger Churches in India was being discussed.

Rajah Manikam, later Bishop but then Secretary of the NCCI, had written an article at this time[24] based on replies which had been received by the NCCI from churches in India to a questionnaire prepared by the International Missionary Council (IMC) on the missionary task, and which were fed into the Whitby Conference.

One of the important points he makes in that article, and that he would certainly have wanted to share with the committee, concerns the new confidence evident in the Church. There was now a sure awareness of the centrality of the Church rather than the Mission, and a marked national consciousness. The Church was the Indian Church, no longer isolated in the Indian setting. It was in the national movement, and had taken the crucial decision to claim no communal safeguards in the constitution. No longer could there be justification for it to be identified with a foreign ruling power.

As far as missionaries were concerned, they would be regarded as guests in the country, not any more as 'agents of an imperial power or vendors of the religion of an alien ruler'. Dr Manikam, having spoken positively about the continuing place for the missionary within the Indian Church – a point which the NCCI made both in 1944 and 1946 – expressed the opinion, accurately as it turned out, that there would likely be for some time to come opposition to the foreign missionary in India. There were, he said, many difficulties still to be overcome if there were to be genuine fellowship between missionaries and their Indian colleagues. Integration or devolution was essential, and he said how thankful he was that a number of Missions had handed over direction and control; among the problems that were still present, however, were racial discrimination, salary inequalities, and property ownership.

Manikam also pointed in his article to the possibility that the Indian Government, after Independence, might well take over or otherwise interfere with medical and educational institutions at present run by Missions. The churches in India would have to be alert to the likelihood of that occurring. Already, he said, some grants-in-aid had been seriously reduced, and elsewhere conditions introduced for the receiving of grants.

In August, some months after the Indian delegation had visited Edinburgh, reports were received about the appeal Dr E. C. Bhatty of the NCCI had issued to the Christian community asking for help with the great relief programme in Delhi, where communal tension between Hindus and Muslims was running high. By this time the Christian community was recognised as a force for reconciliation, and the Government appealed for assistance. There was an overwhelming response.[25] The way in which the Christian community answered the call to serve in the national emergency, so quickly and so effectively, and to act as reconcilers was profoundly significant both for its own self-image and for its effect on Indian public opinion. It marked the coming of age, it might be said, of the Indian Christian community.[26]

IV

We come now to China and the Report of the Commission jointly appointed by the Church of Scotland and the Presbyterian Church in Ireland.

Whereas in India, in 1947, the challenge to the Church came from its new setting in an independent secular nation, and the need to find its true identity as an indigenous Indian Church within a responsible partnership with Churches abroad, in China the challenge was the stark issue of survival. The Church both in Manchuria and Ichang required urgent help from its friends abroad in order to repair the damage of the War years, when the Japanese were in occupation, and to tackle the immediate problems arising from the civil war waging around them.

In response to an invitation from China, the FMC joined the Presbyterian Church in Ireland in sending out a Commission,[27] the first of the Commissions mentioned earlier. The Irish delegates confined their visit to Manchuria, while the FMC delegates included Ichang in their itinerary. The Commission arrived in Mukden at the beginning of April 1946. They spent three weeks there. The Ichang visit followed, and lasted a week.

In their report to the FMC on their return, the Commission spoke of the seriousness of the situation, mitigated only by the extraordinary resilience and courage of the Christian community. The political and economic position was desperate, and prospects for mission in the future were not hopeful. Their impression on their arrival in Mukden was of a derelict city. Everywhere there were destroyed buildings. Factories had been stripped of their machinery by the Russians, China's former allies, and for great numbers of the people there was neither work nor wages. The shops were closed, and there was little or no traffic. Although the Kuomintang was still in control of the city, and of the line between it and Peking, much of the countryside round about was now in the hands of the communist army. There was no electricity, and with mining areas in communist hands supplies of coal had run out. Water no longer came through the taps and had to be carried. Hyperinflation was weighing dreadfully on the poor.

In the midst of this, however, the Church was very much alive. The Commission spoke of throbbing, vibrant life in the Christian community; with men, women and children crowding into the churches to worship. They remarked also on the energetic enthusiasm for evangelism. The Church was making up for time lost during the Japanese period, by pushing out into the city and the countryside to set up churches and preaching stations. The Commission was much impressed by the steadfastness and courage of the Church ('God is truly in our midst' was said again and again), and by its eagerness to recover lost ground.

'That the Manchurian Church should have survived 14 years of Japanese occupation, including four years of complete isolation is wonderful,' wrote John Stewart, a China missionary and one of the commissioners. 'That it should be so full as it is of life and vigour is a miracle. The Chinese Christians in Manchuria put that miracle down to the direct action of God.'[28]

The Church was clamouring for the return of the missionaries who had been absent for so many years. 'There is no doubt at all about the welcome,' the Commission said, 'that awaits the missionaries when they come. "What is the earliest date they can arrive?" we were asked over and over again. "Cannot they come sooner?" And frequently when faced with problems of reconstruction that obviously called for much financial outlay, "It is people we need more than money," was the comment.'

The picture that the Commission gave of the situation in Ichang was not markedly different from that in Mukden, although the problem of reconstruction was if anything worse. Nine-tenths of the city of Ichang had been destroyed.

The Commission was deeply impressed by the magnificent work done by Forbes Tocher and Helen Wilson, both of whom had returned to their duties straight from internment. Institutions had been re-opened, and urgent repairs undertaken.

The financial cost of dealing with the aftermath of the War years, both in Ichang and Mukden, was enormous, a burden made all the more daunting by inflation which had reached alarming proportions. It was estimated that it would now require ten times more sterling than it had pre-War to cover the same amount of work. The FMC was anxious to give all the help it could, but had to recognise the severe limits beyond which it could not go. The most pressing need was to send staff, and that it set out to do. In July 1946 an approach was made to a number of former China missionaries inviting them to consider returning by the autumn. What should be done in the future about finance and staffing was left over until the situation in China clarified.[29]

By the beginning of 1947 many of the missionaries had returned both to Mukden and to Ichang. There were still, however, a large number of vacancies. In the beginning of February a cable was sent from Mukden asking for the return of four men and ten women missionaries, for three new ordained missionaries, one new pharmacist, and for the appointment of one new woman evangelistic missionary, and one new nursing sister. Requests for missionaries also came from Ichang. The FMC's response was disappointing. It was in the position to send less than half the number of people asked for.[30]

Encouraged by the resilience and strength of the Church, by its warm welcome, and by the freedom the Church now enjoyed to live its life and to develop its institutions – in contrast to what had happened under the occupation – the missionaries, as soon as they arrived, set about the task of helping in every way they could. For them, as for the Church, it was a time of new beginning and of hope. There were huge problems, but there was no thought of doing other than working and planning for the future. In face of the appalling difficulties, the Church moved ahead with rebuilding.

The missionaries were much more optimistic about future possibilities in China than were the Commission and the FMC, whose thinking was dominated by the civil war, by the certain victory of the communists, as they saw it, and by the virtual impossibility of continuing under that regime. W. Y. Chen a former General Secretary of the National Christian Council of China, writing in the *International Review of Missions*, shared the more sanguine view held by the missionaries. The Church, although a tiny minority, he said, had an influence in society under the Nationalist Government out of all proportion to its size. There were great new opportunities for evangelism, and for service in the name of Christ. The Government was urging the Church to commit itself to the task of 'spiritual and moral reconstruction', and the NCC had launched a Three Year Christian Forward Movement in response.[31]

The supportive attitude of the Kuomintang, the National Government, to the Church, to which many references were made, encouraged the Christian community to look to the future of the Church and its mission with expectation, and the fact that Madam Chiang Kai-Shek was a Methodist Christian was no inconsiderable factor. The increasingly close alliance between the leadership of the Kuomintang and the Church, it has to be noted however, by no means overruled the uneasiness many Christians felt about both the competence and honesty of Chiang Kai-Shek and his party.

Whatever people felt, it was nonetheless a fact that the National Government, immediately after the war with Japan, did provide an umbrella under which it was possible to live with some approximation to normality and to begin to plan. That was how it was certainly at the beginning of 1947 which finds the Church and the missionaries at work together picking up the threads, and following again well tried and accustomed routines. The Church was now thoroughly immersed in the task of restoring the institutions of mission, the schools and the hospitals, that had been run down or destroyed, of bringing new life to theological training, and building up again the organisation of trained evangelists upon which evangelism and teaching the faith to the people had so much depended. Having faced steadfastly and courageously the many serious difficulties pressing in upon it, it was now head down in all the detail that rebuilding demanded.

It is interesting to note in the urgent requests sent to the FMC for help, and in particular for the sending of missionaries, the recommendation that no missionary families should be permitted to go, because of the existing conditions, did not have the agreement of the missionaries at work alongside their Chinese colleagues. They were getting on with the job, and had accepted the conditions as a 'normal' part of it.[32]

The Manchuria Mission Conference, consisting of the missionaries from both the Church of Scotland and the Presbyterian Church in Ireland, met regularly throughout 1947, five times in all, its meeting in January being the first since the end of the war with Japan.

A word must be said about the place of the Conference in the life of the Church in Manchuria. Historically it was the structure in China by which the two Mission Councils, the Scottish and Irish, did their work, and through which they related together to the emerging indigenous Church. The Mission Councils accepted decisions of the Conference as theirs, and it was those decisions jointly reached that they forwarded to their committees in Scotland and Ireland. By 1935, as the process of Mission/Church devolution progressed, the Conference came to exercise less and less executive power. It had become a body for policy discussion, making suggestions or putting forward criticisms to the Synod, the ecclesiastical authority, and to the Mission Councils.

The Japanese occupation saw the role of the Conference change, and the process of devolution reversed. Because Synod and its committees were no longer able to meet as previously, the Conference took on an authority which did not properly belong to it. This was recognised by the Church as a necessity which would be reversed when the situation changed. By 1947 the Synod again assumed its rightful place, with Mission Councils now discarded.

As in the past, missionaries were members of the Synod, and could belong also to the Synod Executive and to other Synod Committees. Since one of the functions of the Conference had been – and this was continued – to provide a place for missionaries to discuss mission policy, and also for the briefing of those who were members of the Synod Executive, the Conference remained an influential part of the Synod structure. That being so, there was always the danger that missionaries would exercise more power than was desirable within a free indigenous Church. As it turned out, some missionaries indeed, who had served under the interim system, found it difficult to adjust to one which did not allow executive action.[33]

Unlikely as it would seem in the circumstances of that time, questions about the relation between Missions and the independent Church that were also in the forefront in India, became lively issues. The result was the passing of a new Constitution for the Conference, in November 1947, in which its remit was clearly restricted to matters most immediately affecting missionary service as such.[34] By then the political and military situation had changed considerably. It was clear that the communists would soon enter Mukden. At its December meeting the Conference agreed to make a statement about the situation to the committees in Scotland and Ireland. In their statement the missionaries said:

> We may find ourselves in communist territory in the not too distant future .... No one can legislate for the possible contingencies that may arise, nor can we say what opportunities there may or may not be for

Christian work. As a Mission, however, we feel that it is our duty to carry on what Christian work we are doing as long as this is possible.

The response of the FMC was that 'the continuing of service must in present circumstances be a matter for individual decision'. It cabled permission for any missionary to leave Mukden who so desired, and it agreed that no further missionaries be sent meantime.[35] The year which began with such optimism on the part of the missionaries, ended with the sad possibility that again, six years after the last departure, they would be forced to leave. Their decision, however, was to carry on as long as possible, and they replied to that effect.

V

Africa, to which we now turn, had by 1947 reached a new stage in its development. Its schools and colleges had produced many highly intelligent men and women who were aware of the opportunities opening up to escape from the constrictions of 'the old ways', and who were anxious to give a lead. There was a large number also of young people for whom the war had provided a chance to travel and to extend their experience. Nationalism, one of the consequences of the widening of horizons, had become a powerful force, and the new attitudes of self-confidence spurred it on. The time was ripe for radical change.

'Africa for the Africans just like India for the Indians. That's something that must be right in the foreground of our thinking about Africa today. Another is their thirst for education.'[36] In an interview given shortly after her return, that is how Mrs Monteith, one of the commissioners whom the FMC sent to West Africa, summed up her impressions. Another observer spoke of the 'tumultuous pressure toward the betterment of life' that education was seen to bring. And 'pressure' was a key word. The pressure was on to meet aspirations – social, political, and economic – at a level beyond the practical possibility of quick achievement, and to do so with impossible speed.

It was, as the FMC's report to the General Assembly of 1947 notes, a dangerous time for Africa. The gulf between aspiration and what was immediately possible was widening perilously, and there was mounting frustration. In the potentially explosive mix piling on the pressure, racial tension was an increasingly obvious factor. The riots that broke out in August of the previous year at Lovedale, South Africa, only too clearly indicated the dangers. If, as was being said, a new Africa was being born, then there were signs that it was not going to be an easy birth.[37]

(a)

The FMC had sent Commissions to Africa, in 1946 and 1947; the first of the two Commissions having gone to the Gold Coast, as it was then called, and then to Nigeria. The second went to Central and South Africa.

The centenary celebration of the beginning of the Church's Mission at Calabar in Eastern Nigeria was the occasion for the Commission's visit to West Africa. In their report the commissioners spoke of lively churches. Both in Nigeria and the Gold Coast, Churches had come into being which could point to remarkable achievements, that were a vigorous force in the community, and were forward looking. The Church was increasingly concerned about 'untouched areas': in the Gold Coast the Presbyterian Church was eager to stretch out to the Northern Territories; and in Nigeria, the Presbyterian Church of Biafra was planning to widen its work in Ogoja Province, as part of its centenary effort. In the Gold Coast, in particular – where, in addition to the Church of the Gold Coast, the Ewe Presbyterian Church (developed from the work of the Bremen Mission) was at work in eastern districts and in British Togoland – the Church, said the Commission, was 'strong, growing, self-governing, self-supporting, missionary minded'. It was a Church that had increased in the previous 25 years by as much as two to three hundred per cent.[38]

As they moved about in West Africa, the commissioners were constantly aware that this was an acutely critical time for the Church. 'It is apparent,' their report says, 'that the Church in West Africa is standing at the first big cross-roads of its short history.' The Church was having to come to terms with the rising expectations of the people for freedom to run their own affairs, and for education. There was clearly a strongly held feeling that missionaries had too much of a say in the running of the Church and its institutions, and in Nigeria the need for the reorganisation of the administrative system so that Africans might be able to play a more informed and responsible part was becoming increasingly obvious. Not nearly enough had been done in the past, it was being recognised, to train African men and women for senior leadership. The irony was that the demands for change were coming very often from the missionaries themselves who were having to persuade the Church that change was necessary.

It was noted in the Commission's Report that a scheme of training had been before the Calabar Mission Council since 1939, but had not been put into effect for lack of staff. The Commission was now appealing to the FMC to help. 'To make it possible to begin this training,' it said, 'would be one of the greatest services we could render the Presbyterian Church of Biafra at the present time.'[39]

Steps had been taken in Nigeria to involve Africans in the administration of education. An important step forward was the introduction of a Board of Governors at the Hope Waddell Training Institution,[40] which drew it more closely into the structure of the Church, and which gave more opportunity than previously for African participation. Then, to take the place of the Mission Council Conference, a body called the Education Authority was set up. It had an African majority, with representative African teachers and members of Synod outnumbering the missionaries. The new Authority, however, was slow to take effect. One reason given for this, it was being said, was a misunderstanding on the part of the FMC – the title, 'Education Authority', meant something quite different in Scotland. Although the Authority came into being in 1945, the meeting at which the commissioners were present was only its second.[41]

Direct African control was still out of reach. The problem of the shortage of leadership remained, and there was no easy answer. Missionaries had to continue to play a central role. They were needed as teachers in higher education and as administrators. Missionaries too had to go on acting as managers of schools – paying the teachers, and dealing with Government, which constantly refused to meet the cost of separate managers.

The Church found itself facing contradictory needs: to increase its own authority and responsibility, and, at the same time, to look outside itself for leadership. The Church was asking, in consequence of the latter need, for the maximum possible missionary help immediately and in the years ahead. In Nigeria, for example,

Hope Waddell asked urgently for teachers, and from the hospitals, including Itu and Uburu, there were requests for seven doctors.[42]

In the Gold Coast there was not the same problem about leadership. Africans had held responsible positions in the Church and education for many years. All the schools and the training institutions were under the Synod Committees of the Churches, on which sat Church representatives and the Supervisors or General Managers of Schools – African and European. The enormous amount of work done at this time unobtrusively by the Rev. David Elder as Mission Secretary, and as Treasurer for both the Presbyterian Church of Ghana and the Ewe Presbyterian Church, and by David Harker as General Manager for Schools for both Churches, to name just two of the most influential, helped enormously to encourage leadership and to build relationships of friendship when Mission/Church relationships were being questioned.

(b)

In the summer and autumn of 1947, a Commission appointed by the FMC visited Northern Rhodesia and Nyasaland, as they were then called. It then went on to South Africa. The Convener of the FMC, the Rev. G. S. Gunn, had served on the first of the two Commissions, along with Mrs Monteith. On this second, to Central and South Africa, the General Secretary, Dr Dougall, was one of the three commissioners, the others being Rev. Robert Ross and Mr Douglas Benzies, the new Regional Secretary for Central Africa.

Until 1945 the Church of Central Africa Presbyterian (CCAP), which came into being in 1924, covered both Northern Rhodesia and Nyasaland. In 1945 the three congregations of the Church of Scotland mission stations at Mwenzo, Lubwa, and Chitambo in Northern Rhodesia which belonged to the Livingstonia Presbytery of the CCAP, but because of distances had only a tenuous connection with it, became a presbytery on their own – the Presbytery of North Eastern Rhodesia. Immediately after that happened – in fact the next day – the new Presbytery united with the congregations of the London Missionary Society and with those of the United Church of the Copperbelt to form the Church of Central Africa in Rhodesia (CCAR).[43]

With the members of the Commission present the Synod Standing Committee of the CCAP drew up a recommendation for a Federal Council representing their Church and the CCAR in order to work and develop together. Against the background of those events, the Commission, with the agreement of the Mission Councils and the missionaries, made a number of proposals designed to coordinate the work of the FMC in Central Africa – Northern Rhodesia and Nyasaland – across territorial and now Church boundaries. There were three proposals:

1. That the present two Mission Councils be divided into four groups for administration, *viz*: (a) Blantyre Mission Council, (b) Livingstonia Mission Council (Nyasaland), (c) Livingstonia Mission Council (N. Rhodesia), and (d) the United Mission to the Copperbelt (Church of Scotland Committee); and that the Livingstonia Mission Council be retained for legal reasons, but should meet every four years to take account of the isolation of the small group of missionaries in Northern Rhodesia.
2. That a Regional Committee be formed which would have transferred to it most of the powers held by the existing Mission Councils.
3. And that a Regional Secretary be appointed who would reside in Blantyre, Nyasaland.

Basically the intention of those proposals was to prepare the way for the creation of a single united Church of Central Africa which would be responsible for the work of mission in that whole area, while more immediately there was the pressing need to be able to speak with one voice to Government on medical and educational policy.[44]

The Church in Northern Rhodesia, outside the Copperbelt, with which the Church of Scotland was connected, was concentrated in three areas separated by long distances. Mwenzo in the north was 130 miles from Lubwa farther south, and from there to Chitambo was 225 miles. In each of those towns there was a central mission station with a small staff of missionaries, and, in a radius of 50 to 60 miles around, a scattering of village schools which served also as churches. The many congregations in each area, though isolated from one another, were held together through representation on a central session. It was a weak Church, dependent on a few ministers and other leaders trained in Nyasaland, who leant heavily on a small group of missionaries, who were themselves overburdened by the multitude of claims made upon them.[45]

The Church in Central Africa, though all too weak in Northern Rhodesia, was nonetheless firmly established, and was a living and growing Church. In the Livingstonia Mission Council area, the Church, according to the Commission, was 'strongly developed and adequately manned with a well trained ministry greatly assisted by the voluntary work of the eldership'. In Blantyre, however, the age level of the ministers was high. Many of them were ready to retire.

In contrast to the position in West Africa, the Church in Central Africa, in the view of the Commission, needed to be encouraged toward independence. The Mission, it considered, was carrying more weight than was necessary. 'Supervision of the work in some districts should be transferred from direct control of the missionary to a responsible committee of African Church workers chosen by the District Church Council of the Presbytery.' It felt too 'that the Presbyteries of Livingstonia and Blantyre should be invited to take a larger share of financial responsibility for the work of the Church.' Further it pointed to the need to encourage missionaries to become members of the African Church 'and so become visibly identified with it'.[46]

As elsewhere in Africa the pressure was on for more schools. To meet the demand – out of all proportion to the available resources of staff and money – the mission school system was extended to the point of breakdown and missionaries were already overwhelmed with administration. There was a need both to encourage greater Church participation, and to receive more help from Government. The options were considered of handing over the whole system to Central Government, or of preparing it for transfer to 'native authorities', but neither was acceptable. The importance of maintaining distinctively Christian direction in education was recognised as being paramount and could not be guaranteed, if the control of the institutions was not in the hands of Church and Mission. In the event the Commission negotiated with Directors of Education for new or continuing grants.

The Overtoun Institution at Livingstonia was a particularly clear example of the problem facing Church and Mission of maintaining institutions of training. Planned at the end of last century on a large scale that was commensurate with the economic position of the time, but at this stage was totally beyond the ability of the local community to maintain, it was presenting a considerable strain on the resources of Church and Mission.

The importance of Overtoun for the whole development of the Church over the years would be difficult to exaggerate. The Institution had trained a succession of teachers and ministers, builders and carpenters, medical dispensers and midwives, who had settled not only in all parts of Nyasaland, but in Northern Rhodesia and farther afield. The Commission was convinced of the continuing importance of the Institution, provided it was fully used for the training of personnel, and recommended it to the FMC for its support. The actual financial requirement was considerable. Among other things the hydro-electric equipment had to be restored and the water system repaired, the total cost being about £4000, a large sum at that time.[47]

The hospital that was part of Overtoun was promised an annual grant by Government. Other hospitals run by the Mission were assured of support also. The Commission in discussion with Government officials found them ready to recognise the significant contribution that the Mission was making to medical services in the territories. Government was now prepared to give grants to cover running costs and salaries, where there was assurance that there was no overlapping with other hospitals, and that our medical work fitted into the general plans.[48]

The FMC was involved also in the Copperbelt, a place of great need and enormous opportunity, which lay along the border between Northern Rhodesia and what was then called the Belgian Congo. It was there as a member of the United Mission to the Copperbelt, which included the Universities Mission to Central Africa, the Methodist Missionary Society, the London Missionary Society, and the United Society for Christian Literature. There was the closest co-operation among those bodies, except that the UMCA had to work separately where churchmanship was concerned. In every other respect they worked as one body, even being joined by the Roman Catholics for educational work. The missionary staff were seconded by their societies or churches to serve in a team under the auspices of the British Committee in London and with the guidance of a Field Committee in Northern Rhodesia.

The Rev. George Fraser, the leader of the team, was seconded by the FMC. In an interview while on leave he appealed urgently for nine more missionaries to join the team – six men and three women. The fact alone that young men in their thousands were crowding into the Copperbelt from Northern Rhodesia, Nyasaland, Mozambique, Tanzania, other parts of Africa and from Europe, many of them staying for weeks or months and then moving on, made this a very important area for mission. The Commission indeed was led to make this observation about its significance: 'Without underrating the importance of the work in other areas we want to put on record our opinion that this is the place of supreme importance today for the Church to exert its most far-reaching influence on the Central Africa of tomorrow.'[49]

(c)

From Northern Rhodesia and Nyasaland, the Commission moved on to South Africa.

The work in which the FMC was involved was scattered over a very large area under three Provincial Administrations: the Transvaal, Natal and Cape Province. The South Africa Mission as a result found it difficult to work as a team, and their task was made all the more difficult by decentralisation through Governing Councils of Institutions such as Lovedale – one of the most distinguished institutions in South Africa – and through Hospital Boards. Difficult though its task was, the Mission Council however was the only body which could ensure some possibility of holding together the various interests, medical and educational, and of enabling the Bantu Presbyterian Church, with which the FMC worked, to influence policy for the upbuilding of the life of its people.

Among the many factors affecting the mission of the Church in South Africa, none was more pervasive and obvious than the grievously destructive phenomenon of racial discrimination. It cast its shadow everywhere. A statement by the South African Institute of Race Relations put the situation like this:

> In our view there are serious symptoms of mounting discontent .... In these circumstances it is clear to us that the Bantu people are not only losing patience with the responsible authorities, but, what is worse, they are losing confidence in the good faith of Europeans. We feel bound to issue a warning that, if the situation in the field of race relations is allowed to deteriorate further, it will before long reach a stage in which the voice of reason will not be heeded.[50]

The commissioners could see the effects of racism everywhere they went. 'It is literally impossible,' they wrote in their Report, 'for missionary and African to talk together, for Mission Council or Presbytery to meet for business without attitudes and actions being affected by the racial situation.' They could see the strain that all this was bringing upon both the European missionary and the African, but were encouraged nonetheless by what was being achieved by them together. In the view of the Commission, the racist situation suggested that 'the continued presence of the missionary in the African Church was more necessary than the FMC sometimes believed'.[51]

The Bantu Presbyterian Church was clear that it wanted more missionaries to work with it. In order to improve its administration, it was anxious to have a Church office set up in Umtata, and asked for a missionary to act as Secretary, the intention being that he would guide Assembly Committees and, among other things, have responsibility for Church finance. The Business Committee of the Assembly, and a number of Presbyteries, were asking too for more District Missionaries. The specific request was for one in each Presbytery.[52] In order further to encourage a closer relationship between Mission and Church, the Commission suggested that the Business Committee be enlarged to include three missionaries, one of whom might be the proposed Church Secretary.

In the light of the current serious shortage of ministers in the Bantu Presbyterian Church, the Commission discussed also the training of candidates for the ministry. At the time of the Commission's visit, one out of every ten of its central congregations was vacant. Fifteen new appointments were needed, but only three candidates were in training at Fort Hare. It was pointed out that the cost of training was a major problem, and that larger bursaries would go a long way to help. More basically, however, there was the obstacle to recruitment itself of the discouragingly low salary the Church was able to pay to men of suitable educational background.

In the work of the FMC in South Africa, well-established institutions of education and healing played a prominent part. The recognition of them as a public service by the State, and the consequent financial support they received from it, was a considerable benefit. The FMC's financial contribution had indeed become minimal. The institutions were now largely self-governing, and a large proportion of their staff were being recruited from South Africa and on normal professional terms. The FMC, however, continued to appoint the most senior staff, and therefore to influence policy.

The increasing size of the institutions and the fact of their support by Government led the Commission to question how far they had been able to maintain their specifically missionary character. In general the Commission would seem to have been satisfied on this account. Even Lovedale, the largest and most prestigious of all the institutions, well-known throughout Africa, and visited only that year by the King and Queen and the two princesses, which could well have been judged as most open to the possibility of losing its missionary characteristics, was still firmly the 'Missionary Educational Institution' at Lovedale.[53]

VI

The FMC began the post-war reassessment of its missionary task as soon as the war was over. A Deliverance of the General Assembly of 1945 on the Report of the FMC pointed to the decisive stage that had been reached in the missionary enterprise. George Gunn, the Convener of the FMC, writing immediately after that Assembly, expressed the concern of the Committee to awaken the Church to the urgency of the hour:

> There is now no time to be lost in getting ahead seriously with what is the Church's appointed business – to bring the Gospel, with all its individual and social implications, to 'all men in all the lands'. The Church must now play its part in the Christianizing of the recon-struction of the world …. No one else can or will play this part; and, if the Church does not do so, God's judgement upon the Church will be that it will have no choice but to retreat into the background of irrelevance and stagnation. It is not the first time in history that God has shown the miracle of His mercy by asking a weak Church to carry a new, heavy load.[54]

Two years later, in making what was widely regarded as one of the most notable Foreign Mission speeches ever made in the Assembly, George Gunn appealed to the whole Church to do its duty:

> The proverb about cutting our coat according to our cloth applies only if there is no more cloth. But there is money enough in the pockets of Church members not only to do what is now asked, but to sow the seed of truth in many wide areas we have not even touched. In some

minds there seems to be a most unfortunate and wholly misleading distinction between the Foreign Mission Committee and the Church as a whole, with a corresponding resentment when the Committee appeals to the Home Church to do its duty. But foreign missions are not just a fad of the Committee; and the full weight of responsibility must be laid where it properly belongs, upon the shoulders of the total membership of the Church.[55]

Although there was a positive response from the General Assembly to George Gunn's eloquently put challenge and appeal, it was clear from the way he argued, and from amendments to the Deliverances he supported, that there were differences of opinion in the Church about the Foreign Mission Committee's position.

At this stage in the Church of Scotland's foreign mission activity, questions were being asked about its place in the total life of the Church. Was it really as central as was being argued? Now that Christians in the 'mission fields' were claiming their independence and were assuming leadership, why was it necessary to continue to send missionaries?[56] In the light of all the demands, financial and otherwise, that were being made on the members of the Church at home, could the Church afford the luxury of this overseas commitment, even at the current level, never mind what was being projected?

However ill-informed some of the questioning might be, there was no doubt of the need to look afresh at the FMC's programme of work and at its priorities. There were many questions to be asked and many choices to be made. One of the major issues facing the FMC was the relative emphasis to be given to the increasingly costly programme of running Christian schools and colleges. Education played a very large part indeed in the FMC's work. The Committee was involved within Africa and Jamaica alone in over 2000 schools, and in the 18 'fields' in which the FMC worked it was involved in education at many different levels. In India, for example, missionaries were teaching in five Arts Colleges at University level, and in Manchuria and South India were engaged in the training of graduate doctors, and nurses. The administration of all those institutions made heavy demands on the time and energies of the missionaries, and the financial cost also was high. The question was asked about the relation of all this educational work to the central purpose of the mission. Was it necessary? What bearing did it have on the proclamation of the Faith and the building up of the Church?

There was no question about the cost of education to the FMC. It took up a considerable proportion of its resources, but it was, the General Secretary argued on the FMC's behalf, a crucial and central aspect of its work:

> The Church is surely right in giving much thought and effort to the provision of an education which deserves the name of Christian. It does so from a sound instinct ... because [Christianity] refuses to separate so-called secular from so-called religious knowledge .... It shows the Church's concern for man as a whole in society. It affirms by practical deeds the fundamental relatedness of the Gospel to every aspect of the community's life... In a word, it is the effort of the Church to reconcile the divided mind of western civilisation as it impinges on the life of Africa and Asia.[57]

In making no apology for the FMC's commitment of resources of personnel and money to education within the missionary task, Jim Dougall was consistent with the FMC's holistic view of mission, which he shared and did much to further.

This understanding of the wholeness of mission, expressed here in the holding together of the tension between evangelism and education, was also to be seen in the FMC's plea for mission to be regarded as one – at home and abroad. The Committee's concern, as its Report to the General Assembly made plain, was not to claim an exclusive share of the Church's attention on the grounds of its being the Foreign Mission Committee, but to help the Church to take the word and reality of mission into its daily consciousness and habitual attitude. Many in fact would gladly have dropped the word 'Foreign' altogether.[58] The Home Organisation Department of the FMC made every effort to emphasise those points in its publications and in the conferences it prepared; a task it patiently continued to pursue in the years that followed.

CHAPTER 3

Realignment and Retrenchment
(1948-1952)

I

THE world in which the FMC was at work during the five year period from 1948 was a world of violence. Everywhere, it was being said, there was an undertone of fear.

The period began with the death of Mohandas Karamachand Gandhi on 30 January 1948, at the hands of an assassin. Happening so soon after the traumatic events of India's partition and the genocidal massacres that followed, the violent death of Mahatma Gandhi, who had been an almost universal symbol of peace and reconciliation, had a profound and powerful effect.

Although Gandhi's death deeply affected first and foremost his own people, the consequences went far beyond India. Statesmen and other public figures across the world reacted to the news with tributes and appreciations. Gandhi had touched the conscience of millions, and his death had been widely sensed, in the strangest way, as having 'spiritual' significance. As a writer close to the events of that time wrote perceptively a few days after the assassination: 'The full meaning of his life may not be clear to many, but the importance of its mystery is recognised.'[1]

Many in India – Hindus, Muslims, and others – turned to the Christian community for comfort in their sense of bereavement. Principal Kellas of Scottish Church College, who was called upon to take part in several services in commemoration of Gandhi, wrote: 'It was to the Christians that Indians turned in the hour of their bewilderment and grief, and to the hymns of the Cross of Christ .... Never in our time have the Bible and Christ been so real in India. The people are looking to the Christians.'[2]

Many belonging to other faiths had seen in Christianity things that reminded them of Gandhi and his life, and were drawn to it. The selfless action of Christians, during the bloodletting in the cities, their protecting and sheltering of neighbours irrespective of religion, and their effective role as reconcilers, had helped in the eyes of many to make Christianity a more acceptable and valued part of Indian life.

Gandhi's practice and style of life had had a marked influence too on the Church and its mission. We shall have reason to comment on that later.

During this period, however, it is more the communism of Stalin and of Mao that will be before us, than the non-violence of Gandhi.

February saw the Soviet Union's takeover of Czecho-Slovakia, and in June began Stalin's blockade of the Western Sector of Berlin and the cutting of its electricity supply. There followed the remarkable Anglo-American airlift to Berlin, which continued night and day till May the following year. The forming of the West German State took place and the setting up of NATO. It was an anxious time, with the fear of war becoming daily more acute, a fear deepened by the news in 1949 that the Russians had the atomic bomb – they exploded their first in September of that year; and that the Americans were working on the hydrogen bomb, reputedly a thousand times more powerful than the bomb dropped on Hiroshima. Meanwhile in China, Mao Tse-tung, at the head of his communist army, at the beginning of November 1948 entered Mukden, and on the first of October a year later in Tienanmen Square, Peking, declared the establishment of the Chinese People's Republic.

A year late, Communist China, with a 'voluntary army', moved into Korea in support of the North Koreans, defeated a South Korean force supported by the United Nations. By the autumn of 1951 the United Nations forces re-established themselves on the 38th parallel, and armistice talks began. A tense period of virtual stalemate followed during which there was a distinct possibility that nuclear weapons would be used. Again the fear of world war rose to the surface. The General Assembly of 1953 was speaking of the dire threat of war.[3] In July 1953 the Korean war came to an end, though the tension between the North and the South continued.

Communism – Russian and Chinese – had become a major force in the world. The chairman of a General Assembly Commission on Communism made the point in presenting to the Assembly the Commission's Report. In his address he said:

There was in operation a global strategy which in 35 years had succeeded in dominating 800 million souls, a third of the world's population, and was busily engaged day by day in a coercive system of 're-education' of the masses in communal ideology.

There was a sense, perhaps a perverted sense, in which communism was the most vital and dynamic ecumenical movement in the world at present.[4]

Returning to 1948, there were the crucially important events in the Middle East when, as we have seen, the British Mandate over Palestine collapsed and it became essential to find a solution to the Arab-Jewish conflict. A plan was agreed by two-thirds of the membership of the UN, including the USA and USSR, to create separate Jewish and Arab States, and to give Jerusalem international status. The Arabs refused to accept the partition of what they regarded as their land, but the plan was accepted by the Jews.

Before the plan could be put into effect, conflict began between the two sides and continued over the remaining months of the Mandate. On 14 May 1948 the British High Commissioner, with the last of his staff, sailed from Palestine, and the Mandate ended. The State of Israel was proclaimed on that same day at a ceremony in Tel Aviv. Within eight hours of the launching of the new State military units from Jordan, Syria, Egypt, Lebanon and Iraq began to invade. The Arab armies had some early successes, but by the end the Israelis held a third more territory than they would have had if the original partition plan had been accepted. After a series of truces, hostilities finally ended in January 1949. Although open warfare ceased, there was no real peace. Propaganda war and terrorist and counter terrorist attacks continued.

In Africa during this period there was an increasingly strong movement towards independence in several countries where the FMC was involved. There was also in some places a marked increase in racial tension. In February 1948, with serious riots in the Gold Coast, the official inquiry gave as the underlying cause African frustration with the slowness of change, recommending rapid advance toward responsible government. In 1949 the Governor set up a committee under Mr Justice Coussey to devise a new constitution to that end. The new constitution, as recommended in the Coussey Report published in 1950, was accepted. The Legislative Assembly was to be wholly elected, and the Executive Council, to operate ministerially, was to have a large African majority in its membership.

Kwame Nkrumah, with his new Convention People's Party (CPP), which he set up in the middle of 1949, protested against the

revised constitution, declaring that nothing short of self-government *now*[5] would do. During disturbances in January 1950,
Nkrumah was arrested for sedition. When the CPP was returned
with overwhelming popular support in the election held under the
new constitution in 1951, Nkrumah was released and he and his
colleagues given leading posts in the new administration.

In nearby Nigeria the movement toward independence was
more gradual. Its size, the differences among its three regions, and
the need to balance their interests, necessitated the development
stage by stage of a federal system, with autonomy in the regions. A
federal constitution came into effect on 29 February 1952, having
an elected Assembly with an African majority. Under the new
constitution Sir Francis Ibiam, as he was styled at that time, and
who served as a missionary doctor in the Calabar Mission, was
elected a member of the Eastern House of Representatives.

In 1952 Central African Federation – the proposed federation of
Nyasaland, Northern Rhodesia and Southern Rhodesia – which was
being vigorously opposed by African interests, became a pressing
issue. Since the Church of Scotland was directly involved in the
protests against Federation, the matter deserves detailed discussion;
we merely refer to it at this point.

There was a close connection between the movement for
Federation in Central Africa, supported by European settlers in
Southern Rhodesia, and the situation which led in 1952 to the
declaration of the Emergency in Kenya. As in Southern Rhodesia,
many of the settlers in Kenya were convinced of their right to direct
and control affairs. Some among them spoke of an East and Central
African Federation under European leadership.[6] Their entrenched
power, their often arrogant assumption of privilege, along with
what was felt as the painfully slow progress toward Kenyan independence, and above all the continuing occupation by settlers of
territory the Kikuyu regarded as their ancestral lands, in what had
come to be known as the White Highlands, made the violence
that brought so much suffering virtually inevitable.

It is sad to note that the system of 'enclosure' begun in the 1930s,
which had the effect of preventing Africans from farming or living
in their own lands except as labourers, was not recognised at the
time as being morally reprehensible. It has to be noted too that it
was not immediately seen to have been one of the causes of Mau
Mau, among the complexity of factors involved.

Racism, obvious enough in much of the support given to Central African Federation, and in Kenya, was blatantly present in the thinking, attitudes, and actions of the National Government that came into power in South Africa in May 1948 under Dr D. F. Malan. From that time on South Africa was to follow a policy of apartheid and of domination by the white 20 per cent of the population.

In line with its policy, Malan's Government passed, as early as 1949, the Prohibition of Mixed Marriages Act, which made marriage between whites and non-whites illegal. The Population Registration Act was passed in 1950, which set guidelines for deciding a person's race. In the same year there was the Immorality Amendment Act that extended the prohibition on sex between whites and Africans to include sex between whites and all non-whites, and the Suppression of Communism Act, which gave enormous powers to the Minister of Justice. Finally, again in 1950, the Group Areas Act was passed, legislating for the residential separation of the races, seen by many as the cornerstone of apartheid.

II

Against the background of a world torn apart, socially and internationally, by destructive divisions, by strife and violence, with the threat of war never absent, and the effects of World War II still present, the coming into being of the World Council of Churches (WCC), inaugurated in Amsterdam on 23 August 1948, was seen by many, in the Churches and beyond, as a sign of hope. The World Council of Churches brought together 147 Churches, from 42 different nations, many of which had been enemies in the recent war. 'The great new fact of our era', to which Archbishop Temple had referred in his enthronement sermon, had become visible. The Church was now seen to be worldwide as never before, with a structure of unity that might well enable it to witness, in unity, and service worldwide, and to bring reconciliation in the name of its Lord.

Although the importance of what took place in Amsterdam in 1948 was obvious and few would have wished to deny that it was a 'historic hour',[7] contemporary descriptions of the event were notably restrained. At the meeting itself there were those who were disappointed by the lack of speeches that might have expressed the greatness of the hour and caught the imagination. It was, however, a meeting with an immediate practical objective, which required more than anything a realistic and matter-of-fact approach.[8] The representatives of the Churches were there to look together at the nature of their calling as Church, and to see how best to fulfil that calling together. In the end they had covenanted with one another in fresh commitment to God, and declared their intention to stay together.

Amsterdam will be remembered for many things: for the 'battle of the titans' – the controversy between Karl Barth and Reinhold Niebuhr about theology in the context of society and politics;[9] for important statements about racism; and about the just war; but without doubt it will be remembered most for the very fact alone that men and women representing Churches in many different nations, of different denominations and confessions, which had for so long misrepresented and misunderstood one another, had met and agreed to go forward together.

Amsterdam was a significant beginning, but it was only a beginning, and there was a long way to go. To those who were from what came to be called the Third World – they were a small minority of the membership – the Assembly was parochially Western. Its programme, reflecting the interests of the Older Churches and the post-war problems of the West, failed to take seriously the needs and interests of other continents.

Although there were a number of distinguished leaders attending from outside the West, they found it difficult to get the hearing the contributions they could have made and which their presence deserved. The fact that their experience in practice of ecumenicity – unity and mission – outstripped that of most people from the West went unrecognised. Many had served in ecumenical institutions, and in Christian Councils where Churches of different traditions had worked harmoniously together for years, and of course some were themselves members of united Churches, including the Church of South India (CSI). It was no wonder that many of them were impatient with what they saw as the complacency and backwardness of some of the thinking that took place in the sections and was reflected in reports.[10]

Many from the Third World left Amsterdam at the end of the Assembly feeling that somehow they were out of place there, that they were pressed into a mould of thought, political and theological, that was unreal and had little validity for them. All along indeed they felt that the WCC failed to take the world outside Europe and America seriously. They were not included in the planning committees that had been working since 1937, and they were afraid that the WCC would go its own way without learning from the insights of the Third World, and of the missionary movement.[11]

The General Secretary of the FMC, Jim Dougall, was one of the delegates from the Church of Scotland to the First Assembly of the WCC. In an article he wrote on his return he confirmed the opinion that the WCC was a 'predominantly Western institution':

> In theological scholarship, political interest ... the WCC was thinking in terms of Europe and America. The East meant Russia, not China or India, for most of the delegates who met in Amsterdam. Communism was the Soviet threat to Berlin or the paralysis of the free society in other parts of Europe.[12]

He wanted to point out, however, on the positive side, the presence of delegates, many for the first time of the Younger Churches in a worldwide gathering of Churches, and the useful contribution they made: 'They counted a lot by their presence, and when they spoke they were listened to with attention.'

For him and so many others, the International Meeting at Whitby in 1947 – the year before the WCC Assembly – had opened up a vision of Churches across the world working together in mission as partners. Many delegates at this critical moment after the war recognised that the opportunities for mission were immense. The next few years were crucial and everything possible had to be done to develop partnership and to strengthen the Churches newly emerging from the work of the missionary bodies of the West.[13]

Some in the missionary movement were afraid that the coming into being of the WCC would bring a static and institutional element which would weaken the dynamic that was so much part of the activity of mission. On his part Jim Dougall could see the danger, but nonetheless recognised in the formation of the WCC a new opportunity, as he put it, to 'overcome the dualism which relegates missions to one group while the Church as a whole goes on as before'. If those with a vision of mission played their part within the WCC, then the danger could be overcome.

The FMC, as a committee of the Church of Scotland, was influenced in the most direct way by both the IMC and WCC, on both of which it was represented. Against the background of those international meetings the FMC had renewed its efforts to encourage the Church at home to enter with new urgency into mission worldwide, within the worldwide Church, and this in face of the daunting fact that neither the number of missionaries nor the full financial support for which it appealed to the Church was forthcoming. The FMC recognised too that it had to come to terms itself with what only slowly began to be seen as a whole new understanding of mission, in which Western based Churches and societies would no longer hold the pivotal position they had held for so long.

In 1950 the FMC appointed a group to reflect on those factors and other practical missiological issues, including the centrality of the Church and the primacy of evangelism. The group prepared a Statement of Policy (FMC Minute 522) reassessing the work being done and proposing Realignment.

The Statement, having been put before various meetings in India during the visit of the Delegation to which we shall refer, was presented to the General Assembly in 1952.

While continuing to give priority to the role of the missionary, the Policy Statement emphasised the central place of the indigenous Church in the carrying out of evangelism. Special importance was to be given to the training of the membership of the Church locally, and to the theological education of the ministers. At the same time serious notice was to be given to the ongoing debate about the part the institutions should play if new weight was to be given to the Church and evangelism.

In the discussions leading to the Statement there emerged also the importance of unity and necessity to see its relevance for mission:[14]

> Competing congregations in the same town or countryside,' it was being said, 'may be a scandal in the literal sense of the word. If we at home do not feel it so, it may be because we have not had laid upon us the burden and constraint which is felt by the Church when it is alive to the hunger and need of the non-Christian world at its doors.[15]

The point that mission and unity must be seen together was a major concern of the next IMC meeting, which was held at Willingen, Germany, in July 1952, where related topics were the local Indigenous Church and the Missionary Calling.

At that conference the voice of Christians coming from outside the West was heard more loudly than four years before in Amsterdam. In an independent statement, they made clear that they were uneasy about the way in which the words 'Mission' and 'Church' continued to be used in the West, and sensed that attitudes were more unchanged than would appear: 'We should cease to speak of *missions* and *churches*,' they said, 'and avoid this dichotomy not only in our thinking but also in our actions. We should now speak about the mission of the Church.'[16]

It was a crucially important point that was being made, and one that revealed the long way that the Churches and missionary bodies in the West had to go in understanding and practice.

Willingen in hindsight can be seen to have been a conference of great significance for theological reflection on the nature of Church and Mission, and for missionary practice. Its affirmation, for example, that the missionary movement has its source in the Triune God himself,[17] has been determinative of much later thinking which has emphasised that mission is the Mission of God, the *Missio Dei,* and that mission belongs to the very being of the Church itself. The statement of Willingen that 'there is no participation in Christ without participation in his mission to the world', has been remembered – and forgotten – many time down the years.[18]

In this period of influential conferences, mention must be made of two student conferences run by the Student Christian Movement (SCM), which were to have long lasting effects. The first, following a tradition of large quadrennials, took place in Central Hall, Westminster, in 1948, bringing together 2700 delegates from 33 different countries with a panel of speakers which included Bishop Hans Lilje, Pastor Niemoller, Reinhold Niebuhr, Visser t' Hooft and M. M. Thomas; and the second, a Scottish Conference which included Lesslie Newbigin, Bill Stewart, David Carmichael, and Keith Bridston, was held at Wiston, near Biggar, in 1952. At that time the SCM was to a considerable extent in the van of ecumenical thinking and practice, and many who were present at one or other of those conferences played their part in the cause of unity and mission in the years that followed.

III

The visit of a delegation to India and Pakistan was an important stage in the realignment process of the FMC. The delegation arrived in Bombay on 8 October 1950, and left the Indian subcontinent in March 1951. It consisted of Jim Dougall, Betty Walls, Associate General Secretary, and John Kent, a parish minister and the Joint Convener of the Asia–Sub Committee. During their visit the Statement of Policy[19] was widely discussed with individuals and groups, with the intention of its being interpreted, developed and tested, before being generally applied.

By this time in India and Pakistan it was clear that the era of foreign missions, led by missionaries from abroad, was on the way out. Progress toward integration, as agreed at the Nagpur Conference of 1947, was now well advanced. Mission Councils, one by one, had formally agreed to integration and were implementing it step by step. For example, in Madras by October 1948, Boards and Committees of the Diocesan Council had been set up ready to do the work of the Mission Council when integration came into force;[20] the Constitution of the Board of the Santal Church Council[21] was given approval by the FMC in February 1950. In October 1952 the Bengal Church Council of the United Church of Northern India assumed responsibility for the work of the Mission Councils of the London Missionary Society and the Church of Scotland.[22]

The visits of the delegates took them to Western India, the Punjab, Rajputana, Madras, Calcutta, Santalia, Eastern Himalaya, and Nagpur, enabling them to meet the missionaries and representatives of the Indian Christian community, and of seeing the life of congregations, and the working of institutions at first hand. In Nagpur they attended the triennial meetings of the National Christian Council of India; in the Punjab, in Ludhiana, the General Assembly of the United Church of Northern India; and in the South, the Madras Diocesan Council of the Church of South India; all of them meetings which helped them to hear the views of Church leaders, and to take part in policy discussion.[23]

The delegates were impressed by the Church in the places they visited. Despite the many problems it faced – in the South, famine; in the North, flood; in Hyderabad State, war – the Church was patently alive, well, and in some areas, such as Madras and Jalna, growing rapidly.

By the public at large, and to a considerable extent by the Church itself, it was 'the Mission', however, that was seen as important. The institution, regarded by most as 'the Mission', overshadowed the Church; and the Church, if not actually despised, as it largely was by the general public, was certainly not given the respect that was its due.

The delegation, and the Church leaders whom they met, shared the position taken by the Policy Commission about the centrality of the Church. The educational and medical institutions had a very important part to play, but in no way could they be allowed to take over the rightful place of the Church.

A question was being asked about the effectiveness of the institutions, and about the high proportion of the FMC's resources – of its personnel's time and energy, and of its finance – that was absorbed by them. The conclusion was reached that it was essential for their effectiveness as instruments of the Gospel that they should have as high a staff ratio of Christian to non-Christian as possible, and as far as the schools were concerned should have a high proportion of both Christian staff and students. As it was, to call many of the institutions 'Christian' was, it was thought, to stretch the word too far. In the Sialkot area of Pakistan, for instance, there were five boys' high schools with a roll of more than 3000, of whom less than 500 were Christian;[24] and in the Madras area, outside the city itself, there was a similar situation.[25] Overall, in those and in other areas, very often less than half the staff would be Christian.

The delegation expressed its conviction that the answer lay in the closure of many schools and a concentration on a few. They believed this would not only make a lively Christian influence in a school more possible, but would also involve a considerable saving of money, and the setting of more people free from the extra burden of administration.[26]

The delegation made a similar kind of judgement about the colleges. It seemed clear to them that it was necessary to make every effort to make those institutions clearly and unambiguously Christian, by cutting down the number of students, and increasing the proportion of Christian staff.[27]

Many of the recommendations that the delegation made were on the face of it sensible. The trouble was, however, that many factors obvious to those most involved at local level were not adequately taken into account, and that the proposed scheme was in practice inoperable. Sometimes that was made clear in discussion, but not always. More often than not the delegation may have heard a 'yes', when 'yes' in practice was not intended.

Although the thinking that led to the policy of realignment had taken – with the utmost seriousness and respect – the identity of the Indian Church, and the need to move away from a foreign mission centred and managed operation to one centred in the Indian Church, in practice the influence of old habits got in the way. There are not a few references to our schools, our colleges, our hospitals, where a lapse into old mission thinking might be suspected.

In the event many schools were closed, and with the agreement of local churches. Often that was done with much reluctance, but in the end seen to be both inevitable on economic grounds alone, and sensible from the point of view of Christian education.

Since what most people saw of the FMC's policy of realignment was the closure of one school after another, for many people in the churches in India that policy looked more like retrenchment. It could hardly have been otherwise. And the same was true of general opinion in Scotland. The FMC was faced with the difficult task not just of communication but of implementing its own affirmations.

IV

While the FMC was engaged in the course of its policy realignment, its work in China, one of the three major areas of its involvement, was becoming increasingly problematic, and by the time the delegation to India had finished its business, the last of the missionaries to China had returned home.

Events in China were in the mind of the policy group, and of the delegation to India. The importance that had been placed over the years on the institutions within the missionary enterprise in China, as elsewhere, and their collapse under the Chinese communist Government, raised questions about the overall policy of the western missionary movement, and about the FMC's current responsibilities and attitudes with regard both to institutions and the building up of the Church in all the countries where it was at work.

The end, as it could be thought to be, of the FMC's work in China, reinforced the view of those who were already arguing that the end of the missionary movement had come, or at the very least was in sight. The FMC had the onerous task of making plain that realignment marked a new and positive stage, that its work was not being run down, and that retrenchment was not in its mind.

In Mukden during the early months of 1948, the missionaries maintained as normal a routine as possible. The Missionary Conference met eight times in the year to conduct its business, giving the January meeting over to the discussion of the Whitby Conference.[28]

By May, however, serious consideration was being given to a possible evacuation before the arrival of the Communist army. On 26 May, after discussion with Chinese colleagues, it was decided that there should be a partial withdrawal of missionaries.[29] By the end of October the Medical College authorities had made plans to move the College to Wuchan,[30] and John Fleming had written to the FMC for a capital grant to cover the expenses of the move.[31] But that decision came too late. Very soon after, Mukden fell to the Communists, and on 2 November 'the Army of Liberation' entered the city. At that time there were eleven Church of Scotland missionaries and their wives present in Mukden, and five from the Presbyterian Church in Ireland.[32]

Meanwhile in Ichang the work of the missionaries went on. Mission Council meeting on 9 October reported on the completion of a building at St Andrews school to be used as a senior middle school. There had been correspondence with the FMC about the middle school development at St Andrew's and about a further one at Iona School. The Council, which had been promised recognition of the schools by the Government, pending the completion of registration, asked the FMC for their support. The FMC's reply was that they should not begin new permanent work in the present situation.[33]

At the same meeting it was reported that the Executive Committee had appointed the Secretary of the Mission Council to be a fraternal delegate at the General Assembly of the Church of Christ in China, which was to meet in Foochow from 18-20 October. At a later meeting of the Council, it was reported that the Assembly had met, and that there had been a delegation of 200 drawn from all over China, most of whom were Chinese.[34]

In April 1949 the Mission Council requested the appointment of four new missionaries[35] and at the same time repeated the request that the FMC support the development of middle schools.[36] The FMC acceded to neither.

Just before the General Assembly of 1949 the FMC received a letter from Ichang saying that the military were evacuating.[37] This was followed by a second letter, dated 22 May, which spoke of the missionaries being cheered by fresh accessions to the Church in Ichang, and by rising standards of Christian giving. It said also that the city was still in Nationalist hands. In July of that year Ichang fell to the Communists.[38]

In Mukden after the communists entered, and for most of 1949, the missionaries believed that they would be able to carry on their work within the framework of the new society. As conditions became much easier in the city, food more plentiful and cheaper, and fuel available once more, there was a feeling of normality. As late as May, for example, missionaries were still serving in the Medical College Hospital.[39] It was not until the autumn of 1949 that it became clear that things were going to be difficult for the Church. It became obvious that there would be serious interference with medical and educational work, and that soon all the institutions would cease to be run by the Church or Mission. In October 1949 it was reported that the Government was going to amalgamate the Christian Medical College with the former Japanese Medical College,[40] and by the end of the year in East Mukden, the Medical College and Hospital and the Girls' School were out of the hands of the missionaries. There was not, however, an immediate universal clampdown. In West Mukden the Boys' School continued, the Woman's Clinic under Rose and Mary Findlay (mother and daughter) developed into a small hospital, and the Theological College set up extra courses.[41]

The Church during this period – 1949 and onwards into 1950 – was described as being very much alive. Although in the countryside churches had closed down, and Christians were worshipping in house groups, in the city there were six presbyterian churches open, with as many as 700 to 1000 present on Sundays in one of them.[42]

At a meeting of the Conference in July, the opinion was unanimously expressed that the presence of a group of missionaries was not a serious embarrassment to the Church. However, at a meeting the following month, Jean McMinn reported that she felt that her presence in the hospital was not helpful to her Chinese colleagues and friends. At the same time, Tom Blakely proposed to send a tentative offer of resignation to test whether the College authorities wanted his services or not.[43]

At the end of March 1950 it was formally recognised at a meeting of the Joint Central Committee for Scotland of the China Christian Universities Association and Moukden Medical College, that the joint control of the College and Hospital by Church and Government, as agreed, had not been effective, that the institution was no longer being conducted under its previous constitution, and was in fact no longer a centre of Christian missionary activity.[44]

In a letter dated 1 May, John Fleming wrote saying that local opinion was tending to the view that the missionaries should leave Manchuria. The reply from the FMC was that they should return home by the summer.[45] On 1 July 1950 the Standing Committee of the Synod met and decided to advise the withdrawal of the remaining missionaries.[46] Less than six weeks later, on 29 August, the missionaries left Mukden. The six remaining missionaries were: Mrs Rose Findlay and Dr Mary Findlay, the Rev. and Mrs John Fleming with their baby daughter, Miss Janie Henderson and the Rev. Jack Weir.

In Ichang, as in Mukden, the soldiers who entered the city were well-disciplined, and there was no interference with the right to worship. The worship hall was left alone, and church activities continued. The middle schools were closed, but two of the primary schools continued under the Council. The hospitals were allowed to carry on, and missionaries continued to serve in them.[47]

In July 1950 the Mission Council approved a proposal to restart a School of Nursing, or at least Nurses' Training Classes.[48] At a subsequent meeting a fortnight later, it was agreed that responsibility for work formerly done by the Council should in future be undertaken by the Presbytery.[49] At its meeting on 4 December 1950, the closure of the Council was agreed.[50] In the same month the FMC sent a letter advising the missionaries in Ichang to make preparations to leave by the end of the year if possible, and at the latest by the end of January 1951.[51]

On 25 February 1951 the FMC received a letter from the Church of Christ in China expressing gratitude for what it had received from the Church abroad through the years – a letter of 'thank you and farewell'.[52]

It was the end of the missionary enterprise as it operated in

China. Decisions would now no longer be made in Scotland, or elsewhere outside China, about its institutions, or about Chinese staff and congregations. It was the beginning of the new stage in the life of the Chinese Church marked by the Three Self-Patriotic Movement, initiated by the Christian Manifesto of July 1950, setting the goal of a self-governing, self-supporting, self-propagating Church.

V

The situation in Africa at this time, from the point of view of the FMC's operations, was in marked contrast to that in China or in India. Although the movement toward independence was gathering momentum, the various countries in which the FMC worked, not counting South Africa, were still under the Colonial Office, which could be depended upon to provide support, and considerable financial and other help, with the running of institutions of service, such as schools and hospitals.

It was a critical time just because of the close ties between the missionary movement and the Colonial Government. On the one hand there were obvious advantages in a co-operation that enabled institutions to continue to be run without interference under Christian auspices. On the other hand, however, there was clear warning that dependence on resources from beyond the Churches was not something that could continue much longer, and that very soon the Churches would have to come to terms with a situation for which they were ill-prepared, in which they would have to find their own resources, or be deprived of the direct involvement in the education of their youth.

(a)

In West Africa the pressure was on for more and better education, and the Colonial Office responded. Two university colleges were founded in 1948, one in Nigeria and the other in the Gold Coast. New secondary schools were started, and funds were offered to missionary bodies if they would in their turn send staff. It soon became obvious, however, that that was going to be a major problem for the FMC. Considerable efforts were made to recruit staff, but with little success. In the last two years – from 1947-48, for example – no male teachers had offered to serve.[53]

In the Gold Coast, where in 1942 a decision was reached to increase the number of children in schools by five times in the following ten years, there was discussion in 1948, though inconclusive, whether to maintain the number of schools already there by that stage.[54] At the same time the FMC had to turn down a request that it start dispensaries run by nurses, again because of shortage of staff.

The place of the Church in the furtherance of education in the Gold Coast continued to be a matter of great concern, as in other parts of Africa.[55] It had begun to be recognised that it might soon be impossible for the churches to control schools in the direct way they had in the past. Shortage of staff was not the least of the difficulties. Under a colonial system, Government increasingly played a dominant role and gave proportionally more in grants for the payment of teachers than did the missionary bodies. Then with the fast approach of independence, it became clear that if the Church were to influence the schooling of young people, it would have to find a way of working in co-operation with the secular powers. The Coussey Report, which was published in the course of 1949, had proposed that all primary schools be brought under the control of local Government authorities. Up until that time most schools had been Church schools, receiving Government grants. In 1948, at the beginning of this period under review, over 90 per cent of all educational work was being done by missions or churches.[56]

Plans by the new Government for educational development, which took effect from the beginning of 1952, included a great expansion of teacher training. Notification was given that there were to be ten new colleges, none of which would be Church colleges; although, if the Churches were able to provide principals and staff for five of the colleges, the arrangement would be for those colleges to have an informal relation with them. The Churches welcomed the energetic interest of the new Government in education, but could see the danger of the quality of education suffering. As far as teacher training was concerned, the FMC agreed to staff being seconded, but only on specified conditions.[57]

At the FMC's African Education Conference, held in Edinburgh in 1949, the point was made that energy that properly should be given to the nourishing and growth of the Church, and its expansion in evangelism, was being given to the running of schools. There was a grave danger that when children left school there might be no vital Church to receive them.[58]

Deciding priorities was a major preoccupation during this period. Not only was there a conflict of claims between education and the needs of the Church, but there were also difficult decisions to be made about the life of the Church itself, and the resources needed for its outreach.

The crowding into the gold fields of Ashanti and the larger towns of workers from the North drew attention to the needs of the people in that area, and the importance of the Church becoming involved.[59] The Basel Mission was already committed, and hoped that the FMC would help. In May 1949 the Mission Council received a request from the Basel Mission for a missionary to relieve one of theirs when his furlough was due. This was in the Northern Territories at Salaga, where they had recently started new work.[60] The Mission Council agreed that that be done. Ideally what was required was the appointment of two ordained ministers, one for the northern territories, and another to work with pastors in the Gold Coast itself, and that proposal they put before the FMC. The FMC's response was for one of the present staff to be relocated to Church work, while indicating at the same time that in the present circumstances it had no funds or staff for work in new territory. At its meeting in October 1949, the FMC agreed that a missionary who had been on the staff of Akropong Training College should work on Christian literature, and work also with pastors in one Presbytery.[61]

In 1950 the Mission Council appealed to the FMC to have a member of staff appointed to work in the North. The tug-of-war over priorities, however, continued. Even as it was asking for help with that work of outreach, it was requesting scholarships for Gold Coast ministers to study in Scotland, and was indicating that if FMC funds would not stretch to both, then 'Council would choose the scholarships as the better way … of strengthening the Church'.[62]

Much attention was being given to theological education and the training of the ministry at this time. One of the issues considered was whether the Churches should press for a faculty of theology in the new University College of the Gold Coast. Professor Norman Porteous,[63] who had been commissioned as a consultant, was of the opinion that it would be advisable, as a first stage, for a department of religion to be set up, which would provide the nucleus for a faculty of theology to be formed later. In the event the decision was for a faculty of theology. At the end of 1951 it was agreed that Trinity College, the joint theological college run in co-operation with the Methodists, should move to new buildings near the new University College.[64]

Meanwhile the place of the Gold Coast Mission Council in the new climate of independence in both Church and State was under discussion. In September 1952 the Mission Council was dissolved.[65] Although the FMC, in response to a question from the Synod Committee of the Gold Coast Presbyterian Church, agreed that the Synod had a right to correspond direct with the Church of Scotland (which was seen as an indication that the Church was no longer under the Mission), it made it plain that in practice communication would be more convenient through a Field Representative of the FMC. Another indication of the desire of the Church to ensure that it was no longer to be regarded as a subsidiary of the Mission was to be seen in questions raised about the stationing of missionaries, which the Synod Committee regarded as a matter internal to the Church.[66]

It was during this period following the abolition of the Mission Council that the Church moved ahead to a fuller real autonomy. The training overseas of Africans for senior administrative posts was bearing fruit. The first African General Manager of Schools was appointed in 1951, and African Supervisors of Schools and future heads of Colleges and Secondary Schools were being prepared or had already been prepared. The African Synod Clerk, the Rev C. H. Clerk, was showing through his personal influence that it was no longer appropriate for missionaries to exercise a control that properly belonged to the African Church.

(b)

In Nigeria, as in the Gold Coast, education was a dominant concern, and there was the same tension that we have seen between education and evangelism. The British Government's policy of encouraging the rapid growth of education in the colonies was increasing the pressure on district missionaries. They were already overburdened with administration, and now had extra management

responsibilities laid upon them. The shortage of district missionaries, and the continuing failure to attract recruits, added to the
problem. It was becoming clear that the running of schools made
such heavy demands on a diminishing missionary staff that there
was less time for the Church to be given the attention it required for
its growth and the deepening of its life.

The many changes taking place in Calabar, although recognised
as having long term advantage, did not make matters any easier. The
reorganisation of the Mission into districts to conform more closely
to the provisions of a Government education ordinance,[67] increased
the burden of the missionaries, while a considerable building
programme also absorbed much time and energy.

The Hope Waddell Training Institution had development plans
for both the school and the industrial department, and was considering the gradual replacing of existing buildings, which were by
now old and in bad condition. Staff shortages at Hope Waddell,
as elsewhere, were a cause of much concern. The failure, for example,
of the FMC to recruit a bursar for the institution was seen as a
major factor leading to student disturbances in 1950. A revised
constitution for Hope Waddell was passed in 1952, which included as
members of the Board a representative of the Synod of the Presbyterian Church of Biafra, and two persons appointed by the
Director of Education.[68] The Rev. John Beattie at this time took
over as Principal from the Rev. Norman Macrae.

Shortage of missionary staff affected every aspect of the work
of mission. The hospitals, including the Itu Leper Colony, for
instance, needed more[69] doctors, and there was a threat of a general
hospital having to be closed in order to fill a furlough vacancy at
Itu. The Leprosy Scheme, included in the development at Ogoja,
which the Government was prepared to support with a grant of
£10,000, might well have come to nothing for lack of staff, if the
Mission Council had not pressed as hard as it did for the scheme to
go through.

At the end of May 1949, the Rev. Neil Bernard, then Men's
Candidates Secretary, was sent as a special commissioner to Calabar
for a period of six months to help Mission Council and the
Education Authority deal with the reorganisation mentioned above,
bearing in mind the urgent problem of staffing.[70] During the course
of his visit, Neil Bernard's remit was extended to include the
medical work of the Mission, and his report includes a section

dealing with it. He was also asked to advise on the Hope Waddell Institute. His Report to the FMC on his return described organisational changes that had been agreed, which were acceptable to the Education Authority, which would ease the burden on missionaries, and would enable wider participation on the part of African pastors and teachers. In this period the Rev. A. K. Mincher served as Manager of Schools, and the Rev. A. G. Somerville as Secretary of the Mission Council, and Clerk to the Synod.[71]

Not unexpectedly, in the light of the movement toward independence in Nigeria, and the cry for self-government now, there was a growing feeling in the Church that Africans should have a greater say in the management of its affairs, and in the running of the schools. Neil Bernard, in his Report, said that he was hearing people in the Church expressing their feelings in this kind of way: 'The Church was independent, but this was just a mockery as they had neither cash nor property; co-operation between Education Authority and the Church was weak, missionaries showed that the Church was inferior by refusing to become ministers and members, and they showed they were more interested in Mission than in Church.'[72] It was, however, to be recognise that there were missionaries actively working for a proper and realistic sharing of responsibility with the African Church.

(c)

By 1948 the Regional Committee for Central Africa had begun to operate. It had recently been set up to co-ordinate the work in Northern Rhodesia and Nyasaland, to prepare for the formation of a single Church in central Africa, and not least to ensure that Government heard from the Church one voice only.[73] The Rev. Andrew Doig temporarily took over the duties of secretary from Douglas Benzies, who took ill in February, having barely arrived in Blantyre, and who tragically died five months later.[74] Neil Bernard became the secretary at the time of the General Assembly of 1950.

The Regional Committee came into being at a critical time for mission in Central Africa. Important decisions had to be made about schools and hospitals and the integration of Church and Mission. There was also the issue of relations with Government which crucially affected Mission policy, and began to be an overarching consideration as the process toward Central African Federation accelerated.

The Government's increasing of salaries of certificated teachers led to serious difficulties for the FMC. The budget could not meet that extra expenditure, and so, in Livingstonia (Nyasaland) alone, ten out of 15 schools formerly supported by mission grants were closed,[75] and in Blantyre a further reduction of educational work was declared inevitable.[76] In a submission to Government, the Nyasaland Christian Council stated that if the Government was truly in agreement that success in education depended on close collaboration between the Missions and itself, then adequate funding would have to be given to cover the salaries of teachers, both African and European.[77]

In the course of much discussion on policy, it was originally thought in Livingstonia (Rhodesia) that the missionary contribution to education should be directed to the post-primary stage, with the Government assuming responsibility for all primary education, thus leaving the Church of Scotland free to concentrate on secondary schools.[78] A year later, however, that view changed, and the Mission Council was now saying that primary education should not, to the contrary, be handed over to Government, or to native authorities, but eventually to the Church, the reasons given being that the Government had no effective plans for handing over, and that the proposal to hand over to native authorities was not practical.[79]

At a meeting of the Regional Committee, held in September 1949, endorsement was given to recommendations of the Blantyre Mission Council[80] that the whole of the present school system be regarded as the concern of the Church, and that the Mission allocate a block grant to cover the cost, the amount gradually being reduced as the Church increasingly contributed. At that meeting it was further agreed, in line with recommendations of the Blantyre Mission Council, and of the Livingstonia Mission Councils,[81] that an educational secretary be appointed, an appointment for which the Government was pressing and for which it was prepared to pay. The intention of the appointment was, among other things, to help plan educational development as a whole, and to liaise with Government. The FMC, which had at first refused the request for such an appointment, finally agreed, and an appointment was made.[82]

In July 1950 the Blantyre Presbytery took a decision to set up an Education Board.[83] Three years later the Mission Council of

Blantyre indicated its willingness to hand over its educational functions to the Presbytery, the understanding being that some matters, including finance, be reserved for its final decision.[84]

In Central Africa, as in other parts of Africa, the enormous demand for education – the pressure that was on for more and better schools – was matched by no less a heavy demand for medical provision, for hospitals and clinics. The Government, under pressure to provide the medical care that people wanted and needed, looked to the Missions for their co-operation. The Commission sent by the FMC to Central Africa had in its report on medical work stressed the need to fit into the general plans for the territories. There was so much work to be done that there could be no overlapping. Collaboration being of the essence, the Missions on their part would work with the Government, and would hope for funding from it to enable them to do so effectively.

Although the expectation was that medical missions would continue to have a place, and that there would be increased Government support, hard decisions, the Commission pointed out, would have to be made about priorities, both because of the FMC's limited resources and the increasing cost of equipping and running hospitals. A choice might well have to be made between doing a few things well and attempting more things badly. The Commission's Report suggested the most suitable use to be made of present hospitals, and went on to say that one of the best services Missions could offer would be 'to increase and improve the training of dispensers, midwives and nurses'.[85]

Relations between the FMC and the Government medical departments in Northern Rhodesia and Nyasaland, and between the FMC and its missionary staff in connection with medical policy, were often strained. The FMC had to ensure that its scarce resources were not dissipated but used to the best advantage for the development of the Church and its mission. In its turn the Government's position was that it could not take financial responsibility for all the work of the Missions that could be regarded as medically essential;[86] while the doctors and nurses who were faced day by day with human need saw every attempt to weaken their work in any way, or to close their institutions, or to hold back funding, as something to be vigorously resisted. As far as they were concerned, policymakers not directly involved in the life and death issues with which they were involved had the least right to make such decisions.

The controversy that arose about the hospitals at Mwenzo, Lubwa, and Chitambo in Northern Rhodesia, provides a good illustration of the kind of tensions that occurred. In the section of the Commission's Report where those hospitals were discussed,[87] it was pointed out that only the hospital in Mwenzo would be included in the Government's medical plan, and since both the hospital in Lubwa and that in Chitambo would be excluded, for the FMC to maintain doctors there permanently and meet the financial cost would be to make impossible other commitments. The opinion of the Livingstonia Mission Council (R)[88] was that the policy agreed to by the FMC Commission and the Government should be revised. The Council asserted that the Government plan put before the Commission, which included the setting up of a hospital at Serenje and at other places, had been altered. As things were now, the nearest hospital to Chitambo, for example, would be 200 miles away, and that was not acceptable. The Council's view was that the medical needs of this whole area required reconsideration, and that the Government should meet most if not all the cost of the medical services needed. The Council went on to recommend that Dr J. Todd enter into negotiations with the Government. In response the FMC advised that no decision should be proposed to Government without the Committee's sanction.

Argument continued for many months between the Mission Council, the Director of Medical Services, and the FMC, over the staffing and running of those hospitals, leading at one stage to the resignation of Dr Todd. At the end, Dr Todd, having withdrawn his resignation, there was agreement that the Government would continue support and the FMC continue to staff the hospitals, both at Mwenzo and Lubwa. The details of the controversy are to be found in the minutes referred to in the notes.

Although the FMC and the Mission Councils in Central Africa gave much attention to the institutions of service, the hospitals and schools, they did not cease to recognise the centrality of the Church and its calling to evangelism. They could see the danger that with the development of medical and educational work, aided by Government, the Church might be neglected, be deprived of its share of the resources that could be available, and its growth in congregational life and outreach hindered.[89]

As it was the Church itself was becoming increasingly aware of its own special identity and calling in the purpose of God within

Central Africa. It was, for example, taking responsibility more and more for the actual building of places of worship, and for the raising of funds to help meet the cost of full-time workers.[90] The centrality of the Church was becoming a predominant feature too in terms of policy.[91] The integration of Church and Mission was high on the agenda of Mission Councils and of the Regional Committee, as was the preparing of a new constitution for the Church of Central Africa Presbyterian (CCAP). The intention was to bring about eventually a single multi-racial Church, which would include in membership both Africans and Europeans, and at the same time end the anomaly of the continuance in Central Africa of an Overseas Presbytery of the Church of Scotland.

The principle of Church/Mission integration, in line with accepted FMC policy as had been hammered out in Asia, was discussed at length in Mission Councils and met with agreement. As far as the FMC and its missionaries were concerned, there were no major obstacles in the way either of integration or of the proposed Church constitution. A difficulty, however, arose in connection with the Dutch Reformed Mission at Mkhoma and its racial attitudes and policies. It was felt right by all parties, except the Dutch Reformed Church (DRC), that missionaries from Scotland and from South Africa should have the right to full participation in the African Church as members, elders or ministers, and be subject to its discipline. It was at this point that the problem arose, for the DRC refused to countenance this provision. A deadlock ensued which threatened a schism in the existing CCAP and the emerging Church, or at the very least a long delay in the implementing of the intended developments.[92]

It was in the Copperbelt, where the FMC was at work with other missionary bodies in the United Mission, and where there was a concentration of Europeans, that the racial issue became a major factor. There was a fear that the Churches might well take shape along racial lines. To help combat this possibility, the FMC in July 1948 appointed the Rev. Gordon Morris, who had been minister in Crosshouse, Kilmarnock, to the European Free Church in Luanshya, where there had been several instances of racial suspicion and antagonism, on the understanding that he would minister both to Europeans and to Africans.[93]

Outside the Copperbelt, Europeans and Africans had worked together harmoniously for years, and racism was not a major issue.

The conference of Europeans at the Victoria Falls in February 1949, held in secret session and to which no Africans were invited, changed all that. At that meeting (at which were present Sir Godfrey Huggins, the Prime Minister of Southern Rhodesia, others from that country, and from Northern Rhodesia and Nyasaland), a proposal was launched on Central African Federation. Later that year Roy Welensky, unofficial leader in Northern Rhodesia, supported the proposal in the Legislative Council, against the opposition of African members. The insensitivity of that conference being held without African consultation, and in the absence of African participation, was offensive to the African people, and to many others, and set the scene for the subsequent deterioration in race relations.

There followed the London Conference of Officials, again without African representation, which recommended the establishment of a Federation. After the Conference there were issued, in June 1951, three Command Papers setting out details of the recommendations, including the membership of a Federal Legislature which gave a totally disproportionate number to Europeans and to Southern Rhodesia.[94]

Although the argument being put forward for Federation was that it would substantially improve the economic position of the Central African States, enabling Northern Rhodesia and Nyasaland to share in the relative wealth of Southern Rhodesia and provide new markets for that country's produce, which would bring benefit to all, the overriding factor, as the African saw it, was the desire of the European to consolidate his own power, and to prevent the African from taking over. The struggle was on between two nationalisms in Africa, one of European origin and the other African. Confusing the issue for many was the fact that Africans, at least at the beginning of the struggle, looked to the Colonial Office in London for help, while Europeans speaking from within Africa, and their supporters in the UK, were suspicious of the Colonial Office because of its traditional stance as trustee for the rights of the African people. Federation, to put the matter baldly, was for many in the European camp a way of limiting African development in the North, and at the same time of getting rid of interference from the Colonial Office.[95]

By this time there was a general awareness in Central Africa of what was being proposed and a mounting fear that what the African had to endure from European dominance in Southern Rhodesia might spread to Northern Rhodesia and Nyasaland: the prohibition of Trade Unions, the segregation in trains, the discrimination in skilled trades, and the need to carry passes. In an article written for *The Herald* of 1952, a missionary working in rural Northern Rhodesia had this to say:

> The Africans in our areas are very suspicious of the scheme and are strongly opposed to it .... They feel that the British Government is betraying them. It had pledged itself to care for the country until they were able to take a greater share in responsible government. With Federation the Africans feel that they will never be given the opportunity in the government of the country for which their hearts long.[96]

And in a Partner Plan letter, another missionary wrote: 'No matter what happens ... the damage has been done, racial feeling has been intensified and there is in the minds of the Africans a distrust of Government and almost everything British, a feeling that never existed before.'[97]

At the next stage, after the Conference of Officials, a conference was held in London in April-May 1952, to which this time Africans were invited. The Conference, based on the three Command Papers, drew up the Draft Federal Scheme. Africans, except for two from Southern Rhodesia, did not accept the invitation to attend, on the ground that they had not been party to the discussion that led up to the Conference, and to take part now would be in some measure to agree to the principle of Federation, which they were not prepared to do. The Draft Federal Scheme was published in June 1952.[98]

Opinion in the Church in Scotland, and public opinion generally, was strongly opposed to the way in which Federation was being pressed upon the people of Central Africa. Many in Scotland, both within the Church and outside, were incensed by the unseemly haste in which the whole affair was being carried out, and were outraged by the view of Sir Godfrey Huggins that the scheme be put into operation whether the Africans agreed to it or not.[99]

The FMC and the Church and Nation Committee played a crucial part in keeping the issue of Federation before the public, and putting pressure on the Government. They could not have done so without the help of the Rev. Kenneth MacKenzie, a missionary in Northern Rhodesia temporarily at work in Scotland as Candidates' Secretary. It was he who painstakingly accumulated the facts that made responsible argument possible, sifting and analysing the various reports and papers that dealt in one way or another with the issue, and making them available in a clear and readily available form for study and action. He worked with the committees of the Church, with the Iona Community, and with student groups, including in particular the World Church Group that met in the house of the Secretary of the Edinburgh Christian Council for Overseas Students, the Rev. Bill Cattanach, where, incidentally, Julius Nyeyere, who was studying history at the University, was a frequent visitor.[100]

To fill out the picture of what was happening in Central Africa there were the regular communications that came from the Mission Councils and from the missionaries who were in daily contact with the African people. Letters to the press, discussion groups, and public meetings with missionary speakers or visitors from Africa, disseminated the information that was gathered and helped to promote active public concern. Among the public meetings was one held in Community House, Glasgow, arranged by the Iona Community, and addressed by Hastings Banda, who was at that time a practising doctor in England. There was also a large meeting held in the Assembly Hall, addressed by five African chiefs, which called upon the Government to appoint an independent Royal Commission.

Against the background of the discussions taking place in Scotland and agreed statements made at public meetings, the FMC passed a resolution. This it forwarded to the Secretary of State for Commonwealth Relations, the Secretary of State for the Colonies, and the leaders of the Delegations from the Central African Territories to the London Conference beginning on 23 April 1952. The resolution said among other things:

> The Foreign Mission Committee, convinced that the decisions of Her Majesty's Government about the proposed Federation in Central Africa between Southern Rhodesia, Northern Rhodesia, and Nyasaland, will be regarded both in this country and in Africa as the acid test of the sincerity of its Commonwealth policy; and having grave doubts about the trends of the present negotiations, records its opinion that there should be no Federation in Central Africa without full consultation with, and the agreement of, the Africans in those territories ...
>
> The committee felt itself under an obligation to emphasise as the primary consideration the achievement of good relationships based on human freedom and justice between the different races among whom the Church is working.[101]

The Church and Nation Committee, with participation from the FMC, also submitted memoranda to the Government Departments. Attention was directed to the unequal representation in the Federal Parliament, to the rigidity of the Scheme which lacked provision for review, and to the need to have the Federal Constitution reviewed at the end of a specified period.[102] The Church and Nation Committee, along with the FMC, also during this time made personal representation to officials of the Colonial Office, had discussion with the Minister of Colonial Affairs, and with the Governor of Northern Rhodesia, which enabled the committees' objections to Federation to be energetically pressed.

Finally the whole matter was brought to the General Assembly of 1952. In an address to the Assembly on that part of the Report of the Church and Nation Committee dealing with international issues, Neville Davidson had this to say:[103]

> Here was a moral problem of the utmost importance. On its just and generous solution might depend the future development of a huge territory of more than 500,000 square miles and more than six million human beings, not to speak of the repercussions upon other parts of the vast continent.
>
> What was the Church to say in view of such a situation? He ventured to suggest that there were two fundamental Christian principles which could guide them: the first being that every man, woman or child, whatever their racial or cultural development, were of equal dignity and worth in the sight of God; and secondly, that every man, woman and child must be given every possible opportunity of developing in experience so as to enable them wherever possible to take their own share in the government and administration of their country on equal terms with their white neighbours.

The relevant Deliverance of the General Assembly on the Church and Nation Report reads: 'The General Assembly noting with interest the movement towards a Central African Federation but viewing with concern the actual proposals now being made, urge that full consideration be given to African opinion and that no scheme be adopted without the consent and co-operation of the Africans.'[104]

(d)

The tension, racial and nationalist, that had arisen in Central Africa over Federation, was closely paralleled in Kenya. During the Second World War, and in the years following, a volatile mix of frustration and anger against the dominance of the European had drawn close to the point of eruption. For many years the Kikuyu not only felt themselves to be excluded from the possession of their own land, but to have their very way of life put in danger. The arrival home of Kenyatta in 1946 saw a quickening of the ferment that was to lead to the Emergency of 1952.

The Kenya to which Kenyatta returned had during the war become a great military camp, filled with European soldiers and airmen, and with young Africans of Kenya who had been enlisted. Demobilisation also brought back young men who had served abroad. The result was a questioning of tribal values, a breakdown of many of the old sanctions, and an exaggerated expectation of achieving the kind of material benefits Europeans enjoyed. For many, close contact only increased an aversion to things European, and for many more these were perplexing and frustrating times.

It was in this setting that Kenyatta exercised his leadership. He encouraged hope of a rapid achievement of independence and economic advancement, and instilled in his growing number of supporters the determination to achieve these things in every way possible. In 1947 he became President of the Kenya African Union, and by 1950 was gathering crowds of thousands to hear him speak.

Meanwhile the Church was taking stock of the new situation. During the war it lost many of its ministers to be chaplains in the forces, churches had to go without ministers, and theological training ceased. Spiritual morale, it was being said, was at a low ebb. The Church, however, was a living presence in Kenya. As was shortly to be proved, it had many dedicated members and potential leaders. In 1943 it had taken the step to become a Church in its own right as the Presbyterian Church of East Africa (PCEA), a Joint Standing Committee enabling close relations to continue between it and the Mission Council. Weak though it may have been, it was open to change, and sensitive to the needs of the time.[105]

Among the compelling needs which the Church faced were those of education, medical care, and training in agriculture. The Church through the FMC and the Kenya Colony Mission Council worked closely with the Government in all those spheres. The Government recognised the force for good that missionaries had consistently been, and the FMC had repeatedly made clear the importance it placed on supporting to the best of its ability institutions of service that the Government helped to set up.

Many examples, within the PCEA as in other Churches, could be given of this co-operation between the Church and the Government. There was the institution for Teacher Training at Kambui for which the Government gave a large building grant,[106] and then, following the Beecher Report,[107] the Government's lifting from Churches and Missions the major burden of financial support by asking from them not money, but members of staff. As far as medical work was concerned, although Government and Mission relationships had earlier been less than satisfactory,[108] by 1948 co-operation was established, and the Government began to subsidise Mission/Church hospitals. It gave a grant to Chogoria for a new children's ward,[109] to Kikuyu for a maternity block,[110] and to Tumutumu for a nurses' hostel.[111] Finally the Government gave support to the Thogoto Agricultural School at Kikuyu.[112]

In addition to its involvement in those institutions of service, the FMC was concerned with Theological Education, the crucial and urgent importance of which it shared with the PCEA and Mission Council. In 1948 the Church Missionary Society (CMS) had offered, at its site in Limuru, to facilitate a joint training scheme for the Society, the Methodist Missionary Society (MMS) and the PCEA. The PCEA Synod, having welcomed the proposal, Council recommended it to the FMC which approved and made a transfer of grants.[113] On 1 March 1949, an ordinands' course was started at Limuru with 15 students.[114] By the end of 1950 a joint plan had been drawn up by which the Church of Scotland and the MMS undertook the erection of additional buildings to house students and staff.[115] A few months later an agreement was reached between the Church of Scotland and the MMS on the one hand, and the CMS on the other, for the forming of a joint Divinity School.[116]

Meanwhile the revival movement, which had become such a force in Uganda, began to have its effect on the life of the Church in Kenya.[117] The Church in Chogoria, in 1948, was the first to experience the transforming impact of the revival, and the effect spread from area to area. In 1949 in North Kambui, the Annual Conference of Church members in the area was marked, we are told, by 'an unforgettable manifestation of renewal in the life of the Church'. Although at the beginning there were Church leaders and others suspicious of the movement because of the sharp criticism many of its followers had levelled against the Churches and because of its 'emotionalism', it was not long before the movement was accepted and incorporated into the life of the Church. Its influence was enormous, so much so in fact that many would see in it the real beginnings of a truly indigenous Kenyan Church. Whereas previously it might have been argued that the Church's faith was a faith copied from ' an imported religion', now it could be seen to be a Church rooted in Christ direct, in African soil.[118]

Among the many effects the revival had in the life of the Church was a renewed sense of the need for true independence within the one family of the catholic Church. When the PCEA came into being in 1943, it had been agreed between it and the FMC that there would be co-operation between them in the maintenance of institutions until the Church was in the position to assume responsibility.[119] With the revival came a fresh impetus on the part of the Church to run, as far as possible, its own affairs. A major consequence of that was the decision of the Synod that the management of schools should in 1952 pass to the Church, something that the Mission Council had been pressing for years.[120] A vision of the unity of the Church accompanied the desire for independence. Division of the two Presbyterian Churches came to be seen as an obstacle to the Gospel and no longer tolerable.

The question was now being asked about the anomaly of two Churches, both having their origins in the Church of Scotland, existing separately in Kenya: the Overseas Presbytery of the Church of Scotland on the one hand and the PCEA on the other. The matter came up at the 1951 Synod of the PCEA, to which the Rev. David Steel, as Moderator of the Overseas Presbytery, had been invited. Speaking of the two bodies, the Rev. Charles Muhoro, the Moderator of Synod, and the first African to hold that position, said: 'Let them not be spoken of separately, we are one Church of Jesus Christ.' David Steel was of the same mind, and could speak in reply knowing that he would be doing so with the support of the vast majority of the Europeans who made up his Presbytery:' … as we had the same mother in the one Church, we were indeed brethren.'[121]

At a meeting of the Mission Council in August 1950, the Secretary was authorised to approach the Overseas Presbytery suggesting that the relationship between it and the Synod of the PCEA might be re-examined.[122]

In April 1952 the General Secretary of the FMC reported that the Overseas Presbytery had decided to petition the General Assembly for leave to negotiate with the PCEA and the United Church of Northern India, which had set up work among Asians in Eastleigh, Nairobi, in the hope of securing one united organisation for all races in East Africa. The congregation of St Andrews, Nairobi was apparently, he said, in full agreement with the views of the Kirk Session, which had been clearly set out in a declaration of purpose. The recommendation, which was approved by the FMC, was that the Committee should give its support when it came before the General Assembly.[123]

The declaration of purpose prepared by the Kirk Session of St Andrews in support of the petition read as follows:

> There should be one Church (in East Africa) with no distinction based on race or colour.
>
> We pledge ourselves to work towards one Church of East Africa.
>
> Our first step shall be to seek a basis for union between the Overseas Presbytery of Kenya and the Presbyterian Church of East Africa.[124]

The Overseas Presbytery petitioned the General Assembly of 1952 for permission to enter into conversations with the Presbyterian Church of East Africa with a view to creating a united Presbyterian Church, including St Andrews, thus paving the way for a larger church union with the Anglicans and other non-Roman Catholic Churches. The Petition went, according to the rules, through the Colonial and Continental Committee.[125]

The Report of that Committee to the General Assembly was less than encouraging. The development in British East Africa, said the Report, has caused the Committee 'some perplexity', and, making no reference at all to the actual purpose of the Petition, went on to underline the Committee's role to care for the Scot abroad, in seeming failure to recognise that the petitioners themselves could hardly be thought to be unaware of the need for that care in presenting their petition. The reference of the Committee's convener to this part of the Report in his address to the Assembly was no more encouraging: 'The Committee,' he said, 'must not be carried away by a popular word or phrase, diverted by an inferiority complex … the well-meaning enthusiast needed to be yoked with the patient and sober realist. The Church had the right to expect a cautious watchfulness in the committee.'[126]

Dr Hugh Watt, who moved that the Petition be granted, had personal knowledge of the situation in Kenya. He had the privilege as Moderator of the General Assembly of dedicating the new St Andrews Church, in March 1951. In doing so, Hugh Watt said that it had earlier been his intention to move the acceptance *simpliciter,* but the Colonial and Continental Committee were not satisfied with that. In the event the decision of the General Assembly was 'that the Crave of the Petition be granted on the understanding that the negotiators, bearing in mind the responsibility entrusted to the Colonial and Continental Committee, keep steadily before it the spiritual needs of the Scots in East Africa'.[127]

The way in which this request from Africa was handled did little to further understanding at a time of great sensitivity between Europeans and Africans in Kenya and elsewhere. Although the General Assembly did not appear to many to have appreciated sufficiently the offence a Presbytery for Europeans caused, and the doubts it raised about racial attitudes, the fact that it granted the Petition did something to help to repair the damage to racial relations caused twenty years before by the introduction of an Overseas Presbytery. It was not forgotten that it was a committee in Edinburgh that introduced the Overseas Presbytery, and against the advice of those on the spot, both African and European.[128]

Six months later, on 20 October 1952, a state of emergency was declared in Kenya in face of the Mau Mau uprisings. During this whole period from 1948, Mau Mau had been at work surreptitiously, beginning in schools under the control of the Kikuyu Independent Schools Association, and the Karinga Educational Association. By 1950 it had become clear that the KISA schools were being used as centres for the administration of the Mau Mau oath. The extent of the penetration of the schools by Mau Mau only came to light after the declaration of the emergency, and it was then that those schools were closed. Many children, whose parents would not allow them to be transferred to Church/Mission schools, where distrusted foreign and European education was given, were deprived of education and further alienated as a result.

Although Mau Mau had been operating for several years, bringing more and more people under its influence, and forcing them to take the oath, which included among other things not attending Mission Schools, swearing to chase the European from Kenya, and denouncing the Christian faith, neither the Government nor the Church seemed to be aware of the critical significance of what was happening, and were taken by surprise. The murder of Chief Waruhiu by Mau Mau because of his opposition, increased the sense of profound shock.

The first mention we find of Mau Mau by the Church is the declaration of the Synod of the PCEA meeting in September 1952. In that declaration, the Synod warned all Church members against having anything to do with Mau Mau, stated that it would excommunicate all who took the Mau Mau oath of their own free will, and appealed to all the Kikuyu people to keep political controversy out of all schools and to allow the education of children to go forward without check.[129] The next few years was a period of much suffering in Kenya.

(e)

It was in a setting of suffering that the Church in South Africa also lived, and pursued on its part the calling to work for the building of the Kingdom. In his book, *Cry the Beloved Country,* published in 1948, Alan Paton presented in the form of a novel a picture of that suffering. It was an accurate picture of what the social engineering of apartheid meant for the lives of the majority of ordinary African people: in the rural areas and in the slums of cities like Johannesburg, and above all what it meant for the black African to be despised or patronised by whites, and to be used and manipulated by them to preserve South Africa as a white-ruled land. The Government of South Africa, in order to preserve, as they saw it, a 'White South Africa, and a sound Christendom', had passed act after act, in total disregard of the Universal Declaration of Human Rights, to restrict non-Europeans, and to oppose integration in any form, arguing that otherwise the European minority would be engulfed and its civilisation disappear.

Expressing the sense of revulsion that many in the Church and outside felt about what was happening in South Africa, the General Assembly of 1949 passed the following Deliverance of the Church and Nation Committee – the first, as it would turn out, of many dealing with South Africa to be passed in the coming years:

The General Assembly, viewing with grave apprehension the present policy of the Union of South Africa as regards its native populations, declare their conviction that such a policy is to be deplored, not only as aggravating the problem of race relationships in the Union and beyond it, but as contrary to the teaching and tenets of the Christian Faith.[130]

In South Africa itself the Churches, through the Christian Council of South Africa, continued to work together to strengthen their opposition to apartheid, despite the blunt refusal of the Prime Minister to receive a deputation which would have enabled the views of the Churches to be heard. In July 1949 a conference was held under the auspices of the Council, on 'Christian citizenship in a multi-racial society'. The Statement at the end, among many other points, insisted 'that the Church planted by God in this country is multi-racial and must remain so' and 'that man's essential value lies in his nature as man, and not in race or culture'.[131]

Despite racial tension which affected the life of the Church, as it did everything else, the Bantu Presbyterian Church (BPC) continued to value the contribution made by missionaries from Scotland. As we saw earlier, the Church had pressed the Commission for the appointment of a missionary to serve in the proposed office in Umtata as Church Secretary. The FMC agreed to this appointment, and by the end of 1948 Rev. Robert Kilgour, chaplain at Lovedale, had been appointed by the General Assembly of the BPC. His duties as set out in the minutes of that Church were: the publishing of a Church magazine, secretarial work for Assembly committees, assisting committee conveners and the Senior Clerk, and the custody of titles and records. The BPC General Assembly also appointed him as Joint Treasurer and Junior Clerk.[132]

As we have seen, the BPC was asking also for more missionaries to work in local areas. The FMC agreed that this would be desirable, and provided that the district missionary would not be confined to a parish but would be expected to exercise a larger ministry in his presbytery, then the FMC would do what it could to find candidates.[133]

The appointment of a missionary as Church Secretary, and the review of the role of the missionary in the life of the Church, were important steps in bringing together the Mission, and the life of the Church. Further important moves brought representatives of the BPC on to Hospital Boards[134] and on to a new Emgwali Board of

Management, which would in future report annually to the Mission Council. At the same time the Mission Council requested specific representation on the Business Committee of the Church.[135]

There were three hospitals for which the Mission Council was responsible, separated, like all the work of the Council, by long distances: at Sibasa in the Transvaal, Tugela Ferry in Natal, and Sulenkama in Cape Province. With grants from Government and with donations, some extensive developments were made. At Sibasa,[136] for example, a new hospital block was built for 150 in-patients; and at Sulenkama[137] two new wings were added to the hospital, one for children and the other for patients with infectious diseases. The Chamber of Mines also provided a new nurses home.[138] The main problem in all three hospitals was an urgent shortage of staff, which among other factors caused some anxiety about the ability to continue to maintain the hospitals' missionary character.

As far as education was concerned, the Mission Council had under its auspices a large number of day schools situated in the districts. The numbers given in 1947 were 356 District Schools with 850 teachers.[139] Almost all those schools were Government recognised, and the salaries of the teachers paid by its Education Department. The District missionary over the years acted as manager with general control, including the task of ensuring that the schools like the hospitals retained their Christian character. The pressure for education continued to mount, and by 1950 the number of pupils in the schools had risen by over 20 per cent since 1947. The difficulty of maintaining standards increased, a situation made worse by a shortage of staff.

By 1952 it was clear that Churches and Missions would no longer have the freedom to control education and provide schools for black South Africans in the way they had been doing. The Government was now on the point of taking over, bringing education into line with the rest of their strategy of apartheid. In 1948 a Native Education Commission was set up by Government, and it had now presented its Report.[140] The Commission's main recommendation separated off European education, and removed African education from Provincial Councils and the Churches. An autonomous Division of Bantu Education under Native Affairs, it was proposed, would administer the new arrangement.

In 1953 the Bantu Education Act was passed. To that we shall return in the next chapter.

VI

Jamaica was the last of the major areas of the FMC's commitments to be reviewed after the end of the Second World War. Lewis Davidson, a missionary in Jamaica, was asked in 1945 by a committee of the Synod of the Presbyterian Church in Jamaica to make a survey of the Church. Originally the intention of the survey was to discover the most effective way for the Church to conduct its welfare work, a matter of central importance in Jamaica. It soon widened out, however, to become a survey of the life of the Church as a whole: its inner life as the new community in Christ, its function in Jamaica, and its organisation. The new life, it saw, must 'express itself in education, recreation, work, family life and evangelism, as well as in worship'.

As far as education was concerned the Report it produced emphasised the value of the People's College in Adult Education, and advocated a Mission Centre, built round a Rural Secondary School, which would have a 'diversified communal life'. A special committee of the FMC studied the Report with great care, and was much impressed by it, including the proposal for a Mission Centre.[141]

Early in 1949, on the occasion of the celebration of the hundredth anniversary of the Synod of the Presbyterian Church of Jamaica, the FMC commissioned the Rev. James Munn, who had been a member of the Special Committee, to represent it, and with the Synod's Survey in the background, to discuss with the Church how best the FMC might co-operate with it.[142]

The Presbyterian Church of Jamaica in its hundred year history had long seen itself as a Church with a life of its own not subservient in any way to the Mission. It spoke, for example, of being 'in federal relation with the Church of Scotland'.[143] This was not to say, however, that it did not rely for help on the Church of Scotland and other Churches outside, and in particular on the FMC. The Church in Jamaica was numerically weak and faced many difficulties. The vast majority of its members were extremely poor, and their background of slavery, with its destruction of marriage and family life, had led to severe social ills. (Slavery had only come to an official end in 1834, just 15 years before the first meeting of Synod.) James Munn was deeply affected by the tremendous problems facing the Church, but was clearly full of admiration for the Church itself, for the faith of so many of its people, the rich variety of gifts found among them, and the exuberance of its life. The Church had 27 ordained ministers, not counting missionaries from abroad, and 488 elders.[144] Although the Church was relatively small, the number of communicant members given at that time as 11,522[145] somewhat underestimates the actual strength, for many not counted on the roll worshipped with the Church or were otherwise attached to it.

The Presbyterian Church of Jamaica, though staunchly proud of being Jamaican and independent, welcomed help from abroad, and in a spirit of responsibility asked for it. It made requests to the Church of Scotland, especially for missionaries, and in co-operation with the FMC corresponded with the Presbyterian Church in USA.[146] This was totally in line with its understanding of the unity of the Church, to which it was deeply committed. It was one of the founding members of the Jamaican Christian Council, which at that time included in its membership the Anglican, Methodist, Baptist, and Moravian Churches. The Church, as it saw it, was one, and its mission one. Sharing for the furtherance of the Kingdom was to be taken for granted as an essential part of faith, a vision of the truth which was deeply engrained in Jamaican Christians, and which had been made plain when the Jamaican Missionary Society was founded and had, in 1845, sent Hope Waddell as a missionary to Old Calabar.

The FMC helped the Church in Jamaica over the years by sending missionaries, and by giving grants for particular pieces of work. In 1947 there were eleven ordained missionaries and their wives. All those missionaries, according to the *Sketch of the Field,* were engaged in 'congregational work' scattered throughout the presbyteries. At the same time they exercised special responsibilities within the Churches as a whole: *eg* the care of a Children's Home, the leadership of Sunday School and Youth Work, the Synod Clerkship, theological training, or 'the care of some large and difficult parish'.[147]

The Church in Jamaica was responsible for three Children's Homes with which the FMC was associated in one way or another: the Pringle Home for orphan girls; the Broughton Boys' Home, which included children sent by the Resident Magistrate; and the Farm Home, which provided support and training in agriculture for very poor boys.[148] The Presbyterian Church, along with the Methodist Church, ran St Andrews School for Girls, which had over 350 pupils, a third of whom were boarders.[149] The Principal of the School was locally appointed, regarded as a missionary, and paid for by the FMC. In Grand Cayman, the island north west of Jamaica where the Presbyterian Church had a presbytery of eight congregations, with a communicant membership of 800, a new High School was set up at the instigation of the local churches, and a Church of Scotland missionary put in charge.[150]

The FMC was also involved in the Church's commitment to theological education. For some years training for the ministry was run interdenominationally in St Colme's, a Church of Scotland College. The St Colme's building had not provided adequate accommodation, and as early as 1946 proposals were made to build a new St Colme's on Methodist land at Caenwood.[151] By 1952 the Synodical Council had decided to allocate money toward the building fund, and a Joint Committee agreed that there should be a joint Presbyterian-Methodist College with a Board of Management representing the two Churches.[152] As plans were going ahead for a development of ministerial training and theological education, note was taken of the suggestion in Munn's Report, that scholarships might be provided to enable divinity students to take advantage of the facility offered by the new University of the West Indies only just opened.[153] Among the missionary appointments to which the FMC was committed was that of theological tutor. It was in fact one of the three appointments particularly stressed in the Synod's survey Report of 1945; and at a special committee on policy of the Synod, meeting in 1951, a theological tutor was mentioned first in a list of the 'minimum missionary personnel required for the Jamaica Mission'.[154]

The existence of the Jamaica Mission of the Church of Scotland had by this time become an anomaly. Integration had been more or less a reality for many years. Only a few things remained to be done. In 1951 the Synod's Committee on Policy recommended that all correspondence between the FMC and the Church be conducted through the Clerk of Synod, and that the salaries of missionaries, who would continue to receive the FMC scale, be paid through the Treasurer of the Church.[155] Then in 1952, at a meeting of the Mission Council, notice was given of a motion to disband the Mission Council, and to set up in its place, with the most limited functions, a missionaries' committee.[156]

At Easter 1949, during his visit to the Synod of the Presbyterian

Church, James Munn was present at the ceremonial opening by the Governor of Jamaica of the completed first phase of the Knox College complex, at Spaldings in rural Jamaica.[157] The dream of which Lewis Davidson had spoken in 1945 of a Centre for all-round Christian education, which so excited the special committee of the FMC, and which caught the imagination of so many groups in Scotland who met Lewis Davidson while he was on deputation, was now well on the way to fruition. In 1946 the FMC, at the request of the Synod, appointed Lewis Davidson as the first Principal of Knox College. The Education Centre that was Knox was the brainchild of Lewis Davidson, but it was not just the vision of one man. It came out of the need and the longing of a whole community. It was a venture of faith of the Church in Jamaica. The Church laid out sufficient money – and out of its poverty – to get the project going, and one of its own number, David Bent, an elder of Webster Memorial Church, gave up the security of his job to accept appointment as 'Builder and Bursar of Knox'.[158] In August 1949 Knox College was recognised by Government as eligible for grant-in-aid,[159] and by 1952 several conferences for the community had been held, which were to become such an important component of the College programme.

VII

Up until now we have been discussing relationships between the Church of Scotland and Churches in Asia, Africa and the West Indies, which were independent or were growing into independence, and which had come into being following the activities of the missionary movement. Within the Middle East in South Arabia, in the Colony of Aden and the Protectorate, to which we turn, there was still no indigenous Church. For over 60 years, missionaries from Scotland had worked in that area, making friends as they did so, and winning a reputation among the people for caring service and not least for 'holiness'. The hospital which they ran at Sheikh Othman, in the name of Christ, was well known for hundreds of miles around and had built up for the missionaries a widely spread network of friendly contacts, including close and cordial relations with Government representatives. Despite all their patient, dedicated work, there had been only one convert. Many people became interested in the Gospel, and studied the Bible, but only Ahmed Sa' eed Affara had taken the full step and been baptised. Ahmed Affara became a doctor. Under the auspices of the Edinburgh Medical Missionary Fellowship, he had studied at Edinburgh University where he had graduated in 1938. Before returning to Aden he had spent some months in the hospital at Nazareth run by the EMMF. He then joined his colleagues at Sheikh Othman, to work as a missionary of the Church of Scotland, with his wife Nasta, a Christian from Palestine.

Ahmed Affara's involvement in the South Arabia Mission, with his wife, marked a major step forward. Another important step was taken when Dr Pat Petrie, who had served for over seven years in Sana'a, arranged a scheme with the Aden Government for the training of Arab dispensers in the Protectorate, just before his retirement in 1946, and got it working before he left.[160] By 1947, 24 dispensers had been trained at Sheikh Othman, and 17 dispensaries established in the Protectorate. The dispensers came in small groups of eight at a time, which allowed plenty of opportunity for the staff to get to know them personally. Their training included what Dr Petrie would have called 'character training', in which healing was discussed in the light of the purpose of God, whom they knew as 'the compassionate'. The students were given also the option of attending a Bible class, and Muslims though they were, they chose to do so. A significant influence during their time at Sheikh Othman also came through the regular visits they paid to the homes of the missionaries. The Government supplied the medicines required in the dispensaries, and the transport that allowed doctors and nurses to go out to them from time to time. The presence of those dispensaries scattered widely now in the Protectorate, at distances of 60 to 200 miles from Aden, opened up new possibilities of mission in the interior of Arabia, as the Christian influence of Sheikh Othman spread through the activities of the dispensers, and as missionary doctors and nurses were given the opportunity to meet the people and win their trust.[161]

In October 1949 the challenge came to take a new and decisive step into the interior, when the Shareef of Beihan invited the Mission to send a doctor to serve in his territory for a period of six months. What he wanted, he said, to quote Dr Bernard Walker's account in his *Sketch of the Field,* 'was "a religious – a holy one" who would really take to heart the welfare of the people of Beihan'.[162]

There could be no doubt of the people's need, for the Beihanis were illiterate, disease was rampant, and they were desperately poor. Unhappily at that time the Mission was not in the position to help. The Shareef, however, was not easily put off and again he made his request.[163] Just over a year later, in response to his second request, the Mission Council decided that a visit should be paid. In February and March of 1951, Ahmed Affara, the Rev. James Ritchie recently appointed by the FMC, Louisa Cowie, a nurse, and Mette Kristensen, seconded by the Danish Missionary Society and also a nurse, spent six weeks in the country. They were warmly welcomed and given a house for a clinic. During their time there they treated more than 4000 people and performed 120 eye operations. There were opportunities to visit people in their homes and to speak of the Christian faith. The result of that visit was the decision to open a new Mission clinic at Beihan.[164] At its meeting in December 1951, the Mission Council decided that Louisa Cowie be allocated to Beihan and that Bernard Walker should accompany her in order to establish her in the work.[165]

Meanwhile the work in Aden continued. The Keith Falconer Hospital at Sheikh Othman was receiving patients from all over South Arabia and from Somaliland, and was full to capacity for most of the year. Often its eighty beds were occupied, other patients having to be put on mattresses on the floor.[166] The hospital had many difficulties to contend with, not least the shortage of staff. For much of the time there were only two doctors, and only two or three missionary nurses. Understaffing put heavy pressure on doctors and nurses, for in addition to caring for often very sick people they were training or running refresher courses for dispensers, and travelling long distances to supervise and give support to them in their places of work, while of course having at the same time the administration of the actual hospital. It was part of the cost of being involved in what was rapidly becoming a major programme of outreach into the interior. To offset to some extent the shortage of staff at the hospital, in terms of meeting patients and their 'spiritual' needs, the Danish Missionary Society agreed to appoint an evangelistic missionary to Sheik Othman. The Rev. M. A. Borch-Jensen and his wife and family arrived at the beginning of 1950.[167]

The running of the hospital was becoming more and more expensive as the price of drugs and food went up, and the bill for salaries increased. The Government, however, was contributing to missionary salaries in recognition of the service they were rendering, and the hospital was grateful for help given by the Boys' Brigade and the Life Boys in Scotland, who had just produced a sum of money to allow for the purchase of an X-ray, an operating table, and other medical equipment.

In Sheikh Othman itself, Nasta Affara, who was a trained nurse, with the help of Sister Cowie of the hospital, had restarted a Child Welfare Clinic in June 1947 that had been closed for many years, and had gone on to develop it.[168] Many of the Arab women in Sheikh Othman took a direct interest in the Clinic, as relationships of friendship grew and as there began to be a new openness to the Christian message. Mrs Affara also started the first Milk Scheme in Aden,[169] with the financial backing of the local people. Seventy children came daily for milk, and received at the same time cod-liver oil and calcium, hospital treatment being given to those who needed it. A Bible class for women, which had begun during a literacy campaign sometime before, continued to meet. Sister Bain was helped in the conducting of it by Mrs Su'ad Marouf, Mrs Affara's sister-in-law, who had just arrived from Palestine. Mrs Affara herself continued to take services in the Women's Out-patient Department at the Hospital, helped by others including James Ritchie.[170]

At Steamer Point there was a chaplain appointed by the Colonial and Continental Committee. The Rev. R. A. Baigrie, who was chaplain until his transfer to India in 1948, had worked closely with the missionaries and had taken services monthly in the Mission Chapel. When he left Aden the Mission lost a good friend.[171] On his departure the Danish Missionary Society sent the Rev. R. Madsen to fill the gap and take services. In April 1951 James Ritchie succeeded Richard Madsen as minister of the Ion Keith Falconer Memorial Church in Aden – the arrangement with the Colonial and Continental Committee being that James Ritchie would only be able to give part of his time to the congregation, and might have to be withdrawn altogether if his duties as missionary in charge of all evangelistic work in the Colony and Protectorate demanded it.[172]

In 1948 Dr Bernard Walker had taken over the duties of Protectorate Medical Officer responsible for the running of the scheme of dispensers. In discussion with him the Mission Council had decided to plan a combined training school for one year in the first instance, beginning in March 1949, and that Sister Cowie serve on the staff of the Protectorate Medical Service with accompanying duties in hospital. The principle of co-operation between the hospital staff and the Protectorate Medical Service staff was accepted, and it was agreed that dressers in training should work in the various departments of the hospital.[173]

With Bernard Walker's furlough in 1950 it was hoped that the Government would provide a relief doctor. That did not happen, however, with the result that Dr R. Bertram Smith, one of the two doctors in the hospital, had to take over those duties in addition to his own, only to underline the grave staff shortage. There was an urgent need for more missionary staff, and this was particularly so in the light of the new opportunities that were everywhere opening up.[174]

In 1951, as the work of evangelism developed, the Mission Council turned its attention to the reopening of the school at Sheikh Othman, which had been seen when the Mission was first set up as centrally important, along with the hospital for the spread of the Gospel, and which had been closed because of a lack of Christian teachers.[175] The Council was aware that the FMC put great importance on education. When in April it urgently requested the appointment of an additional doctor for the hospital, the FMC replied that priority had to be given to the appointment of an ordained man with educational qualifications.[176] The hope now was that permission would be given to reopen the school, and the Council made that request. The FMC's reply was that although it was sympathetic to the proposal, in view of the setting up of the new clinic at Beihan, the reopening of the school at Sheikh Othman would have to be postponed.

From the Protectorate Medical Health Service's inception the Government had regarded the involvement of the Mission in it as being on a year-by-year basis. After discussion between the Mission Council and the Government in the Autumn of 1951, continuity was now assured. Instead of not knowing from year to year what the arrangement would be, the Council was now to be given responsibility for the Health Service for a definite period, of six years in the first instance, and was to be fully reimbursed for all its expenses.[177]

In 1952 Bernard Walker left Aden to serve as Medical Superintendent of the Mission Hospital at Tiberias in Israel, and James Ritchie had to resign from the chaplaincy at Steamer Point to allow him to take full advantage of evangelistic opportunities, and to consolidate the evangelistic work of the Mission. The FMC was confronted with the task of finding not just one doctor to replace Dr Walker, but as many as four who were urgently needed to deal with the developments into the interior. When on furlough in the following year, James Ritchie appealed for a chaplain to work in Aden.[178]

VIII

During this whole period an increasing shortage both of funds and of candidates for missionary service was a constant anxiety to the FMC. In 1945, at the conclusion of the Second World War, when it set about re-examining the position, there was a serious shortfall of income against expenditure, and 180 new candidates had to be found to bring the missionary staff up to strength. The decision was made at that time, by Deliverance of the General Assembly, to increase the budget progressively over the next seven years (an increase that would involve a more than 60 per cent rise in congregational givings) and to put before congregations the 'unprecedented urgency for men and women to offer themselves for the service of the worldwide Church through its missionary enterprise'.[179]

Although presbyteries accepted the targets that were given to them, and givings rose annually, the figure of income received at the end of the seven year period fell far short of the envisaged budget for 1952; and, to make matters worse, that budget itself was by that time quite inadequate in face of rising costs.[180] The picture for recruiting was equally disappointing. Although much hard work was done in presbyteries and 199 men and women candidates had been appointed since 1945, there had been during that period a total loss of staff of 240, over 150 due to resignations.[181]

Despite this, the FMC was determined to maintain its work, and to make no radical reductions. Consistently it refused to consider retrenchment, a determination in which it was supported by the Church in repeated Deliverances of the General Assembly – incidentally with the explicit concurrence of the Church's General Finance Committee.[182]

The importance of the Church's involvement in world mission was recognised at General Assembly level, but what mattered more was the ordinary church member's perception. The gap between what was being said at the Assembly, and the actual support in practice that was being given by the Church at large, was clearly a cause for concern. In 1950 the budget had been restricted, so that it was less than in the previous year, with the result that expenditure in some places was reduced.[183] A number of congregations had increased their givings, but a large, though smaller number, were 'down' on the year before. It was a reminder of how much the policy of the FMC in practice was affected by the givings of the membership of the Church. It was no encouragement that the Home Board was facing the same problem. In 1950 those responsible for Church Extension were looking to have to spend three times what was contributed in 1949, and were speaking of 'a crisis and a challenge of the first magnitude'.[184] In 1951 the FMC's budget was increased, but in the next year the budget figure was back to that of 1950. All the indications were that many people in the Church had not yet understood the changes that had taken place in recent years, and did not appreciate the continuing importance of supporting Christians in other lands, in a variety of different ways, and of sending missionaries abroad.

In the rethinking and reassessment which preoccupied the FMC at this time, there could be no ignoring the severely practical considerations of finance and staffing. It was on the initiative of its Finance Committee that the FMC's Special Committee on Policy of 1950 was set up, and it had as its specific remit the fixing of the budget for 1951 and subsequent years, and the giving of guidance on appointments to be made. Although the conferences that the Policy Committee organised in May and June of 1950 dealt with larger questions of theology and mission, and emphasised the concept of realignment, the bogey of retrenchment was always there.[185]

The sad failure of the Church to respond adequately with finance to the enormous opportunities that were being opened up for world mission, and to the great needs that were so apparent, was matched only by its failure to recruit men and women, suitable and in sufficient numbers, to serve as missionaries overseas.

One of the many factors leading to the problem of recruitment, and possibly one of the major factors, was the growing recognition that missionary service was just one form of Christian service among others. Generally it was no longer seen as a special or heroic form of Christian obedience. At an SCM Overseas Conference, held in Sheffield at the end of 1951 and the beginning of 1952, attended by about one hundred students considering work overseas, a marked change was observed in the approach to questions of Christian and missionary vocation. As far as students were concerned there was no real distinction between the vocation to full-time paid service of the Church overseas and the Christian vocation in Government service or in business.[186] Writing about the Conference, which he had recently attended, Malcolm Duncan, who later became a missionary in Pakistan, commented that whereas in the past the Christian vocation of those going abroad in secular occupations had 'long been acknowledged, but sometimes rather patronisingly, as if it were a second-best to direct missionary work, today it is seen to be in the forefront of the Church's mission'.[187] There was a feeling present too at this time that the missionary enterprise as such, like the colonial system, which it was said to parallel closely, was outmoded. For many students, otherwise committed to Christian service, and ready to serve overseas, missions were out.

Not all who might have served overseas as missionaries but who decided otherwise, did so for those reasons. Conditions of service and the low level of remuneration were influential factors, factors which were beginning to be seen at the same time to affect resignations. The fact that missionaries were badly paid, and doctors, nurses, teachers, and even ministers, might well find themselves at a disadvantage in terms of employment on their return home, was sufficient to dissuade some at least who might otherwise have considered offering their services; and the difficulty – some would say the impossibility – of living on a missionary allowance (it was considerably less than the minimum stipend, and that itself was regarded as inadequate),[188] where there was no other income, was certainly one of the factors leading to resignations. Some who had no private source of income, or were not given some support from relatives, had to choose between resignation or going into debt. In many instances, of course, it was probable that a man or woman would have been willing to accept those conditions if it had been felt that missionary service was a sufficiently weighty option.

The FMC was committed to the view that mission was the responsibility of the whole Church, and not just to one missionary group or to one department. There was no going back on the insight that the whole People of God was called to participate in mission, and the missionaries themselves were the last people to want to diminish in any way the vocation to mission and service of lay women or men, not least because so much of their effort was given to helping the Church where they were to encourage that very thing. To see missionary service, however, within the setting of lay Christian vocation, brought obvious difficulties. There was in practice a distinction to be made between service under the Church, as institution and organisation, and service as an individual within a secular structure. The issue was beginning to become obvious in the schools in Kenya and West Africa, and in the colleges in Asia, as the pressure for education mounted, and as governments, schools and colleges more and more looked for teachers from the West. The question was being asked about the role in terms of mission of Christian teachers who went out under auspices other than the Church. They were paid quite differently and at a much higher level than the missionaries, and they served under quite different regulations. In particular, the question was being asked about their place within the Church Overseas in its partnership with the Church of Scotland.

As far as partnership was concerned, the FMC was clear that the missionary relationship was distinctive. In its Report to the General Assembly of 1952, it made its position plain: 'There must surely be a profound distinction between the relationships of Older and Younger Churches which are only linked by the casual and informal contacts of individual Christian laymen, however open their discipleship, and those Churches which are bound together by the presence of a missionary group on a solemn contract of service, offered, supported and guaranteed by the Older Church and accepted, integrated, and commissioned by the Younger.'[189]

The concept of partnership is one that we shall be exploring further in the next and subsequent chapters, as well as the role of the missionary.

CHAPTER 4

Cry Freedom
(1953–1959)

I

THE move to bring Northern Rhodesia, Nyasaland and South-ern Rhodesia into a Federation that caused such bitter feeling among the African people upon which it was being imposed, took a further step forward.

In January 1953 an official Conference on Central African Federation, held in London, issued the final Federal Scheme. Six months later, despite continuous protests from the African people, and consistent lobbying both in Africa and the UK, Central African Federation was put into effect by Order in Council. Although every attempt failed to delay or to stop Federation, the pressure put on the UK Government, including pressure from the Church, had some effect. In the scheme as it was finally implemented, a number of alterations were made, designed to safeguard the rights of the African people. Among the most significant of those were the central place that was to be given to the African Affairs Bureau: the pledge in the preamble that the two protectorates – Northern Rhodesia and Nyasaland – would remain under the care of the Colonial Office 'so long as their people so desire'; and, most important, the provision made for a review of the Constitution after not less than seven and not more than nine years.[1]

Although at the beginning of the Federation there was an appearance of satisfactory progress, with clearly recognisable eco-nomic results, the perceived success and harmony were deceptive. For one thing the African people themselves gained little from the economic advantages of Federation, and for another it was respect and freedom they wanted above all else, and that they could ever more clearly see, was not on offer. As the years went by, one after the other of the hard-won 'safeguards' went by the board, including a 'packing' of the Bureau that made a farce of it, until finally the African people were left in no doubt that Federation was an iniquity that must not happen. With the Declaration of the State of Emergency in Nyasaland in March 1959, the break-up of the Federation began.[2]

As increasingly in Central Africa feelings of anger and frustration mounted against the European, with his presumptions of superiority, in South Africa the seeds of animosity and racial tension continued to be sown. In 1953 the Bantu Education Act drove a further wedge between the races, weighing the balance still more against the black majority (we shall be looking at the implications of the Act later for the Church's work of education). In the following year Malan resigned as Prime Minister and was succeeded by J. G. Strijdom. The change brought no let up in the movement towards full segregation, and the policy of white domination. His successor, H. F. Verwoerd,[3] who took over in 1958, strengthened the movement even further. During the War, when he was editor of *Die Transvaler*, he had shown his hand by his support of the Nazis and his attitude to the Jews. He was the architect of the Bantustans, which led to the mass migration of thousands from their homes during this period.

During Verwoerd's premiership, Nelson Mandela emerged as a leader in the black nationalist struggle against apartheid. In 1952, having led a campaign on behalf of the African National Congress, he was given a suspended prison sentence and banned. On the expiry of the ban, Mandela reappeared and was involved in forming an Alliance Congress to combat racism. At the meeting of that Congress in 1955, the 'Freedom Charter'[4] was drawn up and adopted. In December the following year, in response to the Charter, regarded by the Government as communist and revolutionary, Albert Luthuli, the leader of the African National Congress, Mandela, and 154 others of all races, were charged with treason, and the great treason trial began which lasted for five years and ended with the acquittal of all the accused.

Meanwhile the ferment of nationalism, appearing all over Africa, boiled over into violence in Kenya in the prolonged Mau Mau uprising. Jomo Kenyatta was imprisoned in April 1953, and many thousand Kikuyu were sent to internment camps. The emergency declared in 1952 remained actively in force for the next five years.

During this whole period the Gold Coast became the focus of attention – and of encouragement for those who looked forward to the time when colonial rule would end in Africa, and the people would be free to rule themselves in their own lands, without European interference. Kwame Nkrumah, the leader of the party that won the election in 1951, became, immediately on his release from prison, the Leader of Government Business – *ie* Prime Minister, a title formally given to him the following year. After overwhelming victories in two subsequent elections, in 1954 and 1956, at which Nkrumah's party stood for independence, now Ghana, as it came to be known as, achieved independence on 6 March 1957, as a Dominion within the Commonwealth.

Nkrumah was present at the Afro-Asian Conference, held at Bandung, Indonesia in April 1955, which marked in political terms what came to be called the 'Third World'. The meeting together of representatives of more than twenty states which had gained their independence from colonial power had an enormous symbolic significance. It proclaimed, or so it seemed, both the end of colonialism, and the beginning of an era when the non-aligned nations, belonging to the camp of neither the two great powers – the Americans nor the Russians – would be free to work without hindrance for the solving of their problems, and the building of a new world. Bandung greatly influenced Nkrumah, and it was in the spirit of Bandung that in Accra, in 1958, having become recognised as a statesman of international standing, he set up, with Tom Mboya of Kenya as chairman, the influential All Africa People's Conference, the first of its kind, at which representatives of nationalist movements in 28 African countries met.

In 1956, the year after Bandung, Abdul Nasser of Egypt, who was similarly influenced by that conference, took the step of nationalising the Suez Canal, leading to a direct confrontation with the British and the French, to the British invasion of Suez, and to military engagement with Israel, whose access to the canal Egypt had illegally forbidden. Britain's intervention in Suez was a humiliating failure, which served to underline what had become apparent by 1947, that Britain's day as an imperial power was over.

Jawaharlal Nehru, whose action in leading India to independence in 1947 was one of the first signs of the 'wind of change' that was to blow not just over Africa but over every part of the old colonial world, was the inspiration behind the Bandung Conference. He played a major part there. A conference of newly-freed nations meeting to look at the future, which now they could have a share in shaping, could rightly be said to be, for him, the fulfilment of a dream.

Nehru, for years prior to Bandung, was committed to a non-aligned position in foreign affairs,[5] seeing himself as having a role to play in a world polarised by the two great powers. In an address given at Colombia University,[6] during an official visit to the USA in 1949, he had made his position clear. The objective of his foreign policy was, he said, 'the pursuit of peace, not through alignment with any major power or group of powers, but through an independent approach to each controversial or disputed issue'. His concept of Panchsheel – the five principles of co-existence which gave content to that objective – became, in different versions, part of the orthodoxy of the Non Alignment Movement (NAM), post Bandung.

During the Korean War – which continued until 1953 – Nehru refused to be cajoled by the Americans into supporting their position, and on his return home from his American visit India gave formal recognition to the new China. (A month later incidentally the UK followed suit.) In June 1954 Chou En-lai, the Chinese Prime Minister, visited New Delhi. In a joint statement signed at that time 'the five principles of peaceful coexistence' – Panchsheel – were incorporated, including, it is interesting to note, two which Mao Tse-tung had used in a speech setting forth the basis of the foreign policy of his new regime.[7] In October of the same year, Nehru paid a return official visit to China. In the following year he flew to Cairo to meet Nasser, with whom he formed a cordial relationship, and in April of that year received the North Vietnamese leader in Delhi. That same month he flew on to Bandung. After Bandung, Nehru paid an official visit to the Soviet Union, a visit which was returned by Krushchev and Bulganin in November of the same year.

While the Western and Eastern blocs continued to confront one another, and to build up enormous arsenals of nuclear weapons, there was always the fear that the unthinkable would happen and the trigger be pulled. After the death of Stalin, in March 1953, it looked for a time as though a change for the better might take place in the Cold War. In February 1954 the foreign ministers of the USA, USSR, UK and France met in Berlin. The fact that contact was made, and that there was 'no undue acrimony', gave some hope for the summit meeting of heads of governments then being proposed. In July 1955 the meeting of heads of government took place in Geneva, and seemed to go well. It was reported that 'there was a welcome absence of propagandist oratory, and 'it seemed that a new spirit had entered into international relations'.

Unhappily when the foreign ministers met again some months later it became clear that the gap between them was wide and not to be bridged. The verbal attacks made by Bulganin and Krushchev on Britain during their visit to India shortly after, 'inflaming old resentments', as the Church and Nation Report puts it, did not encourage hope that the Cold War was coming to an end.[8] Then in 1956 – under the cover of the Suez crisis – the Soviet invasion of Hungary occurred, which deepened suspicion and hardened animosities all the more.

During the Krushchev regime, however, there were several signs of a change in the political climate. In 1959, for example, there were clear indications of a desire for greater openness in international relations. In Geneva a Three-Power Conference took place concerned with the limitation and inspection of nuclear weapons, and in February of that year Harold MacMillan visited the Soviet Union.

In this whole period, dominated by so much that was destructive, there were hopeful signs. One of the most obvious signs was the liberation of peoples from colonialism. The fact that so many new and independent nations had emerged from countries formerly ruled by colonial powers marked a major step forward in the history of the world. It was no small thing that perhaps as many as 500 million people in the old British Empire had become completely self-governing.[9] A remarkable and hopeful corollary of this movement for liberation was the number of new independent states which chose to be part of the Commonwealth of Nations, with Queen Elizabeth, whose coronation was celebrated in 1953, as its Head. In the ten years from 1947 the following independent nations joined the Commonwealth: Ceylon, Ghana, India, the Federation of Malaya, and Pakistan.

II

The Second Assembly of the World Council of Churches took place in Evanston, Illinois, USA from 15-31 August 1954. In the run up to the Assembly, the Central Committee met in Lucknow, India,[10] for ten days from 31 December 1952. Principal T. M. Taylor of Aberdeen was present as one of the two delegates from the Church of Scotland. John Fleming and John Kellas were there as guests. The Lucknow meeting's function was to prepare for the Evanston Assembly, but its significance went beyond that. It was the first meeting of its kind in Asia, and it had focused world attention on the Church in that continent. The fact that Dr Radhakrishnan, the Vice President of India, addressed the Central Committee, and Jawaharlal Nehru also took the opportunity to speak, stressed the importance attached both to the holding of this meeting in Asia, and to the membership of the Asian Churches in the WCC. In the discussions that took place on the theme of the Evanston Assembly, particularly where those led to questions directly related to Unity and Mission, Asian delegates played a leading part. They were meeting in the Third World, on their home ground as it were – no longer in the West – and against a background of newly won independence. The difference that made was noticeable. They were speaking, it was being said, with new confidence and conviction.

In Lucknow, immediately preceding the meeting of the Central Committee, a Study Conference for East Asia was held on the same theme of Hope as that of the World Council. The theme of Evanston was Christ – the Hope of the World; the Study Conference's theme Christ – the Hope of Asia.[11] To study the theme of Hope in the setting of the Third World, where poverty and all the ills of the disadvantaged – disease, malnutrition, illiteracy – were endemic, and where at the same time a vision was being given, with the emergence of political freedom, of a new future for the masses of the people when they would be free of the injustices from which they suffered, was to ensure at the very least lively and relevant discussion. And that is how it was.

Dr Charles Bhatty, Secretary of the National Christian Council of India, who was present at the Study Conference, put its underlying assumptions in this way:

> In terms of hope, what the Asian peoples need is an assurance that God has not abandoned this world, that He so much loves the man whom He has created in His own image that He will not leave the world to its own devices. He must continue to redeem man and thus consummate His plan of redemption. The Asian people must know that God is working steadily toward the establishment on this earth of His

Kingdom, in which justice and love will prevail and in which there will be equality of opportunity and social status, adequate social security, respect for human personality in terms of the New Testament, a new sense of values in terms of human relationships.[12]

The Study Conference emphasised the active presence of God at work among the poor. In his Report Bhatty continues:

When our Lord comes He will ask us whether we lived under the sovereignty of His will. He will ask us where were our deeds which were inspired by a living hope. The Asian people are in desperate need of a Message of hope which tells them that there is a living God who cares.

★ ★ ★

The Church's mission forbids it to drift or flee before the events of our time. The Church is in the world and, as the Lord of the Church identified Himself wholly with mankind, so also must the Church …. The Churches must become the voice of the voiceless.[13]

Although the Second Assembly of the WCC[14] at Evanston saw the Third World taking a more prominent place than at the Amsterdam Assembly, it still remained far too Western. Jim Dougall, who was present, spoke about this on his return much as he had after Amsterdam:

The WCC … does not as yet represent the Universal Church of the missionary expansion. It is too western in personnel, thought and method. Some of the Indian Churches made an impressive contribution, notably the Church of South India, but Africa – the continent of the greatest missionary contribution – was very poorly represented.[15]

Western attitudes and modes of thinking continued to prevail. Individuals from the Third World made their mark, intellectually and by the cogency of their contributions, but all in all it was the Western world that set the scene. Charles Ranson, Secretary of the International Missionary Council, in a Plenary Address said:

The western world, with its needs and preoccupations, is still regarded as the world which really matters. The rest provides a colourful geographical fringe. We have hardly begun to understand what it means to belong to a Church which is worldwide. We tend to think and plan and work within our narrow cultural boundaries. The work of the Church beyond these familiar frontiers is, for many Christians, an exotic growth, an interesting but alien affair.[16]

Western Churches may have shaped the agenda of Evanston and influenced what took place there in a way disproportionate to their true weight, in terms of faith, obedience and service, but it would be wrong not to recognise the creative part the Churches of the Third World in fact played. A growing partnership between Churches of the West and the Third World could be discerned that promised to provide opportunities, not open before, for a sharing of vision, talents and gifts. Third World Churches clearly had much to give. Their position as minorities living in the midst of people of other Faiths, the pressures upon them of poverty, endured in their own life and shared with those around them, and the constant demand laid upon them to communicate the Gospel both in words and action, led them to understandings and practices which challenged many of the preconceptions of Western Churches. In face of the gigantic task confronting the Church in a world so full of need, Third World Churches were in the main impatient for change, and increasingly uneasy with sterile theological positions which got in the way. Their concern for evangelism which, as they saw it, was seriously impeded by the disunity of the Church, made them, for example, extremely critical of official discussions on unity. Their view was made plain not least in the Section on the Evangelising Church, where the point was made that the Church must deal with these divisions 'with holy impatience, and passionately strive for unity'.[17]

The relation between unity and mission preoccupied both the Churches and the missionary bodies during this period. It had been felt for some time that the existence of two parallel ecumenical organisations, the International Missionary Council and the World Council of Churches, both concerned with unity and mission, was an unnecessary anomaly. The matter had been raised at Evanston, and by 1958, at the meeting of the IMC in Ghana, an actual proposal for their integration was put forward. The Church of Scotland, which with other member bodies was approached by the Central Committee for its views, indicated approval at the General Assembly of 1959. In agreeing to integration, the FMC, along with the other interested committees of the Church, were expressing what was seen to be the overwhelming feeling of Churches in the Third World.

They shared the view that it was no longer appropriate for independent Churches in the Third World to be represented through an organisation of mission councils, and that to continue along that way was 'to misread the powerful signs of the time'.[18] It was therefore with particular pleasure that the FMC learned that Bishop Lesslie Newbigin had been invited to become General Secretary of the IMC on the run up to integration, and gladly agreed to his secondment from July 1959 for a period of five years.[19]

The integration of the IMC and the WCC was in line with the process of Church/Mission integration and raised no new and fundamental issues for the FMC. What it did, however, was to sharpen the FMC's perception of the distortion that arises from a failure to see mission in a world context, and from the perspective not of one department of the Church but of the Church as a whole. The habit still prevalent of speaking of our mission and our fields could lead only too easily to imagining that the centre of things lay with us, and, as an FMC Report to the General Assembly puts it, 'to see the impulses of power and light radiating always from here into other lands and among other people'.[20] The FMC could see only too clearly the important and difficult task that lay before it to help the Church rid itself of this distortion while maintaining a sense of missionary responsibility. At the same time it saw the need for the integration of three committees of the Church that were responsible for work outwith Scotland: *ie* the FMC, the Jewish Mission Committee, and the Colonial and Continental Committee. As it was, those committees occupying the same building could be dealing with different aspects of the same work overseas without consulting one another. It is interesting to note that at this stage the Inter-Church Relations Committee did not seem to pose the same problem, and was not mentioned.

The FMC had extensive experience over the years of practical co-operation with other Churches and missionary bodies, and worked closely with them within interdenominational organisations such as the Conference of British Missionary Societies. Many of the institutions in Asia, Africa, and the Caribbean, were run by different Churches together, and supported by various missionary societies, and in several places the work for which the FMC had direct responsibility received considerable help from bodies outside the Church of Scotland. Moreover it had experience of working in partnership with Churches which had come about as the result of unions, such as the United Church of Northern India, and the Church of South India. With that experience behind it, the FMC did not have to be argued into recognising that mission and unity belonged together. In the years under review it was in the forefront, both within the Church of Scotland and beyond, in stressing the crucial importance for mission in a world context of Christian unity and in its support for the ecumenical movement.

At the General Assembly of 1957 the convener of the Inter-Church Relations Committee, Dr Archie C. Craig, presented what came to be called the Bishops' Report. It was a report of conversations between delegates of the Church of Scotland, the Church of England, the Episcopal Church in Scotland, and the Presbyterian Church of England, on Relations between Anglican and Presbyterian Churches.[21] At the same time in North India, there took place the publishing of a Plan of Union which had received the approval of the delegates of seven negotiating Churches: including Anglican, Baptist, Congregational, Presbyterian and Methodist – both Episcopal and non-Episcopal.[22] The fact that those two events coincided might have been expected to encourage in Scotland an interest in the advanced stage that had been reached in India toward the goal of unity, and a willingness to learn from it, or at least to underline how action in one country might affect for good or ill attitudes and actions in another. It was with that hope that those who were aware of the negotiations in India did what they could to make the Plan of Union known.

George Appleton, as Secretary of the Conference of British Missionary Societies (CBMS), wrote on its behalf to the General Assembly with the same intention. Listing in his letter the many countries in which Church of Scotland and Church of England personnel worked closely together as colleagues, and the considerable number of union institutions in which both Churches were involved, he pointed out that anything said and done as the result of the conversations in Britain would have an effect on church relationships far beyond our own land. 'We are sure,' he said in closing, 'that those engaged in these conversations ... will be aware of the concern and hope with which the course of the conversations will be followed by the younger Churches and by the missionary agencies not only of the participating Churches but also of the other Churches in Great Britain.'[23]

The weeks preceding the presentation of the Joint Report on

Anglican/Presbyterian Conversations did not augur well for its reception, far less for any consideration of its proposals in the light of events in India. The *Daily Express* ran a vigorous campaign against the Report, and an outcry of hostility mounted, inflamed by long unsettled scores against the auld enemies – the Papes and the English – the accusation being that the Report was a betrayal of the Reformation and of Scotland. It was with the greatest difficulty that the General Assembly was persuaded to send the Report down to presbyteries for study, and only after Dr Archie Craig had been questioned for three hours. In its journey round the presbyteries during the next two years, the Report underwent searching and critical scrutiny, which at the end resulted in only one presbytery giving the Report cordial support.

The final Deliverance of the General Assembly of 1959 on the Inter-Church Relations Committee's (ICR) Report dealing with the returns from presbyteries included an amendment agreed by an overwhelming majority of commissioners. It read in part: 'The General Assembly ... are clearly of the opinion that the Proposals in the Joint Report regarding modifications in the polity of the Presbyterian Churches are unacceptable in that they imply a denial of the Catholicity of the Church of Scotland and of the validity and regularity of its ministry within the Church Catholic.'[24]

The FMC's views on the matter of Christian unity were well known, and comments to be found in its Report to the following General Assembly were apposite to the disappointment many of its missionaries, its members and supporters felt with the previous year's decision. The comments come in a section headed 'Pressure for Unity among the Younger Churches':

> They [the Younger Churches] may not attach sufficient importance to apostolic succession or the parity of presbyters, but is there not a danger that these questions, important as they are, should take precedence over weightier matters – the proclamation of the Gospel, united witness to the non-Christian world.

Then, in a quotation used by Hugh Martin, the FMC Report went on:

> Proportion is as essential to truth as to architecture, and it must be admitted that hardly anyone has more conspicuously failed in the sense of proportion than has the ecclesiastic.[25]

During this period, when the Church at home seemed so unwilling to respond to proposals for change and to lag behind
Churches in the Third World, the FMC maintained its support of
Churches there. The Churches in the Third World were involved in
the momentous movements that were rapidly transforming the old
colonial world. In the midst of that ferment of change, the FMC
sympathised with the Churches in their desire to be free to express
their faith and service in their own ways, *ie* in ways appropriate to
them in their own societies and cultures. It encouraged them at the
same time in their intention to live out in practice the unity which
belongs to the Gospel, in the belief shared with them that unity
would enable them to communicate ever more effectively the
'challenging relevance of the Gospel'.[26]

For more than eighty years as the result of ecclesiastical divisions
in Scotland, there had been two Presbyterian missionary organisations at work separately in the Nagpur area of India. In 1957, by
the welcome accession of the Original Secession Church to the
Church of Scotland, that separation, which had increasingly become
a hindrance to the developing mission of the Church, came to an
end. What had been the Seoni Mission of the Secession Church
came then under the FMC, and immediately thereafter within the
process of integration under the United Church of Northern India.[27]

By 1957 ten years had passed since the process of Church/
Mission integration began. The opportunity was being taken to see
how it had gone. It was plain that there had been a major step forward in setting out the priority, at least in theory, that was to be
given to the indigenous Church over the organisations of the foreign
missionary movement and the leadership of missionaries. Much,
however, remained to be done, particularly in terms of attitudes.
We have mentioned the patronising way in which it was so often
assumed that the missionary movement began and ended in the
West, and that therein lay the source of all experience and wisdom.
The meeting of the IMC in December in Ghana highlighted the
point. It was time, it was said, that the use of such discriminatory
phrases as 'older and younger churches', 'sending and receiving
countries', be discontinued. 'We have to school ourselves to accept
the thought of the one mission of Christ's Church.'[28]

It was in that same year that the Church of Scotland took the
important step of transferring property held by the FMC to the
Churches. Much had been done over the years to recognise the

dignity and integrity of the Churches, and it now remained to put right the anomaly of church property being owned by a foreign body. At the General Assembly of 1957 the FMC was authorised to go ahead with the transfer of property. The relevant Deliverance (8) of the FMC Report reads:

> The General Assembly, in endorsing the policy of integration, grant permission to the Foreign Mission committee to enable it gradually to transfer property in Asia, Africa, and the West Indies, including churches, institutions and missionary residences, to the appropriate legally incorporated bodies, as and when the committee so decides. They instruct the Foreign Mission Committee to take such legal steps, by way of Provisional Order or otherwise, as the Procurator may consider necessary, and they note that the Committee proposes, after obtaining any requisite legal authority, to proceed by Minute for each individual transfer, always provided that the Church of Scotland Trust has been satisfied with the evidence as to the standing of the Trust Association or other body to which the property would be thus transferred.[29]

With legal requirements fulfilled and Trusts set up with the approval of the General Trustees of the Church of Scotland, the transfer of property proceeded – though, in some places, not without delays beyond the control of the FMC which consistently pressed for the transfer to be made.

As will be illustrated in what follows, this whole period heralded a new openness of reflection and discussion on the very nature of the Church and of its mission. Emphasis was given, for example, to the Church as people, to the laity and their training; and to the need for the Church to become more firmly rooted as a community in the culture and language of the people around it. The Church following its master had to identify with the poor and the suffering, and with them pray and work for the coming of the Kingdom. Theological education and the training of the ministry were given a new priority, as also was the training of women for family life, for work in the Church, and in evangelism. Lastly, to name only some of the concerns to which fresh attention was given, there was the recognition of the importance of producing and distributing literature for the nurture of the Church, and the spread of the Gospel.

III

In the Indian sub-continent, both in India and in Pakistan, the movement toward the integration of Church and Mission proceeded stage by stage. By the end of this period the aim, as set out in the FMC Minute of April 1947,[30] was almost universally achieved so far as organisational change was concerned. Work formerly carried out by Mission Councils was now under the Courts of the Church and their committees, and the missionaries who were in control now served under the discipline of those Courts

Most ordained missionaries saw no difficulty in transferring their ministries from the Church of Scotland to the indigenous Churches. For some, however, it was a problem. When a missionary in Sialkot made known to colleagues in 1950 that he wished to do so, there was resistance and some ill-feeling. That he wished to transfer, he was told, would be an insult to his ordination, and would cause a division among the missionaries. By 1955, after Integration, an amicable arrangement was made and he and three others in Sialkot transferred their ministries.

The progress toward integration was quicker in some areas than in others. As we saw earlier, the Mission Board of the Nagpur Church Council had taken the place of the Mission Council as long ago as 1947. Now, after some delay, the process moved ahead again. On 24 October 1952 the Bengal Mission Council met for the last time, and two days later, along with the Mission Council of the London Missionary Society, became integrated with the Bengal Church Council.[31] In the same year, the East Himalaya Church Council took the first step by adopting a system of regional boards to take responsibility for work carried out formerly by the Mission Council, and submitted for consideration a draft constitution of a Central Board. In October 1954 the East Himalaya Mission Council was dissolved, and the East Himalaya Church Board of the United Church of Northern India came into being.[32] Meanwhile, in December 1953, the Punjab Mission Council in Pakistan was dissolved, and the Sialkot Presbytery of the United Church in Pakistan took over responsibilities formerly vested in the Punjab Mission Council of the Church of Scotland.[33] Back in India the Santalia Mission Council and the Church there were making steady progress toward integration, and after a conference chaired by William Stewart in July 1955 a new constitution was drawn up.

In the following year full control finally passed to the Church.[34]

In Madras, the setting of the Church of South India, with so many denominational bodies involved, the process toward integration was somewhat different. Following the union, a Church of Scotland Mission Advisory Committee was set up to exercise some of the functions of the old Mission Council. In 1957 it was agreed that responsibilities carried by the Church of Scotland Mission Advisory Committee should be transferred to the Diocesan Council and then gradually devolved on Area Councils and Committees. In the main this change affected the stationing of missionaries – their posting now being the responsibility of the Church rather than the Mission – and the method of communication between the Church and the FMC. To deal with the few remaining matters not dealt with by the Diocese, a Continuing Church of Scotland Missionary Committee was formed.[35] Then, in August 1957, it was agreed that grants in future be sent to the Diocesan treasurer direct, that money for institutions currently managed by the CSM Treasurer should be handed over to the Diocese, and that securities be passed from the Church of Scotland Trust to the Church of South India Trust Association.[36]

Integration had a bumpy ride in some places. In Rajputana, for instance, where the method used was to transfer different pieces of work stage by stage from the Mission Council to the Church, it took just over ten years from 1951, when the Evangelistic Work Committee was integrated with the Church Council, for full integration to happen.[37]

One of the reasons for the slowness of the process in Rajputana was a fear on the part of the Church that integration would mean less money being made available from Scotland, and that as a result the closing down of schools would be accelerated. In 1958, by which time the Church Council had taken the step of integrating educational work, it was faced with the inevitability of having to close schools, and was in the course of asking the Rajasthan Government, formerly Rajputana, to take over others. Consequently the Rajasthan (as it was now named) Church Council Education Committee recommended that the policy of closing existing work with the intention of opening new work should be discontinued. The Mission Council in its turn expressed the hope that the Church Council 'did not intend to exclude future review of the relative values of existing work and of proposed new developments'.[38] The

Mission Council at a subsequent meeting agreed to ask the FMC to reconsider its minute recommending the setting aside of a percentage of the budget for new work.[39] In doing so it pointed out that to continue that policy, in the light of recent missionary resignations and the curtailment of work, would 'increase the impression that the Church of Scotland was reducing its commitments in Rajasthan with a view to withdrawal'.[40]

The minutes of the February meeting of the Rajasthan Mission Council in 1959 reveal mounting tension between the Church Council and the FMC over integration. The Church Council was incensed by what it saw as a failure on the part of the FMC to ensure that money accruing from property put in trust would be used for Christian service in Rajasthan and nowhere else, and that such money would in fact go to ensure an adequate Central Fund, which the FMC itself had pressed the Church to set up. It asked the Mission Council to pass on its observations to the FMC including the following:'From the remarks of the FMC it is evident that the Rajasthan Church Council is not trusted by the FMC. If that is so, Partnership has no meaning.'[41] Despite, however, the difficulties that had arisen between the Church Council and the FMC, the final step toward integration was taken. Later in that year the Church Council assumed responsibility for medical work, the administration of property, the location of missionaries, the control of other works and assets, and obtained the right to communicate direct with the FMC.[42] Full integration took place in March 1960.[43]

Integration in Western India proved to be the most difficult of all, and was not fully achieved until 1992. A major difficulty was the fact that the Western India Mission of the Church of Scotland included two large cities, Bombay and Poona, and also the rural area of Jalna; and that at the same time it overlapped more than one Church Council – Godavari Valley, Ahmednagar and Bombay. Within those Councils, to add to the complications, there were several mission bodies at work, including the American Marathi Mission from the United States of America and societies of the Church of England, the USPG and the CMS. Several different schemes of integration were proposed for Jalna, Poona and Bombay, separately and together, but found, one after the other, to be impractical. In the end it was the transfer of property that was the greatest obstacle, a stubborn hindrance that defied for well over a generation the best attempts of Church leaders, lawyers and administrators, and many groups and committees, both in India and abroad.

In Nagpur, when the Mission Board of the Church Council was inaugurated, it was written into the constitution that a commission of inspection be appointed every five years. The Commission, consisting of Drs E. C. Bhatty and A. Rallia Ram representing the Church Council, and Dr James Kellock the FMC, met in February and in March 1955. In their Report[44] they recommended an organisation of administration which would be simpler than the one of 1947, and which would make integration more complete. The new arrangement in its final form took affect in March 1958.[45] The four parts of the Council's work – evangelism, medical, educational and welfare – each now had its own board, all the boards together being co-ordinated by the Council's Executive Committee. In the new structure, missionaries no longer had a place on boards or committees of the Council, *qua* missionaries, but only as holders of some office which gave them that right.

Although the integration of Church and Mission in India and Pakistan had in most places been completed in a formal structural sense, the goal of open and responsible partnership between Churches at home and abroad responding together in freedom to the one mission of God, had yet to be achieved. As it was, Churches of the old mission fields were in reality controlled to a disproportionate extent by their 'partners' abroad, on whom they were financially dependent, and whose missionaries, despite their new 'equal' position, continued to have considerable influence. A study paper in preparation for the Commission's visit to Nagpur[46] speaks of 'the "unmeant" but very real, financial dominance from Edinburgh', leading to missionaries being given 'prominence as representatives of the patron Church'; while in several areas, missionaries rather than local leaders held important offices in the Council. That was so, for instance, in Bengal, where the Moderator and the Secretary of the Council were both missionaries, in Santalia where they held the chief offices, and in Sialkot where W. G. Young at integration was pressed to be Church Council Secretary and 'given the task of setting a pattern of writing minutes, filing and correspondence'.

The economic gap between the Church of Scotland and the Churches of India and Pakistan was reflected, in the most personal way, in the glaring disparity between the salaries and the living conditions of the missionaries and their Indian and Pakistani colleagues. The more 'partnership' came to be seen as the 'way forward for effective co-operation in mission', the more that differential grew in importance. Many missionaries were acutely aware of the problem and were anxious to find a solution. Many also who found themselves appointed to positions of authority in the Councils and Committees were embarrassed, and accepted office only with the greatest reluctance. For the most part, missionaries recognised the urgent need for the Church to find its own identity and its own leadership, longed for obstacles brought about by the presence of missionaries from the rich West to be removed, and the continuing overarching and undeniable presence of 'the Mission' to be set aside.

The issue was cogently described in the record of a meeting of missionaries held in January 1959:

> We think that 'the mission' (and we consider that this, in the sense we use it, continues despite integration) with its impressive organisation and structure of institutions, its foreignness, and its influence closely connected to financial power, stands counter to mission. As things are, the Church does not know itself (always it has its eye on what 'the mission' expects it to do or say) and cannot act or speak in freedom. We are still far from a free and equal partnership. The situation is bedevilled by what is sensed as imperialism, spiritual, moral and financial, on the one hand, and by humiliation and a simmering rebelliousness on the other, this despite every effort we make in personal ways on both sides.[47]

During this period basic questions were being asked about the direction in which the missionary enterprise had been going. Roland Allen's writings were remembered and re-read, particularly *The Spontaneous Expansion of the Church*. Mission in stark contrast to his position had become a centrally managed operation working through a complex structure of committees, heavily dependent on outside help. The reality was very far from his concept of the Church called to mission as a community of people dispersed in society.

The Rev. William Young, later to become a bishop in the Church of Pakistan, and who had worked for integration, reflecting on integration some years after the event, could see weaknesses not recognised at the time:

As I look back on it now I can see that the integration scheme had its drawbacks .... It involved a multiplication of board and committee meetings. This meant that less time was available for pastoral and evangelistic work. I well remember Dr William Lillie's advice: 'Avoid committees – they are of the Devil!'[48]

The Commission appointed to study the situation in Nagpur in 1955, sensitive to those kind of questions, looked with approval at the steps being taken by the Rev. George and Dr Mary More to find ways of breaking away from the dominant missionary structure.[49] George More had served for some time as a pastor in the small country town of Wardha, and from there had moved to an outlying village called Allipur, where he and Mary set up home in a house supplied by the village, and in which Mary, with George's practical help, opened a pre-natal, post-natal clinic. From the very beginning, village elders and leaders had not only been consulted but gave assurance of support, and that was forthcoming. Not long after the work with women and children began, and people were coming from scores of villages around, George and Mary found themselves being called to help sufferers from leprosy, who were coming in from far afield every market day. A leprosy clinic began to operate – at the door of their village home.

The village of Allipur lay close to Gandhi's ashram of Sevagram in an area where the people were very poor. Gandhi had chosen that site with the poverty of the people and their great need in mind. By moving into Allipur village with its poverty, and taking the decision to live among its people, sharing their conditions, as far as they were able, the Mores were taking a major step toward a form of missionary service which many at this time had seen to be a priority. They found themselves too increasingly in sympathy with the Gandhian involvement, and friendships developed with a number of Christians and others belonging to Sevagram – Murray Rodgers and Marjorie Sykes among them.

The next stage was the decision of the Church Council to allow the Rev. Manohar Londhe to move to Allipur with his family, and later the agreement of the FMC, with the consent of the Church Council, that the writer, at that time the Council Youth Worker, and his wife Alison with their family, should join the others in a community of service.[50]

The Allipur Community, as it came to be called, had the far-sighted support of Dr David Moses, Principal of Hislop College.

David Moses arranged for the sale of a college bungalow in Nagpur, to cover the cost of building simple village style accommodation for communal meetings of the Community and for guests.[51] He had seen clearly from the outset the importance for mission of this Community, and continued to use his influence to encourage the Church to participate in its activities and to learn from it.

By the end of this period the Community had a house for each of the families, two communal buildings, a chapel, a plot of land, and a well with an overhead tank supplying water to the buildings and irrigation for crops and orange trees. The Community led a simple, basic way of life appropriate to the way of the village. They shared a common budget, had meals regularly together, had a discipline of prayer, morning and evening, in which intercession was offered for the village, and for the Church, in which prominence was given to prayer for people by name, and for particular problems and issues.

The work of the Community consisted of service within the village, and the running of training projects for the Church. From the beginning efforts were made to improve the health of the village, in terms of hygiene, nutrition, child care, sanitation, and clean and adequate water supplies, and always with the agreement and active help of village leaders. The clinics were run with the support of the *panchyat* – the village council – and the improvement of wells and the digging of new wells carried out with their participation. Youth conferences recruited from youth fellowships in Nagpur and district, and of different denominations, were held at the Community, and as the years went on, seminars and study conferences took place for specific groups of lay people, elders, medics, journalists and others, including mixed groups from Hislop College. Many visitors also, singly and in groups, came to see what was happening and to share something of the life of the Community.

The Allipur Community continued to be influenced by the Gandhian movement and learned much from the Basic Education Centre at Sevagram, the Hindustani Talimi Sangh, which followed Gandhi's scheme of 'education for life', and from the ashram's life of community.

Basic education during this period was encouraged by the Government across India, and was welcomed by the Churches. Mission Boards and education departments keen to develop this pattern of education sent members of staff to Sevagram and other Gandhian institutions for training. The FMC's involvement with the Gandhian movement was further strengthened when in 1958 it agreed to send one of its missionaries to the All-India Sarvodya Centre run by Vinoba Bhave.[52]

As the new climate following independence had led to changes in primary education, higher education was coming under scrutiny also. The Churches responsible for the running of Christian colleges had to ask afresh what the distinctive function of such colleges was, whether it was possible for them to be effectively different from secular institutions, and how best they might serve India's society and people. Constitutional changes were required, and these were worked out in close collaboration with Government, a process that worked remarkably well. A new constitution for Scottish Church College, Calcutta, which Principal Taylor of Aberdeen University had helped with, came into effect early in 1953.[53] Later that year the new constitution of Wilson College, Bombay, transferring control from Edinburgh to a Board of Governors in India, was accepted by the University of Bombay.[54]

In Wilson College an additional floor was built to allow for the development of science teaching. At the same time a building programme was undertaken at Hislop College, Nagpur, which moved the College out of a narrow site in the old city to a new plot that made possible a much larger building.[55] Space was provided too for a sports field, and the erection of a new student hostel. In 1952 a department of sociology was introduced in the new College, an innovation as important for education in India as the department of journalism had proved to be.

It was a time of much change in the colleges with the retiral of several long-serving and distinguished missionary principals. John Kellas, Principal of Scottish Church College, retired in 1954; two years later, James Kellock of Wilson College, Bombay; and in 1957 Alec Boyd of Madras Christian College, Tambaram. Harold John Taylor of Wilson College took over from John Kellas in Calcutta; J.W. Airan, an Indian Scientist and Educationist, became Principal of Wilson College; and Russell MacPhail of Tambaram, Principal of Tambaram. Lesslie Scott served as Principal of Murray College, Sialkot, until 1956 when he retired to serve under a non-missionary Pakistani colleague. In 1953 William Stewart of Nagpur became Principal of Serampore College.

During this whole period there was a constant demand for more missionaries. The Student Christian Movement of India, for instance, was appealing for 53 missionary teachers from Britain to serve in the universities.[56] Hislop College was asking urgently for two members of staff, Murray Christian College wanted two to teach Chemistry and English respectively, and Scottish Church College was crying out for as many as seven members of staff. This was happening at a time when the Government was tightening its visa regulations, and an official enquiry was being undertaken by Judge Niyogi into missionary activities.

In 1954 the Foreign Mission Committee, along with the United Church of Northern India, became founder members of the United Mission to Nepal, established under the auspices of the National Christian Council of India, and the first secondment was made.[57]

Following a visit to India and Pakistan in 1959, the Rev. Ian M. Paterson had made a number of suggestions dealing with medical policy. A group appointed for the purpose discussed them and put forward recommendations to the FMC. Among these recommendations which the Committee accepted was the closure of St Margaret's Hospital, Poona, which had won a deservedly high reputation since its founding in 1892. That decision, it is to be noted, was made not by the Church but by the FMC, since integration had yet to take place. In its Minute 'the group reiterated the concern of the FMC for the development of rural work, and approved of the work in the Nagpur field at Dhapewada [where there was a clinic run by Dr Peggy Martin] and Allipur, and of the rural outreach from the Rainy Hospital [in Madras]'.[58]

IV

The FMC no longer had direct contact with the Church in China. It did, however, continue to have connection with Chinese Christians. Sister Helen Wilson worked among Chinese in Hong Kong, and the Rev. John Fleming with his wife, Pearl, in Malaysia.

Helen Wilson went to Ichang in 1920 and had been expelled from China under armed guard during the Communist capture of Ichang. During her long period of service there, she went through the troubles of 1927 and was interned by the Japanese from 1942 to 1945. After her abrupt expulsion from China, she worked for eight years in the Rennie Mill Refugee Camp, Hong Kong,[59] among sufferers from the effects of malnutrition and tuberculosis. She retired finally in October 1959.

The Rev. John Fleming was seconded as General Secretary of the Malayan Christian Council in 1951, to fill an urgent vacancy.[60] The influx of missionaries and missionary societies made a strong ecumenical body increasingly necessary, and there was a need for someone of John Fleming's experience to build contacts with the Chinese-speaking Churches in Malaya, and 'to extend the field of recruitment for the Joint Theological College in Singapore'.

For the first few years the work had to do in the main with church extension[61] in the 'New Villages' set up by Government during the emergency, running training courses for church workers in the villages, and producing pamphlets for enquirers. By 1955 there were 120 Christian congregations, 160 full-time workers and 150 part-time; and there were 32 clinics.

In 1956, after furlough and a period of study in Union Theological Seminary, New York, John Fleming returned to Malaya, where half his time was given to the MCC and half as a member of staff at Trinity College, Singapore.[62]

From 1 April 1958, Dr Fleming acted on secondment from the FMC as South East Asia Representative of the Nanking Foundation (see paragraph below), the arrangement being that he continue for the first six months half-time on the MCC staff and give half the year during the three year period of his secondment to teaching at Trinity College.[63] John Fleming's secondment was extended for a further three years after his furlough in 1960. The Rev. Chung Chi-An of Formosa succeeded Dr Fleming as General Secretary of the MCC who in turn became its President.[64]

The Nanking Foundation was the result of a petition filed by American Mission Boards to change the conditions of a bequest allowing money for Nanking Theological College to be used for theological education in South-East Asia. Grants were given by the Foundation to Colleges in Burma, Thailand, Taiwan, Singapore, Indonesia, Philippines, Hong Kong, Japan, and Sarawak, to help with capital grants for new buildings, with staff and scholarships, libraries and text books. Dr Fleming was responsible for advising the Foundation on the annual expenditure of the Fund, and to do so had to get to know the colleges and make frequent visits – which, incidentally, through John Fleming, widened the Church of Scotland's contacts appreciably. In 1957 and 1959, as Director of the

Study Institute Programme, he gathered together theological staffs in a Study Institute to which eminent theological teachers from the West were invited. Dr Fleming was in addition Editor of the *South-East Asia Journal of Theology* supported by the Nanking Board as the organ of a newly-formed association of Theological Schools in that area.[65]

On 14 May 1959, at Kuala Lumpur, the inaugural meeting of the East Asia Christian Conference took place. A structure of committees was established, with John Fleming as chairman of the committee dealing with Church's Life, Message, and Unity, along with Principal J. Russell Chandran of India.[66]

V(a)

In West Africa the centenary of the Ewe Presbyterian Church (soon to be called the Evangelical Presbyterian Church) was celebrated in September 1953. Dr Dougall was present representing the Church of Scotland.[67] On his return he spoke of the 'boundless optimism and confidence' present in West Africa, and indicated how closely that seemed to match the theme of the WCC Assembly to be held in Evanston.

Jim Dougall referred in his report to the movement toward self-government, to economic development, and to the large public expenditure on education. Speaking of the Churches in the Gold Coast, he pointed to the need for youth work beyond what was done in the schools, to the importance of Christian literature and of the training of the laity.

The Ewe Presbyterian Church had given priority, among several of its requirements for their missionary staff, to the appointment of a youth worker, and had requested the FMC to transfer Mr W. G. C. Benton, with his prior agreement, from teacher training at Akropong College. Since the transfer would make new demands on its budget, which at this stage was seriously stretched to the extent that it had to turn down many requests, the FMC was willing to agree only on condition that the Church met the cost of transport and housing.[68] That was a condition, however, that the Ewe Presbyterian Church was not in the position to meet. It was only after missionaries protested against the Church's being asked to pay, and promised to meet expenses from the surplus accruing from the difference between the salaries educational missionaries received from the Government and their missionary allowances, that the transfer was agreed.[69] The missionary youth worker was ready to begin work by the middle of 1954. The importance of youth work was underscored for the Church by the fact that the schools, which had provided its main contact with young people, might soon be taken over by the Government or local authorities.[70]

The surpluses, referred to as Erzuah Balances, were administered by the Missionaries' Committee, which recommended allocations to the FMC, to meet specific needs within the Presbyterian Church of the Gold Coast, and the Evangelical Presbyterian Church. The allocations in October 1954, to give an example, totalled £4250, for projects such as youth work, and for the upkeep of buildings – a figure that may be compared with the total FMC/WFM budget, excluding missionary allowances and expenses of £4838. Taken over a period those balances represented a not insignificant subsidy to the Churches from Government.[71]

In 1953, because of a movement to provide free education for primary school children, the government asked the Training College at Krobo to increase its numbers, and promised a grant to enable buildings to be extended. At the same time new buildings were being erected for Krobo Girls' School, the old buildings now being fully used by the Training College. From 1953 onwards the school was served by an African Headmistress.[72]

Through the Christian Council of the Gold Coast the Churches worked closely with the Social Welfare Department of Government in literacy campaigns, and because of their relatively high rate of literacy the Churches provided many of the volunteers. In an intensive mass literacy campaign referred to in the reports for 1954, a large number of students from the Christian colleges took part.[73]

Programmes of Christian Literature were more advanced in the Gold Coast, because of the work of the Basel and Bremen Missions, than in most other parts of the world where the FMC was involved. One of its missionaries, the Rev. Colin Forrester-Paton, gave most of his time to the work of planning, writing, translating and editing material for Christian literature and literacy campaigns, under the auspices of the Christian Council and the Literature Committee of the Presbyterian Churches. One of the important parts of his work was the editing of a monthly magazine, *The Christian Messenger*, which had a circulation of more than 5000 and was printed in two languages, Ga and Twee, besides English. Colin Forrester-Paton kept in close touch throughout with the Scottish Mission Book Depot and the Printing Press.[74]

The Depot, with its nine branches, was a going business concern. For many years the FMC hoped that the Printing Press and the Depot would become an independent institution in which the two Churches would participate together. The Churches, however, were unable to agree to that arrangement, and in the event both Press and Depot were divided between the Churches, the assets being proportionately shared – the Press in 1958 and the Depot in the following year.[75]

At the end of 1954 the Synod of the Presbyterian Church of the Gold Coast made an important decision to develop further its work in the North, and asked the Scottish and Basel Missions each to provide an additional missionary.[76] In welcoming the decision the Missionaries' Committee indicated that Erzuah surpluses would be available to help toward the costs.[77] This time the response of the FMC was 'yes'. The immediate hope was that a missionary already in the Gold Coast, and with experience, would be willing to go. Colin Forrester-Paton and his wife immediately volunteered, the agreement between them and the FMC being that there would be no going back on the making of a new appointment, and that they would go for a short period only – long enough in order to prepare the way for someone else, and to help whoever that might be to settle in.[78] By the middle of 1956 Robert Duncan[79] with his wife were appointed, ready to go to the North early the following year. It was agreed that the work would begin at Sandema among the Builsa tribe.

By the end of 1956, while arrangements were going forward to purchase land and to contract for the building of a house, the Government was considering the setting up of a health clinic nearby. Mrs Duncan, who was a nurse, had begun a child clinic soon after arriving in 1957, and in agreement with the Presbyterian Church of Ghana pressed for the appointment of a nurse. By the end of the year the work of building relationships with the local people and of teaching at Sandema was well established. Discussions with the Government on medical services were, however, inconclusive.[80]

The period leading up to Independence in 1957 saw a fresh concern in the Churches to reassert their own special African identity, and to be rid of Western ideas and practices, where those had become an obvious encumbrance. It was recognised that the Church rooted in Christ must be planted deep in African soil, and the accusation that Churches were mere spiritual colonies of the West increasingly resented. The Christian Council arranged a Conference on Christian Faith and African Culture in order to face up to the question of adaptation and syncretism.[81]

Denominational divisions introduced from the West became an issue. The visit of the Moderator of the Church of South India, Bishop Hospet Sumitra, in October 1955, provided an opportunity for that to be brought into the open and discussed. In the three days of his visit Bishop Sumitra was able to have consultation with Church leaders, to discuss questions of Church union with the Christian Council, and to preach at a united service when Anglicans, Methodists, Presbyterians, and the American Methodist Episcopal Zion Church took part.[82]

One of the major factors hindering Church union in West Africa was the development of large Western style confessional groupings across national boundaries. Raising that point in discussion after the Bishop's visit the Rev. C. G. Baeta, the African theologian, had this to say:

> When members of the same denomination in different lands enter into close fellowship with each other, does it not check their willingness or desire to draw the different denominations together in their own land?
>
> ... If, as we believe, a denomination is the trustee for some truth or aspect of the truth of the Gospel or the Church, that should be offered as its contribution to the larger experience of the Church just there in the local situation where the total Gospel needs to be preached by a united Church. We are faithful to our stewardship, as the Evanston Report said, our faithfulness will bring us together at the foot of the cross in penitence.[83]

In this period leading up to Independence the Churches in the Gold Coast took stock of where they had come from and the point that they had reached. It was an encouraging story for which they gave thanks. By 1957 the membership of the Presbyterian Church of the Gold Coast was over 40,000, and of the Evangelical Presbyterian Church (formerly the Ewe Presbyterian Church) 25,000.[84]

The Churches were conscious of the contribution made through the Gospel, that had paved the way for the coming of independence.

They were no less aware, however, of what lay in front of them still to be done, among young people leaving school, in relating obediently and sensitively to the cultural setting, and in the active search for Christian unity.

Early in 1957 the FMC received invitation from the Government of Ghana (the new name of the Gold Coast) to be present at the Ghana Independence celebrations on 6 March in Accra. The Rev. J. A. R. Watt, Africa Secretary[85] who had taught at Akropong, represented the FMC. John Watt was warmly welcomed by the Churches in a much appreciated visit. There were visits during this period in the other direction also – to Scotland – equally appreciated. In 1956 the Rev. A. L. Kwansa, Synod Clerk of the Presbyterian Church, visited Scotland. He was followed by the Rev. F. H. Buatsi, Acting Synod Clerk of the Evangelical Presbyterian Church.[86] In the following year the Rev. T. A. Kumi came to Scotland to study methods of evangelism. His visit of several months effected many fruitful contacts. A good ambassador of his Church, the FMC was grateful for his contribution to the missionary cause during his time in Scotland.[87]

Dr Dougall, who went to Ghana for the International Missionary Council meeting in Legon, was present at a service in Sandema on Christmas Day 1957, when the first catechumens were baptised.[88]

The work in the North, in Sandema District, continued to develop. While Robert Duncan built up new congregations in the surrounding area, Colin Forrester-Paton worked for some months on translating a Gospel, along with some psalms and hymns, into Buli for the use of the Church. Alongside the teaching and preaching there was a continuous demand for clinics at Sandema and nearby villages. Mrs Louise Duncan and Mrs Mairi Byers were well qualified to meet this need and, whenever possible, this included teaching on nutrition and preventative health. In this mass education programme, staff could often help with cooking demonstrations and interpretation. After the Duncans' transfer to Tamale in 1964, Doris Hodds, Norma Carlyon and Dorothy Aitken successively continued the clinics in and around Sandema.[89]

The Rev. T. S. Colvin, who had been prevented from returning to Nyasaland, was appointed at the end of 1959 to serve in Tamale in the Northern Territories.[90]

(b)

At the end of 1952 Dr A. B. MacDonald[91] of Itu in Nigeria retired after a remarkable service of over thirty years. In 1927 he had begun to build the Leper Colony which, by the time of his retirement, had become a busy industrial township with a population of over 4000. It relied for its upkeep on a thriving palm oil industry, on the work of 'patients', and on the skills they learned within the community as carpenters, plumbers, or engineers. Itu had become widely recognised in Africa, notably as a place where community, involving care for the whole person, was recognised to be an important part of therapy, giving hope and encouraging regeneration. In his time Dr MacDonald saw thousands of former sufferers from leprosy returning to their homes cured, with self-respect, and with a practical training to help them in their new life.

After a short period in Scotland Dr MacDonald returned to Itu to relieve his successor, the Rev. Bill MacDonald, who was due for furlough. In 1954 Dr A. B. MacDonald was able to see the new hospital, built to replace one burned down in 1949, completed and opened.

By 1951[92] the new drug Dapsone was being used on all patients, proving markedly successful. Also a Leprosy Scheme in Ogoja Province was being developed. At the end of 1953[93] a government grant was received for the scheme and approval given for building plans. In the following year arrangements were made for co-operation with the Mission to Lepers; and the name was changed to Southern Ogoja Leprosy Service. By 1955 further developments were being discussed for the Odubra Division with the British Empire Leprosy Relief Association (BELRA), and with Government for the Yakurr Centre, the latter being turned down on financial grounds.[94] The Leprosy Mission was a continuing support. In its 1957 Report the FMC recorded its appreciation to the Mission for sending a woman doctor to Itu, and a nursing sister to Ogoja. Shortage of staff was a serious problem. In December 1957 the staffing position was so difficult that Dr Alistair MacDonald had to supervise both the Uburu Hospital and Ogoja Leprosy Service, a situation that could not be allowed to continue and that threatened for a second time the closure of Uburu and the jobs of the African staff. At the same time the Nigeria Leprosy Service was asking Itu to take over leprosy control for the greater part of Calabar Province.[95]

The institutions set up by the missionaries, and run by them, had been the primary and chief agents of mission in Eastern Nigeria from the beginning, and so it continued. The Hope Waddell Training Institution, the Itu Leper Colony, the General Hospitals at Itu and Uburu, the Rural Training Centre, and the many schools across the country were still to a considerable extent a foreign enterprise. Although the Church, organised in congregations, had its own independent life, and by 1945 its own constitution as the Presbyterian Church of Eastern Nigeria, the anomaly remained – the Christian institutions, which played such an important part in mission, were not under its control.

By 1953 change began. In July of that year it was agreed to hold a joint meeting representing the Mission Council, the Synod, and Hope Waddell to find ways of working more closely together, by bringing all medical, educational and evangelistic work under the aegis of Synod. At the same time the Mission Council was asking whether the time had come for it to disband and for its functions to be transferred. In May 1953 the Calabar Presbytery of the Church of Scotland signified that all its ministers present were ready to become ministers of the Presbyterian Church of Eastern Nigeria, if Synod invited them to do so, and soon after the FMC petitioned the General Assembly to dissolve the Presbytery of Calabar.[96] At the end of 1954 the Synod appointed a Standing Committee on Evangelism, and assumed full control of Women's work. Joint proposals for handing over to Boards of Synod work being undertaken by Mission Council were under discussion, further important steps being taken in July 1956 when it was proposed that a provisional committee be set up by Synod to prepare a plan of integration.[97] The final scheme of integration was approved by the Synod at its meeting in June 1959. The scheme included constitutions, among others, of the following – Standing Committee, Education Authority, Hope Waddell Training Institution, Uburu Hospital, Itu Leper Colony, Southern Ogoja Leprosy Service. It included also the Missionaries' Committee, which by this time was responsible solely for the affairs of missionaries and for no matters of Church policy.[98]

For the major institutions to be led by missionaries from outside and not by Nigerians, increasingly came to be seen as inappropriate. The fact that Sir Francis Ibiam had been in full-time charge of an institution for many years – and in 1957 Principal of Hope Waddell – was a pointer to what should be.[99]

The issue of Church Union came to the fore in 1953, a further sign of the movement for change. Close co-operation with other Churches and missions in Eastern Nigeria had led to a deepening of understanding, and an inevitable questioning about the unity of the Church and its divisions. The work of the institutions, for example, could be seen to demand all the resources available in the Christian community, if the vast needs and opportunities were to be met effectively. Mission and Unity belonged together. It was recognised too that denominational divisions were an import from abroad which had to be questioned, along with so much else in the quest for self-hood and independence.

In July 1954 the Synod appointed delegates to attend a conference on Church Union to discuss with Anglicans and Methodists the present position on Union in Eastern Nigeria, and to study Church Union schemes elsewhere.[100] At the same time the Mission Council was pressing for an All-Nigeria Church Union Conference.[101] The Synod agreed at its next meeting to invite the Church of South India to send a delegate to Nigeria, who would travel the country and be chief speaker at an All-Nigeria Conference, 'in order to further the cause of union'.[102] The visit would take place from mid-October to mid-December 1955, ending with a three-day Conference. The Moderator of the CSI, Bishop Sumitra, agreed to come.[103]

Having considered the report of that conference the Synod at its meeting in June 1956 resolved among other things the following:

> The Synod regards inter-denominational union as a paramount Christian concern because only so will a witness be borne to the Gospel of reconciliation which the world will not believe till it sees it operating within the Christian Church. Only through union in Nigeria will the Church be able to bear any new power in local and national affairs, and in the evangelistic task that lies so urgently before us.
>
> Synod agreed that if the Churches in Western Nigeria set Church union in Nigeria before them as a goal, their aim should be a united Church of Nigeria. If, however, the Churches in Western Nigeria were unwilling to give up their wider denominational affiliation, the aim of the Churches in Eastern Nigeria should be an Eastern Regional union in the first instance.[104]

Dealing with Church union at its meeting in June 1958 the Synod of the Presbyterian Church of Eastern Nigeria noted:

(a) With satisfaction that the provincial Synod of the Anglican Church had sent a resolution to the Lambeth Conference requesting that machinery be set up to approve a Nigeria Scheme of union, should such a scheme be presented before the next meeting of the Conference.

(b) That no final decision had been reached about the formation of a west Africa Conference of the Methodist Church, but the Methodist Church was confident that even if a Conference was formed it would not be a barrier to Church union.

(c) That the Presbyterian Church in the Cameroons, like the Presbyterian Church of Eastern Nigeria, was in no way restricted by its relations with parent or sister Churches and was fully committed to union.

(d) That copies of the Scheme of union had been sent to the Church of Scotland and the Presbyterian Church in Canada for their information and agreed to inform the missionary committees in Scotland and Canada that the Presbyterian Church of Eastern Nigeria was committed to union and looked forward to its easy consummation.[105]

During this whole period there was a continuing shortage of missionary staff in the institutions, and of ordained missionaries. In 1955, for instance, there was a request for, among other missionary personnel, a builder, three doctors, five nursing sisters, an agriculturist, and a business manager. The effect of the inadequate number of ordained ministers, as was pointed out in 1959, meant for example that important work, such as evangelists' training, had to be postponed while ministers' time was given up to administration.[106]

The most serious shortage of all, however, was the shortage of candidates for the ministry.[107] At one time it looked as though there would be no Presbyterian students in Trinity, the united Theological College. In a Church numerically weak – in 1957 there were only 15,000 communicants[108] – many of the ministers had to look after a score of parishes, and not only was there a shortage of ministers, but the quality itself in terms of education and training was not high.

(c)

In Central Africa, both in Northern Rhodesia and Nyasaland, the movement from mission control to integration was going ahead, and with it the upbuilding of a structure of hospitals and schools under the aegis of the Church. There was at the same time a growing awareness of the importance of strengthening the life of the local Church. Meanwhile there was the overshadowing fact of Central African Federation and the increasing bitterness and racial prejudice it was arousing.

Under the chairmanship of Principal John Baillie, a public meeting on Central African Federation was held in the Assembly Hall in Edinburgh at the end of January 1953, following the London constitutional conference. Paramount Chief Mberwa, a delegate of the Chiefs of Nyasaland, was one of the speakers, as were both the chairman of the Africa Bureau, and a former Minister of State for the Colonies. The meeting had been arranged by the Edinburgh World Church Group, which continued to play a notable part along with other bodies, such as the newly formed Scottish Council for African Questions (SCAQ), not to mention the Churches themselves, in keeping the needs and feelings of the African peoples concerned before the public.

Similar meetings were held in other cities, and there were many letters of protest in the press. In March the House of Commons, at the first reading of the Rhodesia and Nyasaland Bill, approved the proposed federation, and despite the opposition of African representatives the same action was taken in the councils in the Rhodesias and Nyasaland, all European dominated. In Scotland and other parts of the UK the protest continued. In May, on the initiative of the SCAQ, a petition to the Queen was presented to the Secretary of State for Scotland asking that federation be not imposed. The fear, however, that the scheme would be implemented against all opposition, was confirmed as the Government in that same month secured the passage of the second reading of the Bill making possible the Order in Council that brought Federation into being.

The position of the FMC in all this was clear. It unambiguously opposed Federation being set in motion against the will of the African people, and was pressing for a delay. It had been the practice for the FMC to leave political affairs to the Church and Nation Committee, but on this matter felt it necessary to speak. In April 1953 its Convener's Committee adopted a resolution for communication to the Church and Nation Committee, which among other things said this:

At this crucial point in the history of Central Africa the Foreign Mission Committee cannot be silent ... on account of its present close links with Missions and Churches in these two territories [Nyasaland and

Northern Rhodesia] it has a concern on the whole matter which it must make known.

While the committee welcomes the ideal of Partnership which is the declared objective, and recognises the economic advantages of Federation, it is not satisfied that the social and political interests and progress of the African peoples are adequately safeguarded in the present scheme.

The fundamental question is spiritual, not economic. If the ideal of Partnership is to be gained, mutual trust between the races in Central Africa is essential.

African opposition has been minimised as only that of a small vocal minority. The great mass of the people, it is said, either know nothing or are indifferent to the whole matter. The information given to the Committee by its missionaries is that the main draft of the proposals is appreciated by the Africans among whom they work and that the opposition to them is deep and widespread.[109]

The convener of the FMC, in presenting his report to the General Assembly of 1953 reiterated this. Opposition was strong and widespread among the Africans. Federation had created a state of racial tension and was raising distrust of the British Government. 'If Federation were imposed,' he said, 'a special responsibility would lie on the African Church and the missionaries to keep bitterness and distrust from poisoning the whole communal life.'[110]

A Supplementary Report of Church and Nation, dealing with Central African Federation, pointed out that Federation seemed to be inevitable. The related Deliverance of the General Assembly deplored that consent was not achieved, but called on those concerned to give it a fair trial. This led to a vigorous debate. It was argued, on the side of the Deliverance brought by the Committee, that Federation held out a reward not only of material benefit to the three territories, but also the realisation of a fine ideal partnership in a multi-racial state, the basic assumption being that that was still a realisable ideal.[111] The argument, on the other hand, against the Deliverance was that the General Assembly, if they accepted it, would be going back on what they unanimously decided in 1952. 'It was not the primary function of the Church,' it was said, 'to protest and then to depart from the issue when what they had protested against became law.'[112] 'They could not have African interests at heart if they were supporting the scheme .... The Church of Scotland was not to be dragged at the coat tails of the State.'[113] At the end the juxtaposition of the phrases 'deplored' and 'give a fair trial', which had been at the heart of the argument, were retained, and the original Deliverance, with some amendment, was agreed. The 1953 Deliverance reads:

> The General Assembly, noting that Central African Federation seems now inevitable, still deplore the fact that the consent of the Africans has not been obtained; they call for action to be taken by the Governments and all concerned to reassure Africans and convince them of the sincerity of the proposed partnership, and earnestly urge all concerned to give the Federal Scheme a fair trial in the hope that it may prove beneficial to the three territories.[114]

One of the consequences of Federation on the ground, in Northern Rhodesia and Nyasaland, was the damaging of relationships between Africans and Europeans. A senior member of the Blantyre Mission is on record as saying that things were said and done on both sides that would not be forgotten. He wrote:

> Happy relationships ... have been marred and will never be quite the same again .... Although the life of the country is, on the surface, back to normal, there are new tensions and the consciousness of the colour barrier divides as never before.

He went on:

> The work of Church and Mission is made more difficult by this new 'line-up' but perhaps because of our resolute stand against the enforcement of federation we have come through and suffered less than might have been expected.[115]

It was at this time and in this context that Andrew Doig received an invitation from the Governor of Nyasaland to be one of the European Representatives for African Interests on the Federal Assembly. After long discussion, because releasing him from missionary duties was extremely difficult on account of the shortage of staff, it was decided that he be seconded for a period of two years. He himself had seen the overriding importance of accepting the invitation and had gone ahead to do so.[116]

★ ★ ★

The integration of Church and Mission was progressing during this period, and with one exception smoothly, despite sensitivities in relationships and some understandable fears.

In December 1954 the FMC approved a recommendation that a Joint Council be set up in Northern Rhodesia, with an equal number of representatives from District Church Councils and the Missionaries Committee, as a temporary measure until the Church of Central Africa Rhodesia adopted a formal constitution.[117] In June 1955 the Livingstonia (Rhodesia) Mission Council was dissolved,[118] and in October the first meeting of Joint Council was held.[119]

That procedure was repeated when, two months later, Central Africa Regional Committee agreed to recommend that Blantyre Mission Council be dissolved and replaced by a Joint Council.[120] In July 1956, on the dissolution of Mission Council, the Joint Council took over. In October the following year there was a proposal in Joint Council that Synod should undertake work now done by the Council.[121] In April 1959 there was agreement that Joint Council be dissolved and that control previously exercised by it should henceforth be vested in the Church.[122]

In Livingstonia, Nyasaland, the progress toward integration was interrupted. A proposal for the forming of a joint council had been sent down to district councils and kirk sessions. It was rejected, although the proposal which came from the Mission Council was essentially the same as the proposals accepted in Rhodesia and Blantyre. The FMC Report to the General Assembly makes this reference to the Church's rejection:

> Although personal relationships between missionaries and Africans are excellent, there seems to be a fear that this was an attempt by the mission to regain control of the Church, which it had relinquished 25 years ago. When every allowance is made for the deterioration of the atmosphere in recent years, the imposition of Federation, and the position of the European missionary in the Dutch Reformed Church Mission, this lack of trust on the part of African Christians is still a grievous thing for the missionary.[123]

In order to begin to overcome some of the distrust, the Regional Committee recommended that District Church Councils appoint for a limited period observers to attend meetings of the Livingstonia Mission Council.[124] By the end of 1957 the Synod of Livingstonia had agreed that a Joint Council be established, and accepted with slight alterations the constitution proposed by the Mission Council.[125] In 1957 Livingstonia Mission Council was dissolved and the constitution of Joint Council approved.[126] Finally it was agreed by the

Synod of Livingstonia that full integration would take place on 1 January 1960.[127]

The movement toward the integration of Church and Mission was seen as a step on the way to the formation of a new and united Church of Central Africa. In Northern Rhodesia, by the end of 1954, an encouraging stage was reached between the London Missionary Society, the Church of Central Africa in Rhodesia, the Barotse Synod of the Paris Evangelical Mission, and the Church of Scotland in framing a basis of union and form of constitution. A ministry appeared possible that would be undivided by racial differences, and it appeared likely that the English speaking congregations in the Copperbelt would accept the proposed constitution.[128]

Progress toward union proved to be slower than anticipated. The Paris Mission were opposed to union being effected too early, as they saw it, and wanted a delay of ten years. In this they were at odds with their missionaries at work with the Barotse Synod. The hope was that the Mission in Paris might be persuaded to alter its view.[129] By 1956 a Draft Basis of Union was drawn up between the Church of Barotseland, the Church of Central Africa in Rhodesia, and the Free Churches in the Copperbelt, and a Draft Constitution of the United Church presented. Representatives of the Methodist District were present in the negotiating committee as observers. The year 1958, suggested as the date for the inauguration of union, was not acceptable to the Paris Mission. The intention was to go ahead without the Barotseland Church if that had to be.[130]

On 26 July 1958 the union of the Copperbelt Free Churches and the Church of Central Africa Rhodesia took place;[131] and in September 1959 the Church Union Committee met, representing the new United Church of Central Africa in Rhodesia, and the Methodist Church in Northern Rhodesia, with observers from the Anglican Diocese of Northern Rhodesia and the Paris Evangelical Missionary Society. It was agreed that there should be an exchange of visits and of information between the Synod of Barotseland and the other Churches. Various amendments also were made in the Interim Constitution.[132]

Both the movement for the integration of Church and Mission, and for the unity of the Church, like the protest against Federation, were expressions in one way or another of the African's desire to be himself, to be free from outside domination, and from structures that were foreign and disruptive.

* * *

During this period an analogous yet in the long run an ultimately contradictory movement began, namely Lenshina or Alice.[133]

It began among the Bemba people in Northern Rhodesia. In 1953 Alice Mulenga Lenshina had undergone a powerful spiritual experience which led her to believe that, having died, she had been brought back to earth again by God with a special mission. She came from the village of Kasomo in the Lubwa district and was a Church member. She was a deacon and entitled to preach and at the beginning she said nothing contrary to the teaching of the Church. Only later, as she began to preach against the Church and its connection with Europeans and foreign missions, was she then compelled to leave. The Africans, she believed, had one God and the Europeans another. Her calling, as she saw it, was to build a Church which was truly African, to purify it, and to combat witch-craft.[134]

The Lumpa Church which grew up around her expanded rapidly, so that by the end of 1956 it had 100,000 adherents, and the churches founded by the missions, Presbyterian, and Roman Catholic, were being drained of members. As the mining companies gave permission, many of their churches were being built in the Copperbelt. The Lenshina movement became a peoples' movement drawing followers from far and wide. They came to her village to see her, to hear her preach, to have spirits exorcised, to make confession of sin, to have assurance of cleansing, and to join in the spontaneous singing of Bemba hymns which contrasted so vividly with the translated and stilted versions ordinarily used.[135]

In the phenomenon of the Lenshina movement, which erupted out of the frustration of African people as Federation was imposed upon them by dominant whites, many basic issues were being raised and questions asked. Most basic of all, as a General Assembly Report puts it, was 'how to pray for and work for a Church which the African people feel to be their own and not a foreign importation, and for an African ministry which understands, better than any missionary can understand, what goes on in the African mind and how its deepest longings and fears can be brought into captivity to the obedience of Christ'.[136]

The events in this area brought to a head a question which had been raised many times in policy discussions, and not only in Africa.

It concerned the amount of time and energy the missionary had to give to the administration and management of institutions, instead of the care and teaching of people. Again and again missionaries were complaining that they had no time to give to what they had come out to do.[137] They felt sometimes that they were indistinguishable from government civil servants – and that unhappily is how they were often regarded. The fact that mission schools, colleges and hospitals were so tied up with government made that inevitable.[138]

The fresh recognition that was being brought by the Lenshina movement, that much more attention had to be given to the building up of the community of the Church, to pastoral care and teaching – and in relation to the special insights, characteristics, and difficulties of the African people – coincided with the increasing problem of the staffing of institutions, and their financial support. Institutions were being closed or handed over to government. As that was happening, what looked on the surface like retrenchment seemed to be turning out, however fortuitously, to be more like the realignment the FMC was asking for. The missionaries, and the Church with them, free from the 'encumbrance' of institutions as it had often begun to seem, were beginning to ask basic questions about the role of the missionary and the task of the Church: what was the Spirit saying to the Church?

The change took place as happened, for example, at Chasefu in Nyasaland in 1953, when no missionary could be found to serve in one of the schools. The Government stepped in, intimating that unless a missionary could be found, the school on grounds of inefficiency would have to be closed or taken over. The result was that the Mission Council ceased to manage the school.[139] Or, as happened in Northern Rhodesia in the same year, decisions about the future made by the Director of African Education led to the cancellation of Mission Council's plans for secondary education in Lubwa and to the downgrading of education there. It was clear that Mission Council could not go ahead with its own plans, which differed from the Government's, without the Government's financial support, and that was not to be forthcoming.[140] As changes were being forced upon Councils and education committees of the Church, as a consequence of a shortage of missionary staff (there were by this time only three fully trained men missionary teachers in the three Central African Fields, two of them being on the point of retiral) and the inability of the FMC to provide the necessary funds, many missionaries and others were convinced that the time had come for a decision to be made one way or another about the Mission's continuing to run schools. The Rev. William Bonomy, who had served since 1946 and had suffered the burden of having to manage 31 district schools, some of them a hundred miles away from the town where he was based, was one who was pressing the issue:

> Without more staff it must give up many of its schools. He asks if it is not wiser to tell Government now rather than wait until its hand is forced? Is it not better for the African Church in the long run that the missionary should be able to concentrate on the pastoral and evangelistic side of his work, so helping and training his African colleagues in the upbuilding of the Christian community even if this means that the schools go over to Government and Local Education Authorities?[141]

A summary of educational developments in the period under review is given in an Appendix to FMC Minutes.[142]

★ ★ ★

During this period many primary schools were transferred to local authorities. In 1956 it was agreed that the management of primary schools in Northern Rhodesia, other than those in mission stations, should be handed over. In coming to that recommendation Northern Rhodesia Joint Council had in mind these considerations: that the management of schools was causing the Church to have a wrong view of its nature; that it would benefit by being forced to rely on other means than the schools for its evangelism; that management was preventing ordained men from making a worthwhile contribution to the spread of the Gospel; that in the Copperbelt, where the Missions no longer managed schools, missionaries were free to do more effective work in them; and that such a move would be in harmony with the FMC policy of realignment. In its turn the FMC, in agreeing to the recommendation, 'noted with concern the grave situation created by its inability to provide adequately for the management of the schools', and then went on to say that it had made its decision 'not merely because it had no alternative, but because it believed that at this stage the Church in Central Africa would be strengthened by ceasing to be preoccupied with the management of schools to an extent far beyond its powers'.[143]

By 1957 the Nyasaland Mission Council had come to see that a transfer of the proprietorship of mission primary schools was inevitable,[144] and indicated to District Councils that it was willing to discuss the hand over of selected schools or groups of schools. In Blantyre, where in 1957 African managers had been appointed by Synod[145] releasing missionaries from managerial responsibilities, the view was that both the schools and the Church profited by the change. In 1958 the Blantyre Council had supported a request from the Education Board of the Blantyre Synod for a grant for new buildings and equipment for the Henry Henderson Institution, Junior Secondary School.[146] In face of pressure from Government to take the schools over, it was agreed to retain control meantime, and to review the position again after five years.[147]

By 1959 in Northern Rhodesia, a complete withdrawal from primary education had been planned.[148] Chitambo School had been closed, and the schools at Mwenzo and Lubwa were to be transferred to local authorities[149] – although in the event upper primary schools at Mwenzo and Lubwa continued. A special committee appointed to look at future policy in Livingstonia (Rhodesia) expressed the opinion that the missions' direct contribution to Christian education was best given through teacher training, and hoped that the FMC would be able to provide staff for the Malcolm Moffat Teacher Training College, near Serenje, which was expected to open in August 1959. The committee believed that the future of Christian education lay not so much in schools run by missions or churches as in Christians, African and European, working within the Government system of education.[150]

In the Overtoun Institution, Livingstonia, Nyasaland, of which Rev. Fergus MacPherson was at that time Principal, the status quo in the Teacher Training College and the Secondary School had been accepted by Government, although without implications for the future.[151] The Women's Training College in Blantyre, which had so many difficulties in finding a site, had become as planned the central institution for the training of women teachers of all denominations in Nyasaland apart from the Roman Catholics.[152]

In the same way as basic questions were being asked about the responsibility of missions for schools and colleges, similar questions were being raised about hospitals. In Livingstonia Mission (Rhodesia), for example, in 1957, there had been a full discussion on medical policy, including the function of Mission Hospitals, their contribution to the evangelistic task of the Church, their financial difficulties, and the amount of work having to be done by hospital staffs. It was minuted that:

> This discussion on medical work revealed that a continuous increase in number of patients attending for treatment in all the hospitals could be expected, which would result in a situation beyond the power of the Mission to finance and staff. Withdrawal from medical work, complete reorganisation, or handing over of hospitals to the Government would then be necessary.[153]

A new hospital was built in 1954 at Chitambo in Northern Rhodesia. It had been erected in an astonishingly short time as a result of the enthusiasm of the local people, who, inspired by William Bonomy and John Todd, gave voluntary labour and contributed financially.[154] Because of new Government regulations it had become necessary in 1959 to run a training hospital at one of the mission stations in Northern Rhodesia, which as a consequence, because of costs and staffing, would have serious affect on other medical work.[155] It was agreed that Chitambo should be the training hospital, and the initial arrangement was that the hospitals at Mwenzo and Lubwa should be closed.[156] If Lubwa had been closed there would at that time have been no doctor between Mwenzo and Chitambo on the Great North Road, a distance of 350 miles. In the event, with the consent of Government which would continue to give grants, it was agreed to keep the hospital at Lubwa for at least a further two years until a hospital planned by Government for Isoka was completed. Medical work was, however, discontinued at Mwenzo, though the Government continued to run the hospital, though at a reduced level.[157] The idea had been to introduce a system of fees for the hospital at Lubwa, as had been agreed for Chitambo, when it became a training hospital. The arrangement, however, was badly received at Chitambo, where the people complained that they had not been consulted, although they had done so much themselves to build the hospital. Relations between the local community and the mission greatly deteriorated; there were many misunderstandings, and the numbers in the hospital dropped. The result was that the charging of fees at Chitambo was suspended, and not introduced at Lubwa.[158]

In Livingstonia, Nyasaland, it was agreed that a doctor be located at Ekwendeni, and that the hospital at Loudon be put in charge of a sister, this in view of the developments around Ekwendeni and the presence of a new Maternity Centre there. The situation at the third hospital, the David Gordon Memorial Hospital (DGMH), was difficult. With the development of medical work in the more accessible area at Mlowe, fewer patients were coming up to the DGMH. A vehicle was purchased as a travelling dispensary, which seemed to be the only way of making this hospital on the plateau effective.[159] Government grants were given toward the cost of buildings at Ekwendeni and Loudon.[160]

Blantyre Council decided to withdraw from medical work in Blantyre, and to concentrate on the hospital at Mlanje. The move was to happen by the middle of 1958, by which time the Medical Department of Government might be able to take over midwifery and maternity work.[161]

★ ★ ★

While those far-reaching changes were taking place, and with accelerating pace, in medical work, education, and in the balance of Church and Mission, there was a growing sense of tension between the African and the European. By 1957 people were beginning to recognise that race relationships, which had received a set-back with the inauguration of Federation, were rapidly getting worse. The passing by the Federal Parliament of the Constitution Amendment Bill in the autumn of 1957, and, following on from it, in February 1958, the Electoral Bill, against the will of the African people, and despite a reference from the African Affairs Board on the ground that it discriminated against the African people, exacerbated the situation. It was strongly felt that the UK, by supporting the decisions of the Federation, had gone back on its solemn pledge to protect the African people.

The FMC in a Deliverance to the General Assembly of 1958 drew attention to the effect of the UK Parliament's approval of measures regarded as discriminatory. African opinion in Nyasaland, it said, had been profoundly disturbed, and it went on to press the Government to take action to restore the confidence of the African in the British people's determination to fulfil their pledge.[162]

Concerned that the Federal Government would build on the gains that it had won to push for dominion status, Andrew Doig moved successfully an addendum to a Deliverance of the Church and Nation Committee. In moving his addendum, Doig reiterated the importance of African opinion. 'I have been conscious anew,' he said, 'of the deep hurt that is inflicted upon them by disregard of their views and by treatment of discrimination in all sorts of ways. I have glimpsed afresh the tremendous possibilities that could open up not only for Africans, but for Europeans as well if my country-men there were prepared to co-operate with the African, and lower the barriers of reserve or prejudice that are holding them back from united action with the African. African opinion matters.'[163] The addendum itself reads:

> The General Assembly, in face of reports of the mounting tension in race relations in the Federation, particularly in the two Northern Territories, call for an assurance from her Majesty's Government, (a) that no further changes will be introduced in the Federal Constitution without proof of reasonable support in the statutory bodies representative of African opinion (that is to say, in the case of Northern Rhodesia, the African Representative Council, and, in the case of Nyasaland, the three Provincial Councils); (b) that no commitment has been made or will be made to the Federal Government which would prejudge the issue of Dominion Status as it comes up for discussion at the 1960 Conference.[164]

The Rev. Andrew Doig resigned from the Federal Assembly as from 23 June 1958.[165]

In July 1958 Dr Hastings Banda returned home from the UK to Nyasaland to lead the independence movement. That December the All Africa People's Conference had met in Accra under the chairmanship of Tom Mboya, the African nationalist leader. Banda was at that Conference which was enormously influential in artic-ulating the feeling of the time that the end of colonialism had come and that Africa would soon be seen to be free. On his return from Ghana in February 1959, Banda headed the Nyasaland African Congress Party and declared his intention to end Federation.

On 3 March 1959 the Governor of Nyasaland declared a state of emergency in the Protectorate and his proscription of the Congress Party. Rioting followed in which some 50 Africans were killed, and many arrested and imprisoned without trial, including Dr Banda.

Many of the elders and members of the Church of Central Africa Presbyterian (CCAP) were members and officials of the Congress Party, and most were in sympathy with its legitimate aspirations.

The fact that that was so and that the CCAP with the support of the Church of Scotland, not itself held in much favour in official circles, had opposed many of the features of the Federation, led to their being regarded with suspicion as a centre of trouble. The refusal of the CCAP to accept a racialist policy (black or white) added to the suspicion, and the same was true of the Church of Scotland, whose policy of integration, including as it was seen the 'granting of self-government to Synods' was frowned upon. Members of the CCAP, and missionaries, faced physical dangers at this time, and were under strain, compounded often by personal relationships poisoned by distrust and fears. Although there was disruption, as happened, for example, when the headmaster and the other African graduate in the Henry Henderson Institute were arrested, mostly in the institutions it was business as usual. Despite the strain there was abundant evidence of people, Africans and missionaries, supporting one another, and working together for peace and reconciliation.[166]

At the General Assembly of 1958, the decision was reached to set up a special committee to deal with Central African affairs, and Dr George MacLeod appointed its convener. Among the Deliverances on its Report to the General Assembly of 1959 were these:

4. The General Assembly recommend that, while some form of close association is advisable, the agenda of the 1960 Conference should afford opportunity for Africans to state and expound their views on the refashioning of government in the Federal area. The General Assembly, mindful of the duties of Her Majesty's Government as the protecting power in the two northern territories, urge that at that Conference full consideration be given to the opinions of the statutory bodies representing Africans – that is to say, in the case of Northern Rhodesia, the African Representative Council, and in the case of Nyasaland, the three Provincial Councils.

5. The General Assembly request H. M. Government that at the 1960 Conference there be no development in the direction of Dominion status for the Federation without the consent of the majority of the inhabitants.

9. The General Assembly, recognising that the time has come for a radical revision of the Territorial Constitution for Nyasaland, earnestly recommend to H. M. Government that effective power be given to the African community in that land, which admits the possibility of an African majority in the Legislative Council.

Finally as an Addendum, which was moved by the Rev. T. S. Colvin:

12. The General Assembly feel that the continued detention without trial of Africans in Nyasaland will make future reconciliation extremely difficult, and request Her Majesty's Government to take steps to have these detainees brought to trial in a Court of Law or released immediately.[167]

In moving the Addendum, Tom Colvin had this to say:

> Since March there has been in Nyasaland a great rounding up of Africans of all sorts and kinds who are detained in detention camps inside Nyasaland, some in Southern Rhodesia, who have now been there for almost three months without charge and without trial .... British justice is at stake in this matter. If they are all rogues and murderers then it is all the more important they be brought before a court of law and judged and sentenced, but if they are not such, if there are innocents in their midst, it is absolutely essential that they be released, and that is why I add this addendum to have these detainees brought to trial in a court of law or released.[168]

Tom Colvin, who was due to return to Nyasaland on 25 June, was declared a prohibited immigrant by the Government of the Federation of Rhodesia and Nyasaland in a letter dated 26 May.[169]

★ ★ ★

The Church during this period of disturbance and change became increasingly conscious of the urgent need for a strong and well-trained indigenous ministry. By 1953 it came to be recognised in Nyasaland that there should be unified training across the presbyteries. Following advice given in the Report of the International Missionary Council Survey dealing with the training of the ministry in Central Africa, it was proposed in 1956 by Blantyre and Livingstonia presbyteries of the CCAP that there be joint theological training at Mkhoma.[170] In the following year the Standing Committee of the General Synod of the CCAP agreed on the constitution of a synodical board to manage the joint college.[171] No agreement, however, was reached on the site, and there was a difference of opinion on the language medium to be used – the Synods of Blantyre and Livingstonia wanted English, while the Mkhoma Synod wanted ci Nyanja. Since it had become clear that no joint training could start in 1958, it was agreed to run a joint course for Blantyre and Livingstonia, in Livingstonia, beginning on 1 May.[172] Later, in February 1959, it was reported to a Committee on Theological Training of the General Synod that the Dutch Reformed Church Mission had offered land for the building of a Theological College in the grounds of Mkhomo Station. It was agreed that an experimental combined course be held in existing buildings beginning probably in 1962 – without prejudice to future siting.[173]

In July 1957 the Livingstonia Presbytery of the Church of Central Africa in Rhodesia, in line with the IMC survey, and taking account of the need for a Theological Training Centre in an urban setting, more spacious, and with higher standards, decided to transfer the Centre from Kashinda. The Copperbelt Christian Service Council had offered to make available a site at Mindolo, and this was accepted provisionally, the possibility being left open of a site in Nyasaland or at Epworth in Southern Rhodesia.[174]

In August 1958 the Presbytery of the CCAR agreed that the Theological College should be in Northern Rhodesia and at Mindolo.[175] In a memorandum prepared by African ministers arguing for Mindolo, it was pointed out that one of the disadvantages of Epworth was the uncertain future of Federation.[176]

In 1959 the WCC awarded a scholarship to an African minister, Joel Chisanga, to study for a year at the United Theological College, Bangalore, India, on the understanding that he serve on the staff of the new united College on his return. The United Church of Central Africa in Rhodesia (UCCAR) would be responsible for his passage and some other expenses.[177]

Dr Ranson, Director of the Theological Education Fund (TEF), set up in June 1958 at the IMC Meeting in Ghana, was present at the Executive Committee of the Synod of the UCCAR in February 1959. At that meeting he said that any scheme to be supported by the TEF would have to be on the widest possible basis and that the proposed UCCAR College would not qualify. A Theological Education Conference held in Salisbury, Southern Rhodesia recommended the setting up of associated theological colleges on a site at Epworth. Churches had been asked to reply to the suggestion within a year. The Synod, unable to come to a clear decision one way or other, agreed that the theological college be transferred to Mindolo meantime, no accommodation being built which required money from overseas, and that Synod begin negotiations with Methodists, CCAP, Church of Barotseland and kindred Churches, with a view to establishing a United College. The Synod agreed that the first year of the course begin at Kashinda, and that the second year be held at Mindolo.[178]

(d)

In Kenya in 1953 the Mau Mau revolt brought terror and fear across the provinces where the Presbyterian Church of East Africa (PCEA) was concentrated. The ruthless barbarism of Mau Mau was directed against the Churches and their institutions, and very many fellow Kikuyu suffered at its hands. Village work of the PCEA was curtailed, schools burnt down, and atrocities perpetrated. By the end of the year at least ten elders, a minister, and 50 women and children had been murdered.[179]

To support the Army in combating the violence a Home Guard was hastily formed, and a great many people suspected of terrorism were rounded up and placed in detention. There had been little opportunity of ensuring that the right people were enlisted, and since many who came forward to serve had reason to hate Mau Mau, it was not surprising that there were frequent reports of false arrests and brutality.[180] It was during this time that Jomo Kenyatta was tried for managing the revolt and, in April 1953, imprisoned.

There followed in 1954 the massive Operation Anvil in which large numbers of Kikuyu, and other tribesmen suspected of terrorism, were rounded up and taken from their homes, causing great suffering to many innocent people.[181] The Churches at this time protested, and an open letter was published by church leaders, in which they stated the need for 'a radical change of attitude on the part of many of those responsible for law and order'.[182] At a broadcast service from St Andrews on the second Sunday of 1955, David Steel preached a sermon on the Slaughter of the Innocents. In it he condemned Operation Anvil and other activities of Government, and narrowly escaped an order of expulsion being served on him.[183]

Despite the violence and the disruption, the life of the Church continued. Pastors went about their duties, and the schools and hospitals carried on their work. Also, despite attempts on the part of extremists among both Europeans and Africans to make the Emergency into a racialist issue, good relations and co-operation between the races to a remarkable extent remained unaffected. Plans were going ahead uninterrupted for the union in one inter-racial unity of the two Presbyterian Churches in Kenya; and Europeans were busy raising money for a church building to be used by African Presbyterians and Methodists in Nairobi.[184] Friendships too built up over the years between Africans and Europeans remained unbroken. Surprisingly also, despite the strong action taken against rebellious Kikuyu under the Emergency, and the vigorous protests which the Churches and others were led to make about the often clumsy and harsh behaviour of the police, Mau Mau patently did not succeed in driving a wedge between the Kikuyu and the Government, or damage the fruitful co-operation between the Government and the Church.

The Government asked the Churches for help in recruiting staff for the centres where Kikuyu men and women were put who had been detained or convicted of Mau Mau offences. The Government was looking for people with 'army or similar experience, a real Christian faith, a sense of vocation, a desire to help the African and assist in the rehabilitation of those who have been misled'.[185] The FMC had agreed to let this be known. By the the middle of November 1953 there was encouraging news of work being carried out by a team at Athi River Detention Camp on which the PCEA was well represented, and at another place by the local PCEA minister.[186]

By the end of 1954 the rehabilitation of Mau Mau terrorists had become a major problem. The movement was still active and deep-rooted and, as the military campaign went on, thousands of Kikuyu continued to be rounded up into camps. There was the difficult and time-consuming task of interrogating those who were being brought in (by 1956 there were 45,000 in the 'screening' camps), separating out the innocent from those judged to have been implicated in Mau Mau and, following that, the double problem of giving help to the innocent, made unemployable, just because they were Kikuyu, and at the same time doing what could be done to reclaim the others. The Government asked the Churches to train youth leaders, to open community centres, and to send chaplains into the camps. [187]

Meanwhile there was a redoubling of efforts to protect Kikuyu who were in danger from Mau Mau. A scheme was started to concentrate the Kikuyu people in stockaded villages with military protection, similar to the practice followed in Malaya, with the intention both of giving security and of depriving Mau Mau of food and weapons. The Church soon began to work in these villages, much as John Fleming and his colleagues were doing about this same time in South East Asia. Mary Montgomery, for example, from Tumutumu, was visiting women's groups, teaching the Bible, and giving instruction on hygiene and handicrafts.[188] The system of 'villagisation', as it was called, soon ran into criticism. Doctors and nurses reported severe malnutrition and there were claims that conditions in the villages were worse than in prison camps. Those in the villages were mostly women, with their children, and they were doing five days' compulsory labour in the week. There was also gross overcrowding in the huts. The Government position was that malnutrition had always been there and that the new style of living in villages had only brought it to light. Church workers, however, believed differently, and made it plain to Government that in their view it was 'villagisation' that was the cause.[189]

Although by the end of 1955 there were signs that the emergency was coming to an end, the problems were by no means over. The Church was receiving reports that, under 24 hour curfew conditions, 'loyalists' and 'non-loyalists' alike 'were subjected to extreme hardship, including enforced work for the whole day with one brief rest, indiscriminate beatings by members of the Kikuyu Guard, and hunger'. Matters like this were brought by the Church constantly to the Government's attention. Meetings between the heads of the three Churches associated with the UK and the Governor, which had begun on a regular basis, added strength to the protests that were being made.[190]

In response to the need to help young people, particularly in the city, a proposal was put to Government for setting up a Social Welfare Centre in the Bahati Location of Nairobi, the Centre to be under the auspices of the PCEA and the Methodist Church, and include the planned new Nairobi Church building.[191] The Government and the City Council agreed, and between them decided on the proportion of funds they would be prepared to contribute. In the event the Churches together – that is to say, the PCEA, the FMC, St Andrews Kirk and the MMS – met rather more than half the capital cost.[192] By the end of August 1955 building was complete, and arrangements were made for the formal opening which took place for the Community Centre in December 1955, and for the Church in February 1956.[193] By the end of 1958 the work in the Centre had developed to such an extent that plans were being made to extend the existing buildings.[194]

The General Assembly of 1952 had given the go-ahead to negotiations for union between the Church of Scotland Presbytery in Kenya and the Presbyterian Church of East Africa. Arrangements went ahead regardless of the Emergency. A negotiating committee had been appointed and by the end of 1953 had prepared a draft constitution. A special committee under the convenership of George Gunn, having studied the draft and reported to the General Assembly of 1955, recommended that approval be given. Since there were details still to be considered the General Assembly, having given overall approval, authorised the Commission of Assembly, on being assured that minor adjustments had been completed, to give the necessary permission for the Overseas Presbytery of Kenya to enter into union with the PCEA. In giving their approval the General Assembly had expressed their joy 'in the prospect of a union of Churches in Kenya, which [would] bring Christians of European and African race into one fellowship of witness to the Lord Jesus Christ and for the extension of His kingdom in Africa'.[195] The inauguration of the Union took place on 11 February 1956.[196] Dr George Calderwood was unanimously appointed Moderator of the General Assembly of the new Church, and David Steel its principal Clerk.

With the inauguration of the new PCEA, bringing together the African, Indian, and European into one Body under a single admin-istration, the integration of Church and Mission had to a consid-erable extent been accomplished. The process toward integration had moved more quickly than in many other places. From 1943 when the PCEA received its first constitution, the Mission Council had worked in close co-operation with the Synod through a joint Standing Committee. Now under the constitution of the new Church full responsibility for the Church's life and evangelistic mission was laid upon the General Assembly and its subordinate courts, and there was no need any longer for a Mission Council as a managing body. On 12 August 1957 the Kenya Colony Mission Council dissolved itself.[197]

The integrated structure of the new Church was designed not only to bring together Church and Mission, but also to hold together the different racial groups. It had moreover to build on what already existed, while allowing for change and growth. The solution was to reconstitute the old Africa Synod as an African Affairs Committee of the Assembly which would coordinate the work of the Presby-teries in affairs specifically African, and through which the FMC would make its contribution to the PCEA, as Mission Council had done in the past. What had been the Overseas Presbytery would be replaced by a European Affairs Committee of the Assembly, parallel to the African Affairs Committee, with a small African representation.

Most of the presbyteries would go into the union without change, but the Rift Valley Presbytery would become inter-racial with European and African Affairs Committees, and there would be a new inter-racial Presbytery of Nairobi, including Kirk Sessions outwith Kenya. The Medical Committee of the old Mission Council would become a Standing Committee of the General Assembly. It was recognised that there would be many difficulties which would have to be ironed out in the years ahead.[198] The administrative division into two main committees divided racially, African and European, was something that could not be allowed to continue, and by 1959 it was being actively reconsidered.[199]

In the process of bringing together Mission and Church, the continuing support and management of the institutions was a major question. The powers of the Mission Council in relation to the three hospitals, at Kikuyu, Chogoria, and Tumutumu, were transferred to a Hospital Board which was directly responsible to the PCEA General Assembly.[200] Close relations with the Medical Department of Government were maintained and the hospitals continued to receive grants from it.[201] The maintaining of the Christian character of the hospitals, along with their staffing and financing, were major sources of concern.[202] In that connection the General Administration Committee of the Assembly gave general approval, in 1959, to a policy statement of the Christian Council of Kenya which advocated among other things: (a) a stage by stage planned financial support from local church and governmental sources; (b) local control by stages; (c) encouraging Christian vocation among African doctors and nurses; and (d) encouraging the local church to take more responsibility, and to help with the recruitment of Christian doctors and nurses.[203]

Increasing emphasis was being given by the Church, as by the Government, on education, and grants-in-aid and other funding continued to be received from the Department of Education. Grants were given, for example, on a 100 per cent basis to girls' schools in Kikuyu, Tumutumu, and Chogoria.[204] The central importance of Teacher Training was recognised, and Government grants were given for this to be developed in those areas and also in the neighbourhood of Nairobi.[205] In those new institutions increasingly independent governing bodies were being set up, with local and Government representation.[206] The ever-present problem was their staffing. Part of the answer was to make local appointments with the help of the Overseas Appointments Bureau.[207]

In the ferment of social change that was taking place with such rapidity in Kenya, it was urgently necessary not just to move ahead with the education of young people as widely across society as possible and reaching high standards, but even more for the sake of the Church and the furtherance of the Gospel to produce a well-trained ministry. The Mission Council and the Methodist Missionary Society in Kenya responded to the need in 1951 by setting up a Divinity School at Limuru.[208] Three years later in September 1954 the Synod had approved in principle a constitution for a United Theological College at Limuru, to be run by Presbyterians, Methodists, and Anglicans, and a few months later it was in operation under a 'caretaker' council.[209] At the beginning of 1957 the African Council noted 'with satisfaction' that an experienced minister from Scotland, the Rev. Oswald Welsh, was being appointed a tutor at Limuru.[210] In 1958, as part of a programme of further training, a minister of the PCEA, the Rev. John Gatu, went to Scotland. He served in a Church extension charge, St Ninian's, Larkfield, Greenock, whose minister was Bill Cattanach. On his return home John Gatu was sent round the Presbyteries to conduct training courses.[211]

In the rapidly changing society of Kenya, it was important that members of the Church should relate what was happening around them to their faith. To help lay men and women to find a theology for life – and incidentally to help ministers also to come to grips pastorally and theologically with the challenges of the day – a Conference and Training Centre was established in the vicinity of the College. The Christian Council of Kenya was the initiative behind it, and resources to fund and staff it came from Christian Aid and the Division of Inter-Church Aid and Service to Refugees of the World Council of Churches.[212]

(e)

In South Africa Dr Malan's Nationalist Party was returned to office in April 1953. The system of apartheid became further entrenched, despite protests from the African people and pressures from outside. The 'Defiance of Unjust Laws' campaign continued, which in September the previous year had led to disturbances at Lovedale and the imprisonment of some of its staff.[213] In Johannesburg Government plans were going ahead for the removal of African families arbitrarily and against their will to 'Meadowlands' on the open veldt ten miles from the centre,[214] while in Parliament measures were being taken one after the other that were racially discriminating, including another attempt to remove the Cape Coloured community from the common voters' roll.[215]

It was in this setting of increasing apartheid that the Bantu Education Bill was introduced and became law.[216] The Act placed all African education under the centralised Department of Native Affairs, thus separating African from European education, making it essentially an act of apartheid. By cutting grants for teachers' salaries and removing all other grants from Christian institutions, it became virtually impossible for the Church to continue to run their own schools and colleges. In the end the decision was made to lease to the Government the institutions: Lovedale, Blythswood, Pholela, and Emgwali, maintaining the hostels of the last two.[217]

In December 1954 the FMC forwarded to the Government of South Africa a Statement on the Bantu Education Act which included the following:

> Our main objection to the Act … is a matter of principle and touches the racial policy on which the Act is based. We hold that, as God has made of one blood all nations, a man's worth in God's sight does not depend on his race or colour. We hold that, because the economic life of South Africa is dependent on the co-operation of the Bantu, the time is now past when they can justly be treated as a completely separate community. We believe that a Christian educational policy must seek to prepare the members of every social group to assume their full share of adult responsibility in the service of the country. We cannot therefore assent to a proposition which seems to underlie the Act, namely that the Bantu have no part or lot in the country of their birth outside the reserves, nor any voice in determining major issues of policy, the consequences of which must ultimately be felt by the humblest member of every group. Nor can we agree to the consequent educational policy whereby the Bantu are to be trained for life in the reserves, no place being found for them in the European community above the level of certain forms of labour.
>
> We believe that in these matters the policy of the Government of South Africa is contrary to the law of God and that therefore it will be disastrous.[218]

A Deliverance of the 1955 General Assembly on the Report of the Church and Nation Committee reads:

3(c) The General Assembly declare once again their sense of profound disquiet at the racial policy of the South African Government. In particular the General Assembly deplore the bringing into force of the Bantu Education Act and other legislation, which involves the indefinite social segregation of Africans and Europeans, and the maintenance of Africans in a permanently inferior social, educational, and cultural status.[219]

The Bantu Education Act did not come into force immediately. There was a period of uncertainty which lasted for more than two years, the Act itself being little more than a skeletal outline, which was only gradually filled in and clarified. It took until January 1956 before it took full effect.

By the end of 1955 the Lovedale Governing Council met for the last time, and Dr R. H. W. Shepherd, its Principal since 1942, indicated that on 31 December he would retire. The closure of Lovedale marked the end of a remarkable era of service with which the FMC had been associated, and which made the name of Lovedale in particular known and honoured throughout South Africa and beyond.[220]

Although Lovedale ceased as an integrated Christian institution, several of its departmental activities continued under the control of the Mission, including the Press, the publishing of the influential *South African Outlook*, which Shepherd continued to edit, and the Bible School. Close connection was maintained with the hospital.[221]

One of the immediate consequences of the Bantu Education Act was the need to ensure that everything possible should be done on the FMC's part to strengthen the Bantu Presbyterian Church.[222] It was agreed at the request of the BPC to increase the missionary staff serving the churches, to station a team of missionaries at the Church headquarters in Umtata, and to provide secretarial and bookkeeping assistance for the General Secretary. After close consultation with the Church, requests were also made to the FMC for missionary appointments at Blythswood, Pholela, the Lovedale Mission and the Lovedale Press, and agreement given.[223] During this time discussion began on the transfer of property to the BPC[224], and on the use of moneys available from the sale of Mission property, which it had been agreed should not be taken out of South Africa but reserved for use there.[225]

In April 1953 the question was raised whether the Donald Fraser Hospital at Sibasa in the Transvaal, one of the three hospitals run by the Hospital Board of the South Africa Mission Council, should continue to be regarded as such but rather as an independent institution. The question arose after Dr Aitken and Dr Pool accepted Government salaries – which incidentally allowed the hospital to continue to receive its special subsidy – and in the light of grants from Government which made support from the FMC less and less essential.[226] The other two hospitals, the Nessie Knight Hospital at Sulenkama and the hospital at Tugela Ferry, continued under the Hospital Board of the South Africa Mission, despite shortage of staff and finance.[227]

Training for the ministry of the Bantu Presbyterian Church was being carried out at the University College of Fort Hare, adjoining Lovedale, an institution that had become over the years one of the Church's most creative and respected in Africa.[228] The Rev. John Summers, who had served in Calabar, was appointed as warden and tutor at Iona House, Fort Hare, in the summer of 1956.[229] Sadly, however, his appointment there was not to last for long. By the following year news came that the Government was to introduce a Separate University Education Bill by which they would be able to take over Fort Hare and fit it into their apartheid scheme.[230] By the end of 1959 the Act came into effect. At its Assembly in September/ October 1959, the Bantu Presbyterian Church agreed in principle to participate in a Federation of Theological Institutions on a site at Lovedale, and approved the action of Lovedale Mission Committee in offering the Bible School for the accommodation of theological students in 1960.[231]

VI

Jamaica in 1953 saw the beginning of the final stage in the movement toward the independence of the Church. The constitution of a Missionaries' Committee had been drawn up which involved the dissolution of the Mission Council, and the handing over of its major responsibilities to the Synod of the Church.[232] In October 1954 the independence of the Presbyterian Church of Jamaica was legally confirmed. The FMC recorded in its minute its joy that the Church 'had assumed full responsibility for the carrying of the Gospel to its own people in continued partnership with missionaries of the Church of Scotland'.[233]

The Synod, recognising that an important new stage had been reached in its progress, took the opportunity to put on record 'its warmest appreciation of and gratitude for all that the Presbyterian Church in Jamaica had received in the goodly fellowship, understanding and ready help of the Mother Church in Scotland'. At the same time it affirmed that it was pressing forward towards self-support. The ministry of the Church was now 75 per cent Jamaican, and achievements had been made in the maintenance of the ministry, and in the total income of the Church. The aim of the Synod was fuller self-support and less dependence on the FMC for staff and financial help.[234]

1953 was also a year of development for Knox College. A Government-guaranteed loan had been used to increase accommodation and the Rothnie Hostel for Senior Boys built. A bookshop was added to the campus, and a printing press – which by 1955 became a Limited Liability Company providing schools with educational supplies, and getting Bibles and Christian literature into the community.[235] Summer Conferences, which were in effect training schools, became a regular annual feature at Knox. The one in 1953, for example, prepared leaders from various congregations for the Family Life Campaign which was held later in the year; while in 1954 the purpose was to prepare for the general election soon to take place. In 1956 the Summer School was attended by delegates from many Government departments, the subject of the conference being 'Children in Society'. The Beattie Hostel for Junior Boys was built in 1954, named after the Rev. J. A. T. Beattie, by that time Principal of the Hope Waddell Institute, Calabar, who helped to promote the founding of Knox; and in 1955 the Margaret Stuart Music Studio.[236] By 1957 the College had 250 pupils with 150 boarders, including pupils from Arabia, Haiti, Cuba, Venezuala, USA, UK and Canada.[237]

In 1954 negotiations for union between the Congregational, Methodist, Moravian and Presbyterian Churches reached agreement that the Association of Christian Churches (Disciples of Christ) be included, the intention being to prepare a draft Basis of Union, and to promote practical co-operation among the negotiating Churches.[238]

The building of a new Theological College on the Methodist Caenwood site in Kingston, in place of the old Presbyterian College of St Colmes – the foundation stone was laid in August 1954 – marked an important step of co-operation. The Presbyterian Church of Jamaica had been looking for a more suitable place for theological training and the Methodist Church offered to let them build next to their own college. Moravians, Disciples and Congregation-alists joined in to build St Colme's Hostel. By the end of November 1954 the negotiating Churches agreed a draft constitution for a Union Theological Seminary at Caenswood.[239] The new Seminary was inaugurated and continued to grow; in 1959 there were 43 resident students.

Various other activities of practical co-operation between the Churches, including joint courses for Sunday School teachers, con-ferences such as the ones at Knox, united action by women of the Churches, Youth Retreats and Rallies for young people, helped to promote understanding and to draw the Churches together. In 1958 a proposed basis of union between the Congregational, Disciples of Christ, Methodist, Moravian, and Presbyterian Churches, was sent down to Presbyteries for discussion.[240]

At a meeting of the Synodical Council, in 1955, the appoint-ment of a Field Secretary was proposed, who would be both Clerk of Synod and Secretary of the Synodical Council, and who would seek to further the cause of Church Union in Jamaica, the unanimous choice for the post being the Rev. Mungo Carrick, a senior mis-sionary who had previously served in South Africa from 1935. In the same meeting it was recommended that the FMC maintain for a period of ten years an 'irreducible' establishment of seven mis-sionaries. The FMC welcomed the first proposal, although expressing concern at the heavy burden carried by Mungo Carrick, but was not able to agree to the second.[241]

The Presbyterian Church of Jamaica was already committed in principle at this time to a programme of development discussed with Professor G. D. Henderson during a visit he had paid to the Island in 1954.[242] The programme, which had not been formally approved, involved considerable financial aid, help which the Synod hoped it would receive from partners abroad, including the Pres-byterian Church in USA. In 1952, following the hurricane, a dep-utation from the Church visited the United States. The Presbyterian Church in USA made a generous contribution for Hurricane Relief, and indicated its willingness to help in other ways if that were needed. The Church continued to correspond with the American Church and was assured that it was still interested in helping. The Presbyterian Church in USA indicated that it wished to be assured of the assent of FMC for direct consultation.

The FMC, with two vacancies on its candidates lists which it was endeavouring to fill, had to make clear that with regret it was unable to maintain the establishment the Church wanted. It expressed the hope indeed that one of the results of the appointment of a Field Secretary would be an eventual reduction in the number of missionaries required from Scotland.[243] The response of the Synodical Council to the minute which made that point was to 'express grave concern at the retrenchment implied' and to give it as its opinion that the minute 'would affect adversely the decision of possible recruits for the Jamaican Field'. It went on to say that it 'considered that a new onus was being placed on the Field Secretary and asked him to correspond.'[244]

The Synod, at a meeting reported in November 1957, decided on the establishment of a Secondary School and a Church at Meadowbrook, a new housing area in Kingston. The demand for education was high and the 'situation had become crucial'. It was proposed to erect the first block of buildings in 1958. The Presbyterian Church would invest whatever funds it had available and an appeal for sacrificial giving in Jamaica had been launched. The FMC had been asked to help. Once more the FMC replied with regret.[245] There had been a serious earthquake in March 1957 which had caused much damage, and it was in face of this additional problem that the Church made its appeal. In a letter of 20 January 1958 the Moderator of the Presbyterian Church of Jamaica expressed himself grievously disappointed that the FMC was unable to help. 'The building of a Presbyterian Secondary School was more than urgent,' he said. 'It was vital.'[246]

VII

The work in Beihan in South Arabia continued to progress. After little more than a year since it began, and during which there had been an interruption because of illness, the news of the clinic had spread widely, and whole families were coming from long distances. Many local homes were visited, but visiting around the area was restricted because the staff at that time had no transport. In February 1953 the Shareef of Beihan made a request for a male mission doctor, a request which he had made before, in 1949, when because of shortage of staff the FMC had had to refuse. This time the reasons for making an appointment were compelling and the FMC agreed.[247]

In April 1953 a doctor, Dr George Morris, whose wife was also a doctor, submitted an offer of service, and was duly appointed to the South Arabia Mission.[248] In February 1955, after a period in Sheikh Othman, Dr Morris with his wife, Margaret, arrived in Beihan to take over from Dr Sidney Croskery, who had served there on a temporary basis.

In March 1953 a hospital orderly in Sheikh Othman and his wife and two daughters were baptised. Because of an increase in the number of Arabs in the Mission, regular Sunday services in Arabic were held. (Some Christian Arabs also attended the services in English at the Keith-Falconer Church in Aden.[249]) At Sheikh Othman, in 1954, the Boys' Club was reopened, with James Ritchie in charge.[250] In the same year Dr Affara was appointed to the post of Protectorate Medical Officer (West) from April 1954, and at the request and expense of the Government the Mission, including nurses of the Danish Mission, continued to provide staff for the Protectorate Health Service. There was an acute shortage of medical staff by the middle of 1954, when a number of staff were due for furlough. A doctor was needed urgently to replace Dr Walker, a second doctor to keep the Keith-Falconer Hospital adequately staffed, as well as a sister for the Hospital, and a sister for the Pro-tectorate Health Service.[251]

At Mrs Affara's child welfare clinic at Sheikh Othman, where Arab women were helping, by 1955 more than 50 babies and toddlers were coming daily for milk, and their mothers were listening to the Gospel. Twelve women and girls were attending the Wednesday evening Bible class. In Beihan there was an expansion of medical work. Over a thousand patients were attending the clinic every month, and about 200 visits a month paid to homes. Meetings for friendship and discussion took place with local people in the doctor's and sisters' houses.[252] In 1956 the gift of an ambulance was received from the United Nations International Children's Emergency Fund.

In April 1956 the Government took over the training of dressers which the Mission had carried out for the last twelve years at Sheikh Othman, and at the same time appointed its own Medical officer. In August 1956 Dr Affara, who had been Medical Officer, was flown to Scotland for an operation in an Edinburgh Hospital and remained on sick leave until the Spring of 1957.

The year 1957 was a particularly difficult one for the staff in Aden. Serious staff shortages, leading to a series of crises, on top of mounting political unrest, not to speak of the climate itself, were piling on the pressure. That local leave to the hills in the Protectorate, which in the past had been a safety valve, was now no longer possible, added to the strain. Happily the FMC recognised what was happening and made it possible for vacations to be taken in Ethiopia and Kenya.

As a consequence of the British Government's action in Suez there had been unrest in Aden Colony and the Protectorate, and some anti-British feeling. Border raids had taken place from the Yemen, religious feelings there and in the protectorate being stirred up by the British Government's intention to set up a Federation of Independent States. There were strong nationalist feelings also which fuelled the flames. One of the consequences in Beihan was that the ruler there came under condemnation for allowing Christian missionaries into his territories, threatening group solidarity.[253]

For some time it had been felt that there was an expressed need for a business manager who would take over from the missionaries accounts, secretarial work, and matters affecting stores and property. The request forwarded to the FMC in February 1956 had been turned down. Three years later the request was repeated. The FMC, although concerned about the staffing situation that occasioned the appeal, did not agree that this was the answer.[254] Finally Gladys Farquar, who had business experience, was appointed as an administrator in 1961.

It was obvious by this time that the staffing question needed to be looked at in the wider context of the work in South Arabia, and with other bodies involved, particularly the Danish Mission. The proposed visit of the Rev. Eric Nielsen of the International Missionary Council to Aden, which was currently being arranged by the Danish Mission, could not have happened at a more appropriate time, and the FMC gratefully accepted an invitation from the Danes to join them in policy discussion with him. Nielsen visited Aden for three weeks in March and April 1958. During his visit there had been agreement that the Church of Scotland and the Danish Mission should be amalgamated and that the purpose should be to establish one Arab Church in South Arabia. The Report of the visit had been studied by a special committee; and at a meeting in Edinburgh in November 1958 of representatives of the Danish Missionary Society and the FMC, this agreement reached was confirmed.[255]

In November 1958 a question raised about building further accommodation at Beihan received the reply that Beihan should not be regarded as a 'mission station'. The Mission Council agreed that in view of the political situation no action should be taken meantime, but submitted that the condition of the present building was 'precarious' and rapid action would have to be taken when the political situation became more stable. The FMC agreed 'that the political situation rendered it inadvisable for the Mission to erect any buildings in Beihan, but had expressed the hope that a way might be found whereby the State made provision of such accommodation as was required by the missionaries for their work.'[256]

At the end of 1958 there was a serious staffing situation at Sheikh Othman, and in particular a need of a second ordained missionary. The FMC remitted the matter to the Candidates' Sub-Committee.

VIII

During this period the FMC, faced with a shortage of money and of staff, increasingly gave to its policy of realignment the appearance of the retrenchment that it consistently denied. At the same time many long held assumptions about the missionary enterprise and the role of the missionary were questioned.

Its Report for 1953 to the General Assembly indicated that although the income received from congregational givings continued to rise, it remained far short of the sum authorised by successive Assemblies. Meanwhile the FMC in order to maintain essential work had to budget for expenditure beyond what it could expect to receive, with the result that reserves were near depletion. As far as staffing was concerned recruiting was not keeping pace with resignations.[257]

The Finance Committee of the General Assembly commenting on the amount of money congregations were retaining for their own use, and the proportionately meagre amount they were giving for the wider work of the Church had this to say in its Report to the Assembly of 1953:

Too often the sums allocated by congregations for the funds of the Committees are no more than 'token' contributions and the General Finance Committee is convinced not only that most congregations can, without hardship, give more generously, but that,unless they do so respond, the work of the Church is in grave jeopardy [258]

The Committee at the end of its Report then went on to say:

> The General Finance Committee, with all respect, suggests to the General Assembly the need for grave consideration of the deeper implication of these material anxieties, *viz.* the extent to which the financial state of the Church may be an indication of its spiritual health. The answer to the problem will not be found entirely in machinery or administration. It must be sought at a deeper level – in those elements of the Church's corporate life which provide the source and inspiration of all its missionary endeavour and Christian liberality. [259]

In the following year at the General Assembly the Finance Committee reiterated the point it made so strongly, and, commenting on Committees' budgets being reduced to 'minimum requirements', said:

> That position must not be allowed to continue, for both at home and in the foreign field opportunities are being lost through lack of the necessary funds. Little, if anything, is provided for expansion or development. The main problem has been to find the means for meeting existing commitments. A Church with a mission cannot justify its existence on such a basis. [260]

In 1945 the General Assembly had given permission to the FMC to ask congregations for £240,000 annually for the combined Foreign Mission and Women's Foreign Mission Funds. There had been a steady increase in annual givings, but by 1954 there remained a shortfall of over £20,000, an amount, by coincidence, almost equal to the combined deficit for that year of the FM and WFM funds.

At the 1956 General Assembly the FMC asked for the authorised amount to be raised to £300,000. It indicated that the annual deficit incurred and the accumulated debt would have been even larger but for the decline in staff numbers of about 70 men and women. It was asking for the amount to be raised in order to increase its staff, and to lift missionary remunerations as near as possible to the level of the minimum stipend. As it was, there remained a considerable differential, and the Report noted that there were members of staff able to continue to serve only by drawing on private capital. It was asking for the amount to be raised also in order to go ahead with new work, and at the same time to develop its programme in

Scotland to generate support. The General Assembly agreed to the FMC's request.[261]

At the General Assembly of 1958 an Overture dealing with a Co-ordinated Appeal to Congregations for the Support of the Work of the Church was sent down to presbyteries under the Barrier Act, the intention being to set up an effective system that would encourage congregations to see the work and the needs of the Church as a whole, and obviate competitive appeals among committees. A Stewardship and Budget Committee would receive budgets from the committees, from which an agreed co-ordinated budget would be prepared, and through that Committee only appeals would be made to the Church.[262]

During this period the number of missionaries steadily declined. In May 1953 there were 319 missionaries, whereas in May 1959 there were 282 – excluding wives in both instances – and the numbers continued to diminish. Resignations were increasing, and it was noticeable that many of those were from missionaries who had served for short periods, the largest group being from people who had served for five years or less. Other missionary bodies with whom the FMC had been in correspondence gave a similar picture. From a study that the FMC had made of missionary resignations over the period 1951 to 1958, it was not easy to discern any simple pattern of reasons for them, although finance or job satisfaction or both certainly seem to have been frequent factors. The urgent need to fill vacancies after the war period might, it was noted, have led to unsuitable appointments, and to missionaries being given responsibilities for which they were unprepared.[263]

There was renewed discussion on the future of missionary service. It was a possibility that in some countries at least, missionaries might not be given entry; and questions were raised at the same time, and among some missionaries themselves, about the desirability of the Churches continuing to rely on the presence of missionaries. The question came to the fore in India when the Home Minister, Dr Katju, suggested in 1953 that missionaries should not be involved in propagating the Faith, and that their activities should be confined to medical and educational work. The appointing in April 1954, by the Government of the State of Madhya Pradesh, of a Committee of Enquiry into Christian Missionary Activities, under the chairmanship of Dr B. S. Niyogi, focussed further attention on the issue.[264]

This 'Niyogi Committee', as it was called, spent two years on its work. It concerned itself not only with missionary activities but with the work of the whole Church in Madhya Pradesh, and in addition took under its purview the total strategy of the Church's world mission. The Committee issued a questionnaire heavily loaded with anti-mission suggestions. It visited all parts of the State where there was missionary activity and called on the public to give evidence. At the end of its work in 1956 it produced three volumes of over 900 pages, giving selections of the evidence and its recommendations. During this time an atmosphere was aroused of suspicion, distrust, and even fear. Part of that was caused by the Committee's own work, part by questions which began and continued to be asked in the Indian Parliament, and part by a press campaign against the missionaries and Christian evangelism. As it soon became clear the Indian Government had no intention of acting on the Niyogi Committee recommendations, in a short while the issue was forgotten in the upheaval caused by the reorganisation of States and the linguistic controversy over the use of Hindi, English and Regional Languages.[265]

During the period when the Niyogi Committee was at work, and in the following months, many public figures of different religious traditions and political persuasions spoke out in support of the Church, of missionaries, and of Christian institutions. Instead of incriminating the missionaries, the result of the Committee was to a considerable extent the very opposite. It gave many people the opportunity of testifying on their behalf. Dr Moses, for example, the Indian Principal of Hislop College, Nagpur, who was interrogated at length, had this to say to the Niyogi Committee:

> Missionaries came from Scotland not as imperialists but as those who were eager to share the best they had. 'Breathe lightly in this College,' he said, 'the very stones and mortar enshrine their spirit and service', and he went on to tell of how the late Tom Gardner had been content to serve under himself for five years without a hitch.

When asked what he meant by witness, he replied:

> 'This I am witnessing to you now of the great thing God has done for me. Everything I have I have received from my Father – life, health, experience, redemption.'[266]

Although the Report of the Enquiry Committee led by Dr Niyogi was in many ways flawed, revealing not just prejudice, but naivete, ignorance and carelessness in regard to facts, nonetheless, despite much of the distortion it contained, there was much in it from which the Church in India could learn. It was, however, sometime before the Church was able to do that. The clumsy way in which the Committee had set about its work had left bitter feelings, and had put the Church on the defensive. The result was that the Church was reluctant to study the Report, the prevailing attitude being either to refute the Committee's findings wholesale, or studiously to ignore them.[267]

On reflection points made in the Report were taken to heart, not least the impression made by the Church – and the truth behind the impression – that the Church in India was shaped, and divided by foreign, denominational traditions, dependent on foreign money, and influenced to the detriment of its Indian identity by foreign connections. A statement in the Report such as this could not long be ignored: 'We share with some of the thoughtful Christians themselves the view that it is highly undesirable for an important community like the Christians to be in some form or other under foreign domination.'[268]

In contrast to the view that there were too many foreign missionaries, it was said at the same time that the FMC establishment was too small, and that many more missionaries were both required and wanted. The FMC's Report to the General Assembly of 1958 said that in so many words: 'Of the desperate need for more missionaries and of the wide variety of opportunity in missionary service there can be no doubt', and went on to quote Dr D. T. Niles of Ceylon, in Scotland delivering the Warwick Lecture, who declared, 'We are simply howling out for more missionaries'.[269]

CHAPTER 5

In All Continents

(1960–1966)

I

AT the beginning of 1960 Harold Macmillan, British Prime Minister, delivered his famous 'wind of change' speech to a joint meeting of the Houses of Parliament in Capetown, in which he spoke of the growing strength of African consciousness. 'It may take different forms,' he said, 'but it is happening everywhere. The wind of change is blowing through the continent.'

That was 3 February. On 21 March the infamous day of Sharpeville occurred when 69 people were killed by the South African police. Further events rapidly followed that showed Verwoerd entrenched in his position, including South Africa's decision to separate from the increasingly multi-racial Commonwealth. As far as the situation in South Africa was concerned Macmillan's words were premature.

But wind of change there was. In 1960, the year arranged for the Review Conference on Central African Federation, the 'Report of the Advisory Commission on the Review of the Constitution of Rhodesia and Nyasaland' (the Monkton Report) was published. It stated clearly that the Federation could not continue without the most radical changes. Also Nationalist leaders of the three countries involved made it plain that they would boycott the Conference unless it were preceded by discussions and decisions on territorial constitutions of the two Rhodesias – agreement having been reached already on a new constitution for Nyasaland. In the event the Review Conference, addressed by Macmillan, opened on 5 December 1960. During a speech by the Southern Rhodesian Prime Minister, Banda and two Nyasaland chiefs walked out, and two days later Nkomo of Southern Rhodesia, Kaunda of Northern Rhodesia, and Banda led their delegations from the Conference in a planned walk-out. The Review Conference was adjourned on 17 December.

At a conference in Marlborough House in London in November

1962 the right of Nyasaland to withdraw from the Federation was conceded, and by the end of March 1963 the British Government had agreed that the Rhodesias should have the same right. By that stage the Federation was virtually at an end. In 1964 Nyasaland (now Malawi) became independent, as did Northern Rhodesia (now Zambia). In Southern Rhodesia the independence of the majority African population was to be delayed. In February 1963 the Rhodesian Front, the party of the European minority, won the election, and it was not until 1978, and after more than twelve years of white rule under the Smith regime, following the Unilateral Declaration of Independence (UDI) in 1965, that the African majority came into its own in the new nation of Zimbabwe.

Although white domination, as in South Africa and Rhodesia, was still in evidence, there was no question but that change was sweeping across the continent of Africa, and that the colonial era in its classic form was over. More and more new flags of independent nations were being unfurled, the latest being those of Nigeria in 1960 (a year when no fewer than 16 African countries became independent), Tanzania in 1961, and Kenya in 1963. The setting up of the Organisation of African Unity at the Conference in Addis Ababa in 1963 put seal to the new era.

As former British colonies and dependencies gained their independence in Africa and elsewhere the Commonwealth continued to play a significant part in international affairs. The warm reception given to the Queen and the Duke of Edinburgh during their visit to India and Pakistan in 1960, and to Princess Alexandra, who represented the Queen at the Independence Celebrations in Nigeria in the same year, were pointers to what it could be and could achieve. In its holding together of people of different races, cultures and religions, the Commonwealth was seen by many at that time as a sign of hope. Words of Duncan Sandys, the Secretary of State for Commonwealth Relations, expressed the general feeling: 'We have an opportunity, if we can but seize it, to touch the imagination of our fellowmen throughout this great association, and with them to fashion it into an even more striking example of co-operation, straight dealing, and civilised intercourse between the peoples and nations of the world.'[1] In 1965 the Commonwealth was further consolidated by the setting up of the Commonwealth Secretariat.

During this whole period the Cold War continued, with the stockpiling on both sides of nuclear weapons, and with the testing of those weapons, confidence being placed on the policy of deterrence. There was a constant danger of war, bringing with it the appalling prospect of nuclear destruction thousands of times worse than Hiroshima, and on a world scale. In October 1962 the world teetered on the edge of that calamity when the Soviet Union and the USA confronted one another over the building of missile bases in Cuba, following on from the abortive American incursion of Cuba at the Bay of Pigs in April the previous year. Russia under Krushchev had been building up an armament of medium to long range nuclear weapons in Cuba, the pretence being that only short-range surface to air missiles were being installed. US air reconnaissance revealed the true state of affairs, and warning was given to Russia. The US had its own missile crews on maximum alert and when Russian ships laden with missiles for Cuba approached a time and a line laid down by the USA, they were ready to go into action. Krushchev stopped the ships, right at the time and on the line laid down, and for four days there were tense deliberations at the end of which the Soviets agreed to withdraw its missiles. Never had terrible war seemed nearer.

Simultaneously with the Cuban crisis India and China were in conflict. There had been border clashes between their soldiers in August and October 1959. On the night of 19-20 October 1962, when the Chinese attacked with artillery, what had been local skirmishes developed into something more serious. By 20 November, when Nehru had felt it necessary to broadcast to the nation, and had asked the USA for help with aircraft, there was fear that China would move almost unopposed through Assam and enter Calcutta. As it turned out it became apparent that the Chinese had no intention of waging outright war. For them it had been solely a punitive expedition. On 21 November the Chinese declared a unilateral ceasefire, and although no negotiations were held and no peace declared, the conflict in practice ceased and the situation returned to what it had been.

After the death of Jawaharlal Nehru in May 1964, and during the premiership of his successor Lal Bahadur Shastri, India was at war again, this time with its rival Pakistan in September 1965, and once again over Kashmir. Happily, although it was destructive on both sides, it lasted for little more than three months. During the conflict Indian forces had reached into Pakistan as far as Sialkot. Under pressure from both the USA and the USSR a settlement was concluded at Tashkent in January 1966.

Meanwhile during this period China, along with the Soviet Union, was supporting Ho Chi Minh and his communist forces in North Vietnam, while the USA became increasingly involved in the conflict in support of the South. By November President Kennedy had dispatched troops to Vietnam, and from then on year by year, under Lyndon B. Johnson, the United States' commitment escalated. A massive bombing of the North began in February 1965. It marked a dangerous stage. From that time on the Vietnam conflict came to be seen increasingly as a major threat to the peace and stability of South-East Asia, and indeed to the peace of the world itself.

The 1960s in the international scene was a time of conflict and violence, but paradoxically it was also a time that generated, in a spirit of extraordinary optimism, a vision of a new world opening up for the masses set free from the shackles of colonialism. The achievement of independence seemed to augur a new era of hope. In 1966, however, the optimism began to falter. In that year Nkrumah of Ghana, such a symbol of the new Africa that was being born, was unceremoniously pushed out of power, the corruptions of his Government, his own dictatorial style, and the absurdities of his religious pretensions, revealed for all to see. At the same time the reputation of the other hero of the new era, Banda of Malawi, did not remain untarnished. He had assumed some of the worst paternalistic features of his colonial predecessors, and beyond that was using power ruthlessly against those with whom he disagreed.

In September of that critical year, 1966, Verwoerd, Prime Minister of South Africa, was assassinated in the House of Assembly, Cape Town. He was succeeded by B. J. Vorster who, as Minister of Justice from 1961, had been noted for his strict application of apartheid laws.

II

In an important paper given in November 1958, in New York, to the North American Advisory Committee of the IMC, Lesslie Newbigin urged the importance at this stage in history, in face of the enormous changes taking place across the world, of focussing afresh on the Gospel, and of recognising that world mission holds the central clue to the understanding of world events. Scientific developments, which had their basic origin in Western civilisation, had spread around the world bringing into being what it was now appropriate to describe as world culture and as world civilisation. The tragic thing is, said Newbigin, 'that, at the moment when the scientific culture which was formed within the western Christian tradition has achieved world-wide expansion and dominance, its unity with the supernatural faith in which it was begotten has disintegrated'.[2] He went on to say: 'The faith ... which finds the significance of human life in the achievement of a new order of human society on earth – is achieving global extension and penetration just at the time when – by the outworking of its own inner falsity – it stands self-condemned in the lands of its origin.'[3]

Lesslie Newbigin in that speech made articulate a question that independence from colonialism, and the dawning hope of social justice for the masses of the poor, was bringing to the fore: how was world mission to be understood in relation to secular movements for liberation? The FMC's Report to the General Assembly of 1960 was concerned with the same issue. 1960 had seen the fiftieth anniversary of Edinburgh 1910 with its vision of a world Christian civilisation, a vision that had so clearly not materialised. Reflecting on what had occurred since 1910 the Report quotes from Newbigin's speech: 'The secularised and distorted form of the Christian faith has transmuted the hope of God's Kingdom transcending history into the hope of a new order within history to be achieved by man's progressive mastery of nature and of his own affairs.'[4]

At the same time as it recognised that issue, the Report confirmed belief in the basic shift that had taken place in world mission from an enterprise originating in Europe and North America to one whose home base is everywhere, a point that Newbigin made in his speech.[5] The formation of the South East Asia Christian Conference in 1959 was a pointer to the beginning of the new era, as also the holding of the Third Assembly of the WCC in India in 1961.

Among the delegates to the WCC Assembly appointed by the General Assembly were the FMC representatives, the Rev. James Munn and Miss E. A. C. Walls. The Rev. John Fleming, Dr Robert Mackie and Principal William Stewart were present as advisers, and the Rev. Douglas Aitken as a Youth Participant.

The Assembly meeting in New Delhi, from 19 November to 5 December, brought together the WCC and the International Missionary Council in one body. Simultaneously it had received into its membership 23 new churches, representing approximately 71 million Christians on five continents; and in the islands of the Pacific, expanding the membership of the Council to 197 churches from 60 countries. The new enlarged constituency of the WCC, which now included the Russian Orthodox Church, with three other Orthodox Churches from behind the iron curtain [sic], and eleven new churches from Africa, had the result of moving the geographic centre of WCC membership from its former American/European axis, southwards and eastwards.

M. M. Thomas, of India, writing of the effect of those changes and of the new relationships they would introduce, had this to say:

> It is a long time since men, even Christian men, have begun to talk of the end of the Vasco da Gama era, and the necessity to take seriously the new self-hood of the nations, religions and churches in the non-western world. But only that which touches the imagination of the leaders and the rank and file of the churches can influence their will and shape policies and relationships. And what New Delhi has done is to give that touch to the imagination of Christian people and bring them a realisation that the old pattern of relationships, which the words 'Mission', 'Christendom' and 'non-Christian world' represented, are dead and gone and that new patterns have to be worked out.[6]

In addition to bringing the basic changes in attitude that M. M. Thomas points out, New Delhi gave a new theological emphasis to the laity and its role. The laity it defined as 'the whole people of God in the world', bringing the concerns of the total mission of the Church into the heart of the World Council. A passage in the Report on Witness illustrates that effect: 'Each stands in his own special place; the missionary in a country that is not his own; the pioneer in new fields of service; the Christian worker in his office or factory or home – each will be conscious that his witness is a part of the one ministry within the whole mission of the Church and that he is the representative of the whole Church.'[7]

The notion of wholeness in the understanding both of the Church and of Mission found expression in the address 'Called to Unity' given by Joseph Sittler of the University of Chicago, based on verses from the first chapter of Colossians, where the phrase 'all things', *ta panta*, is repeated. He argued for an understanding of the Church and its mission which would be undergirded by a Christology that would fully acknowledge Christ's lordship over all things:

We must declare that in him, for him, all things subsist in God, and therefore are to be used in joy and sanctity for his human family .... What is needed is an all-encompassing Christian vision ... with a core of spirituality illuminating economics, politics, and all other areas of human affairs.[8]

Alongside that address of Joseph Sittler on unity, which may in the long term have had a profound effect, there was the important statement on unity issued by the Central Committee meeting in St Andrews in August 1960, and received by the WCC Assembly, which read:

We believe that the unity which is both God's will and his gift to his Church is being made visible as all in each place who are baptised into Jesus Christ and confess him as Lord and Saviour are brought by the Holy Spirit into one fully committed fellowship, holding the one apostolic faith, preaching the one Gospel, breaking the one bread, joining in common prayer, and having a corporate life reaching out in witness and service to all and who are at the same time united with the whole Christian fellowship in all places and all ages in such wise that ministry and members are accepted by all, and that all can act and speak together as occasion requires for the tasks to which God calls his people.[9]

In 'The Message', written to the Churches, the WCC Assembly said: 'Let us everywhere find out the things which we can do together now; and faithfully do them.' At its first meeting held after the Assembly, the Commission on World Mission and Evangelism, as a first step toward acting together, initiated a discussion based on a paper prepared for the Assembly, entitled 'Joint Action for Mission', in which it was proposed that 'Churches and their related missionary agencies in a given geographical area should come together to face together as God's people in that place their total missionary task, and to seek the guidance of the Holy Spirit in fulfilling it.'

The aim of 'Joint Action for Mission' was stated at that time in four propositions:

(a) Advance in the Christian world mission calls for the redeployment of the resources available in specific geographical areas.
(b) A necessary step towards advance in mission in any given area is that the churches and missionary bodies within it together survey the

needs and opportunities confronting them in the area, and the total resources available to meet them.

(c) This process of survey should be followed by consultations of the churches and mission bodies in the area, aimed at securing real and effective redeployment of resources in the area in the light of the agreed goals.

(d) The process of survey, agreement and action in the redeployment of resources for the more fruitful discharge of responsibilities in mission will call for repentance and reconciliation on the part of all the bodies concerned.[10]

The next stage was the convening by the East Asia Christian Conference, in February and March 1963, of three 'Situation Conferences' to promote 'Joint Action for Mission' (JAM). The first of them was held in Madras, at which William Stewart and David Moses led groups, and Betty Walls was present from the FMC. At the end of that year the first meeting of the Commission on World Mission and Evangelism (CWME) was held where careful study was given to 'Joint Action' and agreement reached that there be at least one programme of JAM in each of the six continents.[11] The CWME meeting took place in Mexico City, from 8-19 December, under the chairmanship of Bishop John Sadiq of Nagpur, with Lesslie Newbigin as Secretary. Betty Walls and John Hamilton were two of the eight delegates from the Conference of British Missionary Societies.[12]

In a report some months after the Delhi Assembly, Lesslie Newbigin emphasised the increasing awareness of the world missionary task as an integral part of churchmanship that resulted from the coming together of the IMC and the WCC. The prominence given to world mission at the Montreal Faith and Order meeting had been evidence of that, and the positive effect of integration clearly seen in many other WCC programmes, including the Division of Inter-Church Aid. He drew attention to the disappointing fact, however, that there had not been a corresponding drawing together of home and foreign mission agencies.[13]

In the Message at the end of the meeting of the Commission on World Mission and Evangelism in Mexico, there was this concluding paragraph:

We ... affirm that this missionary movement now involves Christians in all six continents and in all lands. It must be the common witness of the whole Church, bringing the whole Gospel to the whole world. We do not yet see all the changes that this demands; but we go forward in faith. God's purpose still stands: to sum up all things in Christ.[14]

III

During this period the Church of Scotland had taken its share in the modern ecumenical movement, and its work overseas had increasingly been carried out in co-operation with other Churches and missionary bodies. It was no longer possible for any one committee within the Church itself to deal in isolation with many of the issues that were now arising, and organisational changes were necessary if the Church were to respond effectively to the ecumenical vision.

In 1958 the General Assembly appointed a special committee representing the FMC, the Colonial and Continental Committee, Jewish Mission, Refugee Service and Inter-Church Aid, and Inter-Church Relations, along with the Scots Memorial (Jerusalem) Committee, 'to consider means of co-ordinating the overseas work of the Church'.[15] In the following year an Interim Consultative Council was appointed to prepare for the eventual setting up of a Department of Overseas Mission and Inter-Church Relations.[16]

In 1963 a unified scheme had been agreed, and in May 1964 the new Department came into effect. Within the Department a new Committee called the Overseas Council was formed which had within it the FMC (including the Women's Foreign Mission), the Jewish Mission Committee (including the Women's Jewish Mission), the Scots Memorial (Jerusalem), the Colonial and Continental Committee, and the Committee on Inter-Church Aid and Refugee Service. A Women's Overseas General Committee was appointed which had as its convener the Woman Vice-Convener of the Overseas Council.[17]

Following such reorganisation designed to take account of the rapid changes taking place politically in the world and in relationships with Churches overseas, the Church of Scotland had been reassessing the policy decisions made in 1947 about integration (FMC Minute 8799 of 15 April 1947) and the developments in partnership relations that had been taking place. It recognised that the time had come for a full scale consultation to be held with representatives of the Churches abroad with whom the Church of Scotland was in partnership[18], the intention being to go beyond bilateral discussions, and to follow out the implications of 'Mission in Six Continents'.

The Consultation took place from 14-22 September 1965, in St Andrews, and was followed for the representatives by a programme of tours in Scotland over a period of four weeks. Invitations to the Consultation had been sent to all the Churches and Church Councils in whose areas the Church of Scotland shared in mission. Invitations had been sent also to Churches and Missionary Bodies with which the Church of Scotland worked in those areas, including the Conference of British Missionary Societies. Following the reorganisation within the Church there were representatives also from other Church of Scotland committees.

There were 118 members of the Consultation, attending full or part time, including observers appointed by Churches in Scotland: the Episcopal Church in Scotland, the United Free Church of Scotland, the Congregational Union of Scotland, and the Baptist Missionary Society. There were observers also from the World Association for Christian Broadcasting, from the BBC, and from the Press and Publicity Department of the Church of Scotland.

The main work of the consultation was done in four study groups, and in committees dealing with practical relationships, property and finance. The subjects studied by the groups were these: 'The Church and its Mission in the Contemporary World'; 'Building the Church for Mission'; 'The Place of the Missionary and the Christian Abroad'; and 'The Future of Institutions'. In the discussions on mission, in those groups and in plenary sessions, the Report noticed what would seem to be a loss of nerve. It speaks of the confidence that is found in the New Testament both in the plan of God and in the Church's message being replaced by 'uncertainty, fear and mistrust and a withdrawal from the contemporary world'. The stress was on structure and organisation, it says, while Mission remained on the circumference.[19]

There was an important address on 'Joint Action for Mission' by the Rev. R. K. Orchard,[20] General Secretary of the Conference of British Missionary Societies, and in at least one of the study groups, in which a number of examples of effective Joint Action were described, including the Tema industrial scheme in Ghana, Port Harcourt in Nigeria, and Durgapur in West Bengal. There was agreement that there was needed in all areas a survey 'on a joint action basis' of the present day effectiveness of evangelism.[21]

William Stewart gave the opening address at St Andrews. At the end of that address, having spoken of integration and partnership, he went on to speak of the importance of decisions being made together in consultation:

> The whole field of thinking opened up by recent writing on 'Joint Action for Mission' points to this. The missionaries from another land will share in that policy making, but they do so within the Church in which they serve and not as the guardians of some remoter interest. For this reason one longs to see the Church of Scotland willing to be represented much more frequently in active thinking by its representatives who come on visits for that very purpose, and longs to see more responsible thinking from all participants when decisions are taken.[22]

M. M. Thomas, who gave the concluding address,[23] spoke on the dynamism of mission and the meaning of history. As with Newbigin in the address he gave in New York in 1958. M. M. Thomas saw in world mission the clue to world events. 'What we are after,' he said, 'is an understanding of contemporary secular history in the light of the Kingship of Jesus Christ, who holds within His control the whole of history as it moves towards its consummation in His Second Coming. There was an echo too of Professor Sittler's address at New Delhi, as M. M. Thomas went on to say:

> It is precisely within the context of Jesus Christ as the reconciler of all things – of the whole history, of the whole universe as the Epistle to the Colossians puts it – that men can see the meaning of Jesus Christ as the bearer of reconciliation and redemption, not merely for a little part of the soul but for the whole of man, who has been awakened to this new humanity .... Men today are seeking redemption.
>
> When you see that between the resurrection and the consummation all history is in His hands and under His control; then certainly there is confidence in the plan of God. And this is the only way in which we can recover the missionary dynamism which we seem to have lost.[24]

IV

In the Indian sub-continent at the beginning of the 1960s, as in other parts of the world, there was a growing awareness of the need to look afresh at the life of the Church and it missionary calling. At the end of 1959 the FMC commissioned Ian Paterson, who was at that time Asia Secretary, to visit India and Pakistan, to consult and to make recommendations about the involvement of the FMC. On his return Ian Paterson raised questions, among other things, about integration, institutions and evangelistic outreach, which were to continue to preoccupy committees and councils of the Churches in the months and years ahead. Then in September 1961, following a resolution of the Executive Committee of the NCC, the Synod of the CSI set up a Commission to make a survey of the life and work of the Church; the Report of the Commission, entitled 'Renewal and Advance', being published in 1963.

If in the St Andrews Consultation of 1965 it was considered relevant to speak of a loss of nerve on the part of the Church, that is not how it seemed to many a few years earlier. In his report to the FMC on his visit to India and Pakistan, Ian Paterson had given a picture of a Church alive to new opportunities, and ready to take advantage of them for the furtherance of the Gospel.[25] In Pakistan the period before the takeover by Ayub Khan in October 1968 had been marked by graft and corruption, and there was growing disillusionment with Islam. In this situation Christians had begun to be noticed for a difference in the way they lived. Laymen were preaching to Muslims in the bazaars – and were being heard – and there was missionary outreach to Azad Kashmir. Ian Paterson was left, he said, with the impression of a small but virile Church.

In November 1962 the 14th General Assembly of the United Church of Northern India met in Kolhapur, with Bill Stewart as its Moderator. It was a historic meeting because of the decisive resolution made there, without a single dissentient vote, to 'merge its identity in the Church of North India/Pakistan, with those other Negotiating Bodies who also accept the Plan', the plan referred to being the third edition of 1957.[26] At this stage not all the Churches were ready to go ahead. The issue of ministry as understood by episcopal and non-episcopal Churches continued to be a difficulty, as did the problems raised for the Baptists by infant baptism. By 1965, when a fourth edition of the Plan was published, which differed only in detail, misunderstandings had been effectively removed and the way made virtually clear for union to take place.

Although the Church both in Pakistan and in India continued to be dependent to a considerable extent on foreign help, financially and in other ways, the movement for the integration of Church and Mission encouraged a new and strong sense of responsible self-identity. The Churches were proud to be Indian or Pakistani. In most areas the process of formal Church/Mission integration had been completed. Of the remainder, the Rajputana Mission became fully integrated in the Rajasthan Church Council in February 1960[27]; three years later at a special meeting of the Nagpur Church Council the Seoni Church Board of that Council had been inaugurated[28]; in June 1965, the Eastern Himalaya Church Council took over work previously done by an Educational Board[29]; in 1966, in view of the continuing delay in bringing integration into operation in Western India, it had been agreed to set up a Poona Education Board[30]; and later, in 1966, a Jalna Church Board of the Godaveri Valley Church Council.[31]

Formally with integration the Church achieved its independence. There was still however much to be done before the Church in India and Pakistan could truly be said to be free. Integration meant a major step forward toward the kind of partnership in freedom visualised at Whitby and Willingen, but the financial imbalance between the partners continued to get in the way. It was all too often felt that mission bodies who 'paid the piper', whether they were aware of it or not, were also 'calling the tune'. A discussion on Block Grants was bringing the issue to the fore.[32] As he travelled in India and Pakistan Ian Paterson could see that the Church in India and Pakistan was unhappy with the existing arrangement of moneys being allocated to particular pieces of work by a committee abroad, and wished to have a system discussed whereby they would be in the position to make decisions themselves about where and how resources made available should be used. There was, by this stage, general agreement in principle about Block Grants, and it was clear that the time had come for details to be worked out and a decision reached.

In 1961 the matter of Block Grants had come before the India Group within the Conference of British Missionary Societies, with particular reference to the Church of South India. It was seen to have become urgently necessary for missionary bodies supporting the CSI to work together, and to reach a common mind in respect of financial policy particularly in connection with Block Grants. Agreement had been reached to discuss with the CSI the holding of a meeting in India of Secretaries of related Missionary Societies, at which finance and wider matters of integration might be considered. The CBMS was anxious at this stage to explore how a missionary body might be best able to support a diocese as a whole and not simply the work for which before union it had had responsibility.[33]

'Renewal and Advance', the Report of the Church of South India Commission on Integration and Joint Action, was presented to a Consultation held at Tambaram from 30 December 1963 to 1 January 1964. The appeal to Partner Churches and Missionary Bodies was to see the CSI as a whole, with its opportunities and needs, and not to allow their giving of resources to be restricted by historical connections or to traditional purposes. The hope also was expressed that Missionary Bodies would pool their resources and make them jointly available to the CSI. Block Grants were to be regarded as the norm, to be allocated by the Diocesan Executive Committee 'according to the needs of the work throughout the diocese ... subject [only] to any special conditions stipulated by any Missionary Societies connected with that diocese'.[34]

An important working paper entitled 'An Advisory Study', produced by the Commission on Ecumenical Mission of the United Presbyterian Church in the USA, to encourage a re-examination of the Churches' common task in mission, had been published in 1962 and widely distributed for study. The UCNI General Assembly had sent it down to Church Councils for their consideration, and it had been adopted by the East Asia Christian Conference as an official study document. Following on from two consultations, which the UCNI General Assembly set up at the end of 1963, based on that document and on the work of the Madras Situation Conference, the UCNI Integration and Mission Committee met in Nagpur, in January 1964, along with representatives of Partner Churches, including James Munn, at that time Convener of the FMC.[35]

The meeting had before it two main issues. As things were, different Church Councils of the UCNI, and individual institutions, were receiving resources of money and personnel direct from missionary bodies abroad without reference to any central body within the UCNI, thus hindering resources from being most effectively distributed and going where they were most needed. The recommendations coming from the meetings were for missionary bodies abroad to find ways of working together in relation to the UCNI, and for the UCNI General Assembly to set up a committee with overseas representatives to look together at ways and means of serving the Church as a whole irrespective of historical backgrounds. The second issue concerned institutions. For many years it had been recognised that institutions, and the demanding administration necessary to run them, had overshadowed the Church in its local form, in council areas and in congregations, and had become a burden holding back its development. It was being recommended that where institutions were clearly furthering the work of the Church in its mission and must continue, then arrangements should be made for the Church to be set free from their day to day administration.

In Pakistan the question of how resources from abroad should best be used between the local Church and Murray College, in Sialkot, raised the issue of priorities in sharp form. There was general recognition that the College had an important part to play in the mission of the Church. Through it contact was made with many aspects of society and its leadership. It continued to produce graduates whose standards of thinking and integrity were admired. It was however costly to run in terms both of money and personnel. When in 1962 it was decided to appoint to the College W. G. Young, Malcolm Duncan, and Kay Stiven, all of whom were ordained district missionaries working with the local Church, there was a feeling of betrayal among the leadership of the Church Council.[36] Grants for the support of the College were received from the FMC, and from the Reformed Church of the Netherlands. From the autumn of 1963 the Reformed Church had two lecturers in the College, Dr Peter Born, and Dr Thomas.[37]

Missionary bodies in the USA and the UK, including the CBMS, had indicated the need they felt for a fresh assessment of the position and future of Indian Christian Colleges, and were asking for a survey to be undertaken. At a meeting in Nagpur in February 1963 it was agreed to go ahead with the survey, for which the FMC along with others had been pressing.[38]

It was during this time that Dr Radhakrishnan, President of India, who had been a student of Madras Christian College, Tambaram, received in 1963 the honorary degree of LLD at Edinburgh University. In his address he had referred to his debt to his College, and had spoken appreciatively of the other Scottish Colleges in which many leaders of India had been trained.[39] In the previous year Dr Harold John Taylor, who was serving as Principal of Union Christian College, Barapani, after his time as Principal of Scottish

Church College, Calcutta, had been appointed Vice-Chancellor of Gauhati University.[40]

In his Report of his visit to India and Pakistan Ian Paterson had drawn attention to the serious problems facing very many mission hospitals. Because of the increasing cost of running hospitals, the difficulty of maintaining the necessary level of staff and handling adequate resources, it had become necessary to re-examine what was being undertaken. In some places, for example with Bamdah Hospital,[41] or the Kalyani and Rainy Hospitals in Madras,[42] it had been possible to develop existing institutions, whereas closures had to be made in Poona and elsewhere.

The work of preventative medicine, including what was coming to be called community development, had become an increasing concern. It was something to which George and Mary More working among the very poor in Allipur were deeply committed, as was John McLeod in Jalna.[43]

★ ★ ★

During this period considerable advances were made in Theological Education and Christian Literature.

It had been decided at Whitby in 1947 that a fund for theological education be set up, and ecumenically administered, which would enable the Church world-wide to tackle effectively at last what, as long ago as the IMC meeting at Tambaram in 1938 had been recognised as one of the greatest weaknesses affecting the mission of the Church. By the time of the IMC Assembly in Ghana in 1958, four million dollars had been promised enabling arrangements to be made for the fund and its operation. A five-year plan was agreed. The Theological Education Fund (TEF) over the five-year period proved remarkably successful in raising standards, improving facilities, providing text books, giving theological teachers a new sense of vocation, and indicating new methods of co-operation. As a consequence of that success a new fund was set up to run for a further period with a new mandate.[44]

The theological faculty of Serampore College, whose Principal was William Stewart, benefited immediately from TEF, through a grant of $100,000 given for capital development.[45] The United Theological College, Bangalore, also received a major capital grant, and in addition the promise of recurring grants for five years.[46]

The Christian Literature Fund,[47] similar in many ways to the TEF, was inaugurated at the meeting of the Commission on World Mission and Evangelism in December 1963. For many years prior to the CLF, pressure had been mounting in India for a new expansion in Christian literature, and much thought had been given to how that might be done. Following the rapid increase in the Indian population it was calculated that between 1951 and 1961 there had been an increase of 46,000,000 in the reading public, and that there was now a potential readership in India of 125,000,000. Some months prior to the inauguration of the Fund, and after a consultation at Bethel in Germany that had pressed for a decision, an All-India Conference had been held which produced a Report entitled 'From Dialogue to Deeds'. The Conference and its Report stimulated a great deal of interest, with the result that literature agencies in India were poised to take advantage of the opportunities anticipated.

An ecumenical venture of Joint Action was envisaged, and it was to be carried out through the National Christian Council of India, in collaboration with the WCC. The Board of Christian Literature (BCL) of the NCC, which communicated with Christian Literature organisations abroad and which served Literature Committees in Regional Christian Councils across the country, and the Christian Literature Service Association, which did the same, as a professional body, for printing presses, shops, and other distribution agencies, began to hammer out the steps necessary to achieve in practice what was hoped for. To help it do so the Director of the Christian Literature Fund (CLF) made himself available to the newly appointed secretary of the Board and the Association, and generously shared his knowledge and experience, accompanying him for the first weeks around India to various projects, and being present for the first two years at the CLSA annual meeting.

In the year 1966/67 the BCL forwarded to the CLF 28 schemes, the majority of which were accepted and grants or allocations sanctioned. The schemes included two literature centres, several for the strengthening of publishing houses, capital for new literature in Hindi, Tamil and English, schemes for the production of tribal literature, a scheme of distribution training, and a scheme for the publishing of a new category of books designed for people of all faiths or of no faith, secular in topic, but firmly, if unobtrusively written from the perspective of the Faith. During this period 146 different books in 13 languages, and 173 different tracts in six languages, received subsidies.

Of FMC staff, among others, Jim Brodie had been involved in publishing in Nepali; William Young writing and publishing in Urdu; Catriona Somerville serving with Christi Sahitya Prasarak in the running of a bookshop and publishing centre in Maharashtra; and Ellis Shaw in the writing and publishing of evangelistic and apologetic material in Tamil. David Lyon, seconded to the NCC in 1964, as Christian Literature Secretary had been responsible under the BCL and the Christian Literature Service Association for the CLF operation across India, until his appointment and secondment to the Selly Oak Colleges at the end of 1967.[48]

V

The FMC, and the Overseas Council as it came to be called, continued to extend its interests in South East Asia through John Fleming. The third Training Institute for theological teachers was held in Singapore in 1960. Thirty-five attended. The study theme was 'Christ and Culture – the encounter in South-East Asia'.[49] The fourth Institute took place two years later, and included teachers from Japan, Korea, Ceylon, Pakistan and India, in addition to those from South East Asia. Professor John Bennett of Union Theological Seminary, New York, and Dr D.T. Niles took part as guest lecturers.[50] As well as directing those institutes for six weeks each summer, John Fleming for four to five months annually visited colleges in East Asia, and taught at Trinity College, Singapore. He edited the *South-East Asia Journal of Theology*, and by agreement with the Nanking Board became a co-operating staff member of the East Asia Christian Council.[51] In 1965 he visited theological colleges in Thailand, Indonesia, Sarawak, the Philippines, Taiwan and Hong Kong.[52]

In that same year John Fleming, while in Scotland, reminded the Committee of its Minute committing the FMC as a matter of policy to work among the Chinese – FMC 6336 of 18 April 1961.[53] In April 1965 the FMC had received a letter from the Rev. W. T. Hwang, General Secretary of the Presbyterian Church of Formosa, inviting the Church of Scotland to enter into association with his Church, and indicating at the same time particular opportunities of service.[54] Dr Stuart Loudon, a member of the Committee, and Vice-

President of the World Presbyterian Alliance, while representing the Alliance at the centenary celebrations of the Formosan Church, had conveyed the General Assembly's congratulations and good wishes.[55]

In May 1961 it had been agreed to continue the grant to the Malayan Christian Council at its previous level[56], and in response to a request from the Council in 1963 the FMC agreed to underwrite the salary of its General Secretary.[57]

The FMC continued to maintain contact with Hong Kong, although despite its efforts it had been unable find the staff which the Junk Bay Medical Relief Committee had repeatedly requested.

VI (a)

In Ghana during the Rev. E. M. L. Odidja's Moderatorship of the Synod of the Presbyterian Church of Ghana (PCG), creative new relationships were built up with overseas partners. As a token of its appreciation for all that the Church of Scotland and its missionaries had done for it, the PCG sent a cheque in July 1966 to the FMC for £1000.[58] It followed the invitation for missionary ministers to enter the ministry of the Church in Ghana,[59] and was a fresh and significant symbol of the partnership that was desired between the Churches in Ghana and Scotland. At the end of 1961 the FMC agreed to proposals made by the Synod of the PCG for a further step to fuller integration, involving the appointment of a secretary for Inter-Church Relations who would be a 'Scottish fraternal worker' [sic] – the first time that the word missionary was replaced – and the commitment to share in the expenses of overseas staff.[60] In August 1962 the Missionaries' Committee was suspended.[61] The Fortieth Anniversary of the Autonomy of the Synod was celebrated in 1966. In marking the occasion the Synod once again expressed its appreciation of the contribution made by Scottish missionaries. The FMC in its turn thanked the Church in Ghana for 'continued co-operation in mission'.[62]

Colin Forrester-Paton was the first Inter-Church and Ecumenical Relations Secretary of the PCG. As such he had the responsibility for corresponding with overseas Churches on behalf of the PCG, and was in the position to interpret in each direction the mind of the churches in connection with requests or decisions. The Moderator and the Synod Clerk often corresponded also, but copies of letters were shared, and particular matters discussed and agreed. The PCG in this period had new overseas partners – in Holland, USA, and England, and Consultations with Partners began. Alongside that important development the PCG began to send fraternal workers to Switzerland, Germany and the USA. As a Church in its own right the PCG now 'owned' its membership in the WCC, the All Africa Council of Churches (AACC), and the World Alliance of Reformed Churches, sending delegates and studying Reports. There had been a residential meeting, for example, to study the New Delhi WCC, and the Ibadan WARC Reports. Arising from the Church of Scotland side, the St Andrews Consultation was a creative event for the Ghana Church in realising partnership.

The work in the North continued to develop; there were three missionaries working alongside African colleagues. One of the first group baptised at Sandema had begun training for the pastorate,[63] and to mark the third anniversary of the arrival of the first Presbyterian missionaries some 500 people had taken part in a service held outside the Paramount Chief's Court at Sandema.[64] There was pressure for more missionary staff. There had been an urgent request from Sandema for a nurse.[65] The village and agricultural projects started in the North by Tom Colvin led to the formation of a Christian Service Committee under the Christian Council of Ghana to give them support; and help came also from Inter-Church Aid and from Scottish War on Want.[66] The Christian Service Centre in Tamale distributed food and medical supplies during weeks of drought and periods of flooding, and was helping to dig fish ponds, and to build latrines and roads.[67]

In the Volta River area 80,000 people were being resettled from 500 villages in the way of the flooding to take place above the new dam. Fifty new communities were planned, and Church workers were being trained to help.[68] The Ghana Churches provided £1000 annually for this work the remainder being given by Churches overseas.[69]

In 1961 the Christian Council of Ghana set up a Centre on Christian Marriage and Family Life, in line with recommendations of the IMC Ibadan Conference of 1957. The Rev. C. K. Dovlo and Mrs Jean Forrester-Paton were appointed respectively chairman and secretary. The committee became responsible for devising the programme for the annual celebration of Christian Home Week throughout Ghana. It created weekly 'clinics for married couples' in the major cities and ran short conferences for teachers on sex education. In 1966 the Apostolate Department of the National Catholic Secretariat co-operated fully in the Committee's work. In the following year Dr Hugh and Mrs Isabel Douglas came to head up longer courses on Christian marriage for lay and ordained participants, Roman Catholic and Protestant. Later the British Marriage Guidance Council supplied staff to train marriage counsellors.

By 1962 plans were well advanced for the building of a College and Chapel at Legon near the University of Ghana, to rehouse the joint Trinity Theological College, Kumasi.[70] The foundation stone of the new building in Legon was laid at the end of March 1964.[71] The cost was to be met by the Churches in Ghana, by Overseas Churches including the Church of Scotland, and by TEF. By 1965 the move had been completed.[72] Requests were made to the FMC for staff to serve in Trinity College,[73] and for scholarships to support students for theological training in Ghana or in Scotland.[74]

A proposed Basis of Union had been prepared by the Ghana Church Union Committee for study by the Churches. The Union Committee representing the Diocese of Accra, the Church of the Province of West Africa, the Evangelical Presbyterian Church, the Methodist Church, Ghana, and the Presbyterian Church of Ghana, had been in negotiation since 1957. The preface of the basis of union states that 'there is no question of achieving union by one church simply absorbing the others, with its tradition simply imposed on all the rest'. The document goes on to declare: 'The negotiating churches commit themselves to the guidance of the Holy Spirit in working out, in the constitution and in the life of the united church a right relation between the personal responsibility of the bishop in the Anglican tradition and the various forms of corporate oversight in the Presbyterian and Methodist traditions.' It then goes on to say that the agreement to accept the historic episcopate is not to be taken as 'committing the united church to any one particular interpretation of episcopacy'. The document had been forwarded to the Inter-Church Relations Committee of the Church of Scotland.[75] The Committee had to know whether the United Church would remain in full communion with the Churches with which the separate uniting Churches were at present in communion; and whether the FMC could continue to send out licentiates who might be ordained in Ghana, and be admitted to the ministry of the Church of Scotland on their return to Scotland. The view of the ICRC was that the answer to both questions was 'yes'.[76] At the beginning of 1966 the FMC agreed to share the cost of a secretary for the Church Union Committee whom the Methodist Church was making available. Negotiations for union were proceeding, with discussions continuing on the unification of the ordained ministry.[77]

A meeting arranged by the WCC was held in Rhodesia, in 1962, under the chairmanship of Dr Baeta, chairman of the Christian Council of Ghana, 'to build bridges of understanding' between independent Churches and the 'older' Churches. From 28 December of the same year to 7 January 1963, in Nairobi, the first major conference of African Christian youth took place, bringing together about 500 young people from all over Africa.[78] The All-Africa Council of Churches was also formally inaugurated in 1963.[79]

Friction between Church and State in Ghana came to a head in 1962. It had arisen in connection with the notorious inscription on Nkrumah's statue: 'Seek ye first the political kingdom and all other things will be added unto it', to which the Churches and the Christian Council had vigorously objected, seeing in it a further and blatant sign of the idolatrous language which he was encouraging people to use of his person.[80] By this time followers of his had begun to refer to him as *Osagyfo*, 'the Redeemer'.[81] The tension between Nkrumah's Government and the Churches was not new. When the Government put forward a White Paper, dealing with Marriage, Divorce and Inheritance, and proposing changes in the law which would virtually abolish legal provision for monogamous marriage, and remove the rights under customary law of the wives of polygamists, there had been strong criticism from the Churches. The Christian Council and the Presbyterian Church of Ghana which had protested to the Government, arguing that the Government proposals discriminated against women, and would encourage temporary unions, also published a comprehensive reply to the White Paper, setting out its own constructive proposals.[82] Although efforts were made from time to time to ease relations between Church and State – in 1963, for instance, at a dinner to which Church leaders had been invited, Nkrumah having said that he wanted closer contact[83] – tension continued right up to the time when he was deposed in February 1966.

(b)

In 1960 the Federation of Nigeria became a free and independent nation, and in the same year the Presbyterian Church of Nigeria began its independent life. On 18 June the Calabar Mission Council was dissolved, and the Synod of the Church took over responsibility for the work hitherto done in the name of that Council, and of the Church of Scotland Mission.[84] In handing over to the Synod, the Calabar Mission Council had conveyed its 'satisfaction at the good relations which had prevailed between the two bodies'. That sense of good relationships over the years between the Church of Scotland and Nigeria was underlined by the invitation to the General Secretary and his wife to be present at the inaugural celebrations of the Federation as honoured guests.

Sir Francis Ibiam, appointed Governor of Eastern Nigeria, one of the three regions of the Federation,[85] expressed his desire to continue his connection with the FMC. It was agreed that he be regarded as seconded to Government service for a period not exceeding five years.[86] Typical of his thoughtfulness and sensitivity, Dr Ibiam invited Mr James Duffin of the office staff and his wife as his guests to his installation.[87] In 1961 the University of St Andrews, where Dr Ibiam had done his medical studies, awarded him the Honorary Degree of Doctor of Laws,[88] adding to his honours. In the same year, at the Third Assembly of the WCC, he became one of its six presidents, along with Dr David Moses, Principal of Hislop College.

During this period up to 40 missionaries from Scotland, not including wives, were serving in the Calabar region in any one year. By 1966 the number had gone down slightly to 35. In 1960, 18 of those missionaries were serving in schools or colleges, 15 of whom were being supported entirely, and one partially, from Government funds.[89] Of the Church-run institutions where they were serving, the Women's Teacher Training College at Umuahia was administered jointly with the Anglican and Methodist Churches, and the Union Secondary School for Girls at Ibiaku with the Methodist Church. The hospitals, where more than ten of the missionary doctors and nurses worked, were supported financially by the Government, though funding and shortage of staff was a constant problem. In 1965, for instance, there was a serious staffing shortage at the Queen Elizabeth Hospital, run jointly with the Government, and at the Mary Slessor Hospital, where the Church had constantly appealed to the Government for Joint Status in the hope of meeting staffing and budgeting difficulties.[90] The overall problem of staffing may be seen from these figures of 1961 listing vacancies: one doctor, and ten sisters, including three for relief purposes; and these figures from the previous year: four ministers, three men teachers, one woman teacher, one auditor and two hospital managers.[91] In addition to those working in schools and hospitals, there were missionaries involved in agricultural development and in Christian literature. Finally, the FMC/Overseas Council (OC) co-operated in joint theological training with Methodist and Anglican Churches in Trinity College, Umuahia, in which one of its missionaries served.

Over the years the FMC/OC encouraged the Presbyterian Church to send young ministers and others to Scotland for experience or training. In 1962, for instance, Etim Onuk was the first of several studying at New College, in Edinburgh; and in 1964 Ako Oku, a Church Sister, studied for a year at St Colms.

Co-operation between the Churches in the running of institutions, and in many other ways, led to an increasing understanding of the need for union, and an impatience with the divisions which separated them. The Nigerian Christian Council Report at the beginning of this period spoke of a 'growing impatience on the part of local Churches with the perpetuation of divisions that have roots in European or American history ... and a growing realisation of the hindrance in obedience caused by our divisions'. It went on:

> It has been remarked that inter-Church co-operation is observable at four levels of willingness: it is most readily accorded between Nigerian Christians; it comes rather less readily from overseas missionaries; slower still to move in this direction are the home boards of the missions; and slower than all are the home Churches of those missions. Like all generalisations, it is not the complete truth, but there is sufficient truth in it to make us ask whether God is not using us who are the children to lead our fathers in the faith into a new perception of His truth.[92]

On 24 July 1963 the Church Union Committee of the Synod of the Presbyterian Church of Nigeria put before the Synod a Notice of Motion that the Church resolve to enter a united Church on the basis of the Scheme of Union (Third Edition), and that there be an immediate consultation to plan the amalgamation of educational, medical and other work. At the same time a meeting in London suggested that the FMC express to the Synod its willingness to transfer property to the united Church.[93] Meanwhile the Anglican Province of West Africa adopted a resolution urging its member Churches to proceed with Union negotiations, 'in this way asserting its own authority to approve these even if provinces in Britain and elsewhere were slower to make decisions'.[94]

Later, in February the following year, the FMC agreed to a meeting in Nigeria of Africa Secretaries, including those from Canada and Holland, and noted that in the opinion of the Church Union Committee, property transfer should be delayed until after the consummation of union.[95]

In a letter from the Synod of the Presbyterian Church of Nigeria received by the Principal Clerk, it was confirmed that the Church of Nigeria would be constituted on 11 December 1965. It was the hope of the Presbyterian Church, the letter said, that the Moderator of the General Assembly or his representative would be able to attend the inaugural service and visit the Eastern Region.[96] In the event the Moderator of the General Assembly was to be in India at that time and would not be able to be present. The Very Rev. George F. MacLeod would represent the General Assembly in his stead.[97] All those plans were, however, to be thwarted.

Because of the difficulties that had arisen with regard to two congregations of the Methodist Church in Lagos, over the transfer of property to the new Church, the Church Union Committee at an emergency meeting had decided to postpone the inauguration of the United Church.[98] On 24 February 1966, at Onitsha in Eastern Nigeria, the Inaugural Committee met. It reported that the Committee was not able to fix a new date for the inauguration, that efforts to overcome the obstacles would be continued and intensified, and that it was hoped that at the next meeting it would be in the position to set a date.[99]

A meeting of representatives of the Anglican and Presbyterian Churches, held at Onitsha in June 1966, agreed that the two Churches should not go ahead immediately with a union between the two Churches alone, but instead develop joint action between all three Churches as fully as possible.[100]

Further developments were interrupted by political events leading to the outbreak of the Biafra Conflict. By the beginning of 1967, after fruitless meetings between the protagonists of Biafra and the Federation, war had become inevitable. On 30 May 1967, Lt Colonel Ojukwu declared the independence of 'the Republic of Biafra'.

(c)

On 1 January 1960 the integration of the Church and Mission was completed in the Synod of Livingstonia of the Church of Central Africa Presbyterian,[101] followed in November 1962 by the merging of the Missions of the Church of Scotland, the London Missionary Society, and of the United Church of Canada in the United Church of Central Africa in Rhodesia.[102]

During this period the issue of Federation continued to cause anxiety and uncertainty in Central Africa and preoccupy to a considerable extent committees of the Church of Scotland. There began, however, to be hopeful signs. Banda and other detainees were released in April 1960, three months later there was held a successful conference on a new constitution for Nyasaland, and in October an encouraging Report from the Monkton Commission was published.

In the Assembly of May 1960 two important Deliverances, 7 and 11, to the Report of the Special Committee Anent Central Africa were accepted:

> *Deliverance 7:* The General Assembly, while recognising the advantage of some form of association between the three Territories, reaffirm their conviction that no scheme should be retained or developed which does not rest upon the consent and co-operation of the majority of the inhabitants irrespective of race.

> *Deliverance 11:* The General Assembly urge strongly that the delegations from Nyasaland and Northern Rhodesia to the Conference reviewing the Federal Constitution should be such as will be recognised by the African people as their genuine representatives.

As the result of arguments put forward in debate following the presentation of the Committee's Report, four other Deliverances – 5, 8, 9 and 10 – dealing with the different functions of the Territorial and Federal Governments, and with the question of the Territories' right to secede from the Federation, were referred back to the Committee, pending the Publication of the Monkton Report. Dr R. H. W. Shepherd,[103] the previous Moderator, and former Principal of Lovedale, who moved the motion to refer back, was a member of the Monkton Commission and was concerned that the Church should take cognisance of its findings. He had taken exception to what he regarded as the heavily biased attitude of the

Committee to the Government and to those Europeans and others who sought a more gradual and less abrasive approach to the problems of Federation. He clearly felt too, as did his seconder, Brigadier Bernard Ferguson,[104] that Dr George MacLeod, who as the Committee's convener was responsible for presenting the Report (by his persuasive rhetoric) had obscured what was happening, and had misled the Assembly. George MacLeod[105] was at his passionate best that day, and was in no mood to allow his opponents, Colonial and African experts or no, to drown what he believed to be the urgent and authentic cry for justice of the African people. The fact that Kenneth Mackenzie[106] was there to back him up with his experience and his long and careful study of the issues, added weight to his appeal. Although the particular Deliverances that Dr Shepherd wished deleted were not accepted immediately, the bulk of the Deliverances were, and, most importantly, Deliverances 7 and 11 above.

Dr Shepherd in his intervention was anxious to offset what in his opinion was a simplistic and idealistic view of the African position. It just was not true, he believed, that the bulk of African opinion was against Federation. His own experience had been that pressure was being placed on the people to take a stand against Federation against their wills. He asserted that many had been prevented from giving evidence to the Monkton Commission by threats against them and their families. Although there were undoubtedly instances of unwarranted pressure, and while it was important to have pointed out that the right was not restricted to one side only, the weight clearly seemed to lie with those who claimed overwhelming support for the anti-Federation position.

In its Report to the General Assembly of 1961, the Special Committee on Central Africa had compared its Recommendations in the Deliverances that had been referred back with related sections in the Monkton Commission Report. In very many respects there was an identity of view. The Monkton Commission on the one hand argued for the benefit to the whole area of some form of close association, but at the same time recognised that that could only happen by consent. In a Section headed 'General Conclusions' the Commission had stated:

> Certain facts are inescapable. The Federation can continue only if it can enlist the willing support of its inhabitants. The wisdom of Solomon

himself, were we able to command it, would not suffice to make any Constitution work without the goodwill of the people.[107]

Having taken note of the Monkton Commission Report the General Assembly of 1961 adopted the following Deliverances:

14. The General Assembly, strongly supporting the unanimous conviction of the Monkton commission that the Federation must ultimately rest on a general willingness to accept it, and that to hold it together by force is out of the question, urge that this should be accepted by all parties as a basic principle when the Federal Review Conference is re-convened.

15. The General Assembly, believing that there are advantages in the co-operation of the territories and peoples of Central Africa, urge all concerned, and especially those who will take part in the reassembled Federal Review Conference, to seek to discover the agreed form of association which will bring the greatest benefit to the peoples of all races.

In the following year, on 30 October, general elections took place in Northern Rhodesia, under the new Constitution, and went through peacefully, contrary to what some had warned. After bye-elections, which took place in December, a coalition of the United National Independence Party (UNIP) under Kenneth Kaunda, and the African National Congress, was formed to become the first African administration in Rhodesia.

The Marlborough House Conference on Nyasaland held in November 1962 brought independence a major step nearer by its decision to set up a cabinet presided over by a Nyasa Prime Minister by February 1963. Commenting in Parliament on the success of this Conference, Rab Butler paid tribute to 'the realism and statesmanship of the Nyasalanders of all races' to whom the result was due. He went on to refer to the Malawi Congress Party's victory at the General Election which had justified bringing into office a largely African Government, which he said 'continued to enjoy the confidence of the vast majority of people in the Territory, including many of non-African race'.[108]

At a General Election in January 1964 Kenneth Kaunda obtained a sweeping majority with his UNIP, and was installed as Prime Minister, while in May of that year Prime Minister Hastings Banda at a General Election finally paved the way for Independence. In 1964, with Federation ended, the two independent nations of Malawi and Zambia came into being, in July and October respectively.

Although by and large Independence happened smoothly in both countries, it did not go forward without some conflict, and in one instance a major outbreak of violence, in which members of Churches were affected.

From 1960 onwards, as the nationalist movement grew in strength, followers of Lenshina were being drawn away from Alice and the Lumpa Church to Kaunda's Nationalist Party. Though both movements shared a deep rooted nationalist fervour, the 'other-world-liness' of Lenshina and the political activism of UNIP inevitably led to divergence and to conflict. By 1963 Lenshina villages around Chinsali, and up on the Nyasaland border at Lundazi, became separated from the rest of the community, and as they openly spoke against UNIP provoked antagonism. There were attacks on stockaded Lenshina villages, and retaliation from them. In July 1964 the confrontation mounted, with the police ordered to open the villages up and end the segregation. In the violence that erupted there were many casualties, including members of the UCCAR and the CCAP, and sporadic fighting went on almost up to the time of Independence. [109]

In Malawi following Independence, Hastings Banda immediately made sure of his own position of leadership by taking action against rivals or potential rivals, who had emerged as leaders in the nationalist struggle. One of the most prominent of those was Orton Chirwa, a barrister who was a founder of the Malawi Congress Party and had been its first President. Chirwa had stepped aside to allow the older man to assume the leadership of the new nation. He was seen by Banda as a threat and forced to flee the country. Two months after Independence, he and his wife left for exile in Tanzania. Other prominent leaders, who had served as ministers were equally in danger, so that the months following Independence were a time of anxiety and uncertainty. Many of them, and their sympathisers, were members of the CCAP, with the inevitable result that missionaries by their friendships had become suspect through association. Albert McAdam and his wife found themselves in that position. By taking friends into their home who were relatives of ex-ministers regarded as enemies of Banda, they aroused resentment. Although a police guard had been placed at night at the

McAdam's house for their protection, church leaders feared for their safety, and advised that they and their children should leave Malawi.[110]

★ ★ ★

During this period of change in Central Africa, despite the insecurity and the dangers, the Churches were pressing ahead with the pastoral care and education of their people, with outreach, in the training of the laity and of ministers and the management of institutions of service. They were concerned also with Church union. By the time of Independence in Zambia, arrangements for the coming together of the three Churches to be united in the United Church of Zambia – namely the United Church of Central Africa in Rhodesia, the Methodist Church and the Church of Barotseland – were well advanced.[111] On 16 January 1965 the United Church of Zambia was inaugurated at a service in Mindolo at which Kenneth Kaunda read the lesson and Colin Morris preached. Neil Bernard represented the FMC.[112] In Malawi discussions toward union were being held with the Diocese of the Anglican Church. The fact that the Mkhoma Synod had withdrawn from the discussions was a cause of concern.[113]

The renaming in 1960 of the Women's Teacher Training College in Blantyre, serving many of the Churches together, as Kapeni College, after the Chief on whose land the College had been built, had been a significant pointer to the new era of independence in which the Churches were now to work.[114] The College had received major grants from Government,[115] and by the end of 1962 was being run by a committee of management on which were represented the Government, the Council of Churches, and the Synod of the Church of Central Africa Presbyterian.[116] In January 1964, by Government Order, a College Board of Governors had been established, five of its membership of nine being appointed by the Minister of Education.[117] The intention of the Government was to take over education from the Churches (from the missionaries [sic]), with as far as possible retaining their co-operation. In 1962 Dr Banda was quoted as saying:

> In common with others in this country I have the greatest respect for missionaries and religious teachers. I honour and revere the memory of such men as Dr Laws ... and other missionary heroes of this country.

I could never be against them; I would never try to destroy what they built in this country.[118]

At about this same time the Minister of Education informed the Synod of Livingstonia that the Government planned to establish a university at Livingstonia, and would require the whole plateau.[119] In January 1963 agreement had been reached to establish a Junior College at Livingstonia.[120] At the end of 1966 both the College and the Livingstonia Secondary School, which shared the Overtoun Institute premises with it, were operating successfully. The school, though now under a Board of Governors, was still regarded by Government as a Church school.[121]

In 1960 at Serenje[122] (Northern Rhodesia) the Malcolm Moffat Teacher Training College was being built. The FMC had promised to find a woman and a man for the staff as missionary teachers, but unhappily it was a promise they were finding difficult to fulfil.[123] At the same time there were proposals to develop a Secondary School for Girls at Mwenzo, and to build a new building, for which a 75 per cent grant might be available from Government.[124] The UCCAR had been approached by local Christians to resume the management of schools and had asked the FMC whether it would be prepared to help. The FMC with regret had to say 'no'.[125] All schools for which the UCCAR was responsible had been handed over to Government in January 1965.[126]

Turning from educational institutions to medical, by 1960 the misunderstanding between the Hospital at Chitambo, in what was then Northern Rhodesia, and the Lala (Serenje) Native Authority had been resolved. The Authority made a grant to the Hospital, and appointed two representatives to the Hospital Committee,[127] while in the following year it contributed toward the cost of equipping the maternity wing, which had just been built.[128] Meanwhile, the decision was reached to press the Government to take over of the Lubwa Hospital by the end of August 1961.[129] In that same year representatives from Churches in Rhodesia and Nyasaland, dissatisfied with the attitude of the Minister of Health to Christian medical work, were asking for a Commission to be appointed:

1. to consider the role of the medical services rendered by the Church in relation to those provided by the Federal Government; and
2. to make recommendations to the Minister in regard to the ancient

operation of Church hospitals and to advise on the form and degree of assistance needed now, and which be required in future.[130]

At this time the Northern Rhodesia Council was urging the establishment of four nursing sisters at Chitambo and pointed out that if the Hospital were to continue to receive recognition as a training hospital that would be necessary.[131] There continued to be a staffing problem and a letter had been received from the Synod Clerk, saying that he must hear by January 1964 whether appointments could be made. If not training would have to be stopped, which in its turn would have financial implications that might lead to the closure of the hospital.[132] By 1965 the situation had changed. The Government gave recognition and support to the Hospital at Chitambo, and Government grants allowed adequate increases in local salaries.[133] In the same year the Government made a grant to cover 75 per cent of the cost of a Tuberculosis Block for the Hospital.[134] The Synod of the UCZ asked the FMC and the United Church of Canada for help with the remainder.

In Malawi there was a similar shortage of medical staff as in Zambia. The hospitals at Mlanje (90 beds) and Ekwendeni (64 beds) had only one doctor each, and Livingstonia (30 beds) and Loudon (25 beds) had none.[135] The Women's Foreign Mission Committee, the Presbyterian Church in Ireland and the United Presbyterian Church in USA were asked to help. Finance was also a constant problem. While the number of patients increased, Government grants did not.[136] It has been minuted however, in October 1966, that as far as staffing at Mlanje was concerned things had improved. There were now three sisters there, and a fourth, a VSO, was expected.[137] In the previous year the Private Hospital Association of Malawi (PHAM) had been founded, with membership open to any non-governmental medical facility in Malawi recognised by the Ministry of Health.[138]

In both the UCCAR (later the UCZ) and the CCAP emphasis had been given to the training of the Laity and in particular the training of women for the service of the Church. In October 1960 the Synod of the UCCAR agreed to establish a Rural Women's Training Centre at Kashinda.[139] In response to a request for help with capital and recurrent expenditure, the FMC gave a capital grant for each of two years, and promised funds toward annual maintenance.[140] The United Church of Canada contributed too, as had the

Department of Rural Development.[141] The LMS made available one of their buildings, and seconded a missionary, part of whose maintenance was to be met by the Church of Scotland.[142]

In March 1962 the Synod of Blantyre of the CCAP approved in principle the setting up of a permanent Lay Training centre[143], and in the following year the establishment of a Lay Training Centre at Chilema, along with the Anglican Church, under a Board of Management.[144] Two years later, in August 1965, the Synod of Livingstonia, in conjunction with the Seventh Day Adventists, and the Anglican Diocese of Malawi, approved the constitution of a Lay Training Centre at Mzuzu.[145]

The development of lay training accompanied a new concentration on building up the ordained ministry of the Church. There was a serious shortage of ministers in both countries. It was not unusual in many areas to find one ordained minister having responsibility for ten congregations and other scattered groups. There was a need also to improve the level of the ministry in theological education. As it was, ministers were frequently ill-equipped to meet the demands of an increasingly educated younger generation.

In Nyasaland an experimental course was planned, beginning in 1962 with five students from each of the three Synods of the CCAP – a three year course with an additional year of practical training. The intention was to have tutors, with Charles Watt as their convener. The course would be held at Mkhonia.[146]

In Northern Rhodesia the UCCAR resolved to build its Ministerial Training College at Mindolo, the furnishing of the chapel as a project to be undertaken by all the congregations. Money already received from the United Church of Canada would be used for the erection of a classroom block. It was hoped that the Church of Barotseland would send students to the College and that the Paris Mission, PEMS, would provide housing for them and provide a tutor.[147] Representatives of the Churches concerned were to meet the Director of the Theological Education Fund. The FMC had agreed to make a grant of £5000 to be paid over five years.

In the light of proposals for Church Union, recommendations had been made by a joint meeting of the Methodist and the UCCAR for co-ordinating the training of future ministers. The meeting recognised the importance of setting up a union college, if possible in Northern Rhodesia, but agreed there should be close liaison between Mindolo and Epworth College on common standards and curricula.[148]

Meanwhile, in 1961, the TEF made a grant of £35,000 to be divided between the Epworth Theological College and the University College of Rhodesia and Nyasaland.[149] The University College had received a grant from the TEF to help establish a Department of Theology. It had created a Chair of Theology, and had strengthened the theological section of its library.[150]

The first meeting of the Executive Committee of the United Church of Zambia in February 1965 stressed that there was a need for the unification of theological training in the UCZ and that the students from the four presbyteries should go to one college. It was agreed that all matters connected with ministerial training should be referred to that one Ministerial Training College.[151]

The Synod requested the FMC along with the LMS and the United Church of Canada to increase its grant toward the Ministerial Training College at Mindolo, which the FMC agreed to do.[152]

Another step in building relationships across Churches, encouraging a two-way traffic in partnership, took place when two of the General Secretaries of CCAP Synods were invited to Scotland. The Rev. P. C. Mzembe of Livingstonia came to Scotland at the end of February 1960, and the Rev. Jonathan Sangaya of Blantyre early in 1961. The desirability of church workers, both ministers and lay people, being sent abroad for training began to be more and more keenly felt.

(d)

At the beginning of 1962 a Conference on the Constitution of Kenya was held in London, and on 12 December 1963 Kenya became an Independent State within the Commonwealth, with Jomo Kenyatta as its first President. Dr Archie Craig was an official guest of the Kenya Government at the Independence celebrations.[153]

In the Church, African leadership began to emerge into greater prominence. At the end of 1961 the Rev. Charles Kareri, the Moderator of the General Assembly of the PCEA, attended the Third Assembly of the World Council of Churches in New Delhi, representing his Church.[154] The Rev. and Mrs Kareri were invited to Scotland in 1964, where they were present at the General Assembly. To encourage African leadership the FMC was asked to provide financial support for Africans who were becoming available for major posts in the Church, and to make possible more frequent overseas visits. At the same time the PCEA General Assembly was asking for help to cover the cost of appointing an African General Secretary.[155] The FMC responded positively.[156]

The Rev. John Gatu, who was to play such a prominent part in the Church world-wide and in the missionary movement, was the first African General Secretary of the PCEA. He was appointed at the Fourth General Assembly in 1964.[157] In 1961, when the Rev. Donald Lamont was appointed to that post, John Gatu had been made Administrative Assistant.[158] A year later he became Deputy General Secretary,[159] and in that same year was elected Chairman of the Christian Council of Kenya. In 1963 he and his wife were guests of the United Presbyterian Church in the USA.

Pan-Africanism, which had been gaining momentum ever since Bandung in 1955, and Accra three years later, by 1963 reached a new stage in its development. A Conference in Addis Ababa, bringing together 32 independent African countries, set up the Organisation of African Unity. Heralded by a Consultation in Ibadan three years previously, a meeting in Kampala in 1963 of the All Africa Conference of Churches established a permanent organ for mutual consultation of Churches in over forty countries in Africa, and through which in many instances they related to Government.[160]

In the run up to Independence and in the years immediately following, the Church was concerned, as much as Government, to seek for Kenya and the Church in Kenya an authentic African iden-tity, while at the same time accepting the genuine friendship of Europeans and respecting the good they had to share. There was to be an effort to move beyond racism. In 1960 the Kenya Christian Council was proposing to build a non-racial secondary school for 450 boys, which would be partly boarding, the current expenses being met by fees and Government grants, and, as from 1961, by decision of its Board of Governors, the Egerton Agricultural College was to be open to all races.[161] In July 1961 a remarkable and historic meeting took place between African and European farmers in Kenya's Rift Valley to discuss, under the auspices of the Kenya Christian Council, the vital and vexing problem of land tenure and food production. Fifty farmers and Church leaders met at Nakuru, and many who had not been able to come had written expressing their support.[162] Earlier in that same year the General Assembly of the PCEA had directed the Presbytery of Tumutumu, in consultation with the Nyeri Kirk Session and the European congregation, to move toward integration, resulting in the first instance in the setting up of a non-racial Nyeri Kirk Session.[163]

The schools in Kenya associated with the Church played an out-standingly important part both in the development of the Church itself and of the country as a whole. The Alliance High School had as its former pupils many of the leaders of the new Kenya. Half of President Kenyatta's cabinet, it is said, had been pupils there.[164] The Alliance Girls' High School had a similar reputation for excellence. Although the management of schools was transferred to district and local school committees in 1958, the PCEA was strongly rep-resented on those committees and continued to have influence. It had direct responsibility for two teacher training colleges, one for women and one for women and men, and it participated in the management of interdenominational colleges. The Government met the cost of the colleges.[165]

The PCEA continued to be responsible for three hospitals, at Tumutumu, Chogoria and Kikuyu. Staffing was a major problem. If the training of nurses were to be done in each hospital, and up to the level of Assistant Nurse standard as called for by Government, then three doctors and four sisters would be required in each place.[166] A Policy Committee meeting in 1961 had agreed that the Church should continue to train Assistant Nurses and Midwives, that close liaison should be secured on a permanent basis with Government, and that the control of the hospitals should be by elected Commit-tees of Management responsible to the Church. Deep concern was expressed about staffing.[167] Following the Report of a Special Hos-pitals' Commission later that year, it was agreed that Tumutumu be designated as the essential PCEA training hospital, that Chogoria be permitted to continue nursing training and Kikuyu initiate a pre-selection Course, on the understanding that the best candidates would qualify for training at one of the other hospitals.[168]

The FMC General Secretary and Mrs Macartney, who were visiting Kenya at that time, were present at the General Adminis-tration Committee in October 1962. At that meeting the following requests were made to the FMC: that it give guidance to the PCEA on the support it could expect to receive; that it provide a minimum medical staff of five doctors and five sisters for the PCEA hospitals; that it consider urgently the need to appoint non-medical assistant staff; and that it provide bursaries for Africans to study and qualify abroad as doctors and nurses. In its Report to the FMC, its two deputies recommended that it give a clear indication of what staff it could provide 'based not on what it would like to provide but on what terms of realistic recruitment it could with confidence promise'.[169] In response to those requests, the PCEA were informed that it was unlikely in the next four years that more than four doctors and four nursing sisters could be provided.[170]

The General Administration Committee (GAC) of PCEA General Assembly accepted in October 1964 the estimates of senior medical staff that the Church hospitals required a staff in 1965 of eight doctors, eight sisters and three hospital administrators.[171] In April 1965 the grave situation was reported to the Africa and Jamaica Committee of the Overseas Council that only one male doctor could be located.[172] In June 1965 the GAC of the PCEA, realising that it would not longer be possible to run three hospitals, appointed a commission to consider what should be done.[173]

Dr Jack Wilkinson of Kikuyu Hospital had received an invitation from the WCC to attend, in May 1964, at their expense, a consultation to be held at Tübingen on the Healing Ministry in the Mission of the Church.

In 1960 St Paul's Theological College, Limuru, in which the PCEA participated along with Anglicans and Methodists, began a new phase. In that year the Association of East Africa Theological Colleges – covering Kenya, Tanganyika, and Uganda – was set up, with the help of the TEF, and an East African Diploma in Theology was instituted. St Paul's Theological College, Limuru, took part and greatly benefited. With grants which it had received from the TEF and other sources, including a sizeable gift from St Andrews, Nairobi, new buildings were provided including a hall of residence, a dining room and common room, a library and tutors' rooms. The Rev. Oswald Welsh, who had previously been Vice-Principal, and a missionary of the Church of Scotland since 1957, was appointed Principal.

Following a Conference held at Limuru, in July 1961, on relations between the College and the Missionary Societies, a memorandum was prepared, dealing with a number of matters including plans for future staffing and finance. The College would be putting forward a request to the TEF, which would have to be matched by monies from the Churches and the Missionary bodies. It was proposed that they gave in the proportion 50/50, the Anglican Churches and their associated societies giving 50 per cent and the Presbyterian and

Methodist group of Churches the other 50 per cent.[174] The FMC responded to this request by indicating that it would have to be dealt with in terms of a block grant given to the College or the PCEA, with necessary decisions on priorities being made in Kenya. [175]

It was reported in October 1963 that the Association of East African Theological Colleges requested that the Rev. David Philpot be made available as Secretary/Registrar of the Association. St Paul's Limuru were willing to release him on condition that he continued certain duties as Administrative Secretary of the College.[176]

(e)

At the beginning of January 1960 the Government of South Africa, in pursuance of its racial policies, detached the University College of Fort Hare from its affiliation to Rhodes University, reducing it virtually to a tribal college for Xhosa students.[177] The University College of Fort Hare was the offspring of Lovedale, and had become with it the most prestigious and creative centre of education in Southern Africa. Many of Africa's most outstanding leaders were educated there, including Mugabe and Mandela. Fort Hare's closure as a University College was widely regarded as an act of vandalism on the part of the supporters of apartheid to whom the College was anathema. In a strongly worded reference to it, the FMC's 1960 Report says: 'It is difficult to read the speeches and the account of the proceedings at the Final Assembly without a feeling that South Africa is taking one step after another backward into the abyss'; and in his account Adrian Hastings refers to 'the rape of Fort Hare' marking 'the end of an epoch'.[178]

In the Sharpeville massacre in March, during a demonstration against the pass laws, police and military shot dead 60 African demonstrators and seriously injured many more.[179] The news of the event went round the world and was received with horror and intense indignation. The General Assembly's response, having reaffirmed its abhorrence of racial segregation, and having expressed deep distress at 'the tragic events', indicated its desire to make a fresh approach to the Dutch Reformed Church in South Africa, which 'exercises a strongly determinative influence in the matter of racial ideology', and with which it was in full communion.[180]

In December 1960 a Consultation sponsored by the WCC was held at Cottesloe, outside Johannesburg, to which the eight member

Churches in South Africa were invited to send delegations of ten persons each to discuss race relations and their relationship to society. All those Churches were present, including the Bantu Presbyterian Church which had included in its delegation missionaries from the Church of Scotland, and the three Dutch Reformed Churches. It was a remarkable event in that the resolutions framed at the end were acceptable to so many of the DRC delegates, although one of the DRC Churches, the Hervormde Kerke, had withdrawn.[181]

The preamble to the statement released at the end of the Consultation included the following paragraph concerning race relations:

> We are united in rejecting all unjust discrimination. Nevertheless widely divergent convictions have been expressed on the basic issues of apartheid. They range on the one hand from the judgement that it is unacceptable in principle, contrary to the Christian calling, and unworkable in practice, to the conviction, on the other hand, that a policy of differentiation can be defended from the Christian point of view, that it provides the only realistic solution to the problems of race relations, and is therefore in the best interests of the various population groups.

The statement included also the following:

11(1)   We recognise that all racial groups who permanently inhabit our country are part of our total population, and we regard them as indigenous. Members of all these groups have an equal right to make their contribution towards the enrichment of the life of their country, and to share in the ensuing responsibilities, rewards and privileges.

11(6)   No one who believes in Jesus Christ may be excluded from any church on the grounds of his colour or race. The spiritual unity among all men who are in Christ must find visible expression in acts of common worship, and witness, and in fellowship and consultation on matters of common concern.

11(12) It is now widely recognised that the wages received by the vast majority of non-white people oblige them to exist well below the generally accepted minimum standard for healthy living. Concerted action is required to remedy this grave situation.

11(15) It is our conviction that the right to own land wherever he is domiciled and to participate in the Government of his country is part of the dignity of the adult man and for this reason a policy which permanently denies to non-white people the right of collaboration in the Government of the country of which they are citizens cannot be justified.[182]

As soon as the Statement was published, Prime Minister Verwoerd reacted vigorously against the delegates from the two Synods
of Nederduitse Gereformeerde Kerk which had remained in the
Consultation and had supported the Statement. The Cape and the
South Transvaal Synods of the NGK then at their meetings repudi-
ated what was done at Cottesloe, including the section of the
Statement urging common worship and witness, written in direct
opposition to one of Verwoerd's apartheid laws of 1957 which made
segregation obligatory even in church buildings.[183]

Dr Beyers Naude, who had been the leader of the delegation
from the Transvaal Synod of the NGK, at the meeting of his Synod
in April 1961 which was demanding the rejection of the Cottesloe
Resolutions, refused to give way on any single one of them. Two
years later, in November 1963, he became the first Director of the
Christian Institute of Southern Africa, which in the following years
was to play such a significant part in the struggle for freedom and
justice.[184]

Soon after turning their backs on the Cottesloe Resolutions,
the Dutch Reformed Churches withdrew from the WCC. They
remained, however, as members of the World Presbyterian Alliance,
which had in 1960 admitted to membership the three Mission
Churches related to the DRC: the Dutch Reformed Bantu Church
in South Africa, the Dutch Reformed Mission Church in South
Africa, and the Dutch Reformed Mission Church in the Orange
Free State.[185]

From the time when the University of Fort Hare came under
the Bantu Education Department at the beginning of 1960, and
when Iona House was taken over, the work of theological education
was carried out at Lovedale in the former Bible School, under the
name of the Lovedale Theological School.[186] In September 1960
the General Assembly of the Bantu Presbyterian Church agreed to
recommend to the FMC that a site on the Lovedale land should be
given free for the building of a Federal Theological Seminary, and
that the compensation received from the Government for Iona
House be used toward the building of premises.[187] The FMC had
agreed to the free gift of the Lovedale site.[188] On 26 September 1963
the Federal Seminary was opened under the presidency of John
Summers, and two days later St Columba's, the Presbyterian
College.[189] The serious staffing problem continued.

The question of the integration of Church and Mission had still to be resolved. At its General Assembly in September/October 1959 an Integration Committee was appointed with a membership of 15 plus a recommended addition of up to seven from the Mission Council. The Committee was authorised to draw up a document to transfer to the Bantu Presbyterian Church, at an agreed date, functions which had been the responsibility of the Mission Council. At the same time it was agreed to ask Mission Council to increase the representation of the BPC so that it might be roughly equal to the present number of 14 overseas missionaries.[190]

The Mission Council Executive at its meeting in November 1959, after lengthy discussion with no agreement reached, suggested that an interim Joint Council of Church and Mission be appointed instead of the large Integration Committee proposed by the BPC. It was of the opinion that the medical work should be integrated into the Church, but noted that that might be prevented by Government racial policies.[191]

At its meeting in September 1960 the Assembly of the BPC appointed an Integration Committee, which it empowered to meet with representatives of the Mission Council to draw up an agreed constitution for a Joint Council, to take over the work previously done by the Mission Council 'until such time as full integration with the Church was achieved'.[192] The Executive of the Mission Council, meeting in November, thanked the BPC for its decision and appointed its members to the Integration Committees. After a delay, during which a draft constitution was withdrawn and Neil Bernard asked to put in writing matters for discussion, the BPC Assembly accepted a revised draft, which was forwarded to the FMC.[193] The Mission Council met for the last time on 25 September 1963, when it transferred its responsibilities, duties and powers to the South Africa Joint Council.

In a Statement on Medical Policy made at Mission Council, in March 1961, these points were noted regarding Mission Hospitals:

(i)   The recognition of the great need for their continued existence and of the important contribution which they are making to our Christian witness in South Africa.

(ii)   Acceptance of the fact that the continuation of these hospitals must depend on Government grants and subsidies, but that so long as we retain the right and power to appoint the staff for these hospitals, they can fulfil their function as centres of witness of Christ as Saviour and Healer.

(iii)   Acceptance of the principle that these hospitals are the joint responsibility of the Church of Scotland and the BPC and must be maintained as a joint enterprise by these two Churches.

(iv)   Emphasis on the need for an immediate and considerable reinforcement of the staff of these hospitals and an urgent plea for enabling them to fulfil more adequately their primary purpose as centres of Christian healing and of the exercise of the ministry of compassion.

Following on from that Statement, and taking note of a serious staffing situation at Sulenkama, the FMC was pressed to increase its staff of doctors in South Africa to four, in order that two might be located each at Sulenkama and Tugela Ferry.[194]

In reply to a letter from the Government Committee dealing with the Planning of Health Services in Bantu Areas, Dr Aitken stated that the Church regarded its hospitals as important, but could neither add to their number or increase their size. He said, among other things, with uncertainty about Government policy on the continuation of Church hospitals, there was a need for clarification.[195]

At its meeting in December 1964 the Executive Committee of the South Africa Joint Council received a report from its Medical Committee. In doing so:[196]

1.   The Executive welcomed the announcement that in future all capital expenditure on mission hospitals would be paid in full by the Department of Bantu Administration and Welfare, and recommended that the Hospital Boards should co-operate with this Department to secure the improvement and development of our three hospitals to conformity with modern standards.

2.   At the same time the Executive realised that the most urgent need of our hospitals at present was for additional staff and urged that renewed efforts be made to find medical, nursing and administrative staff for hospitals.

3.   The Executive was pleased to learn of the formation of a hospitals Co-ordinating Advisory Committee representative of the State Health Departments, the four Provincial Administrations and the Department of Bantu Administration, and that steps were being taken by this Committee to improve the basis of subsidy for the maintenance of the hospitals in all Provinces.

In 1966 the numbers of beds in each of the three hospitals was:

Tugela Ferry 180, Sibasa 350, and Sulenkama 190. They all at that time had staffing difficulties, but the Government was providing up to 90 per cent of running expenses.[197]

Following the implementation of the Bantu Education Act, the educational buildings at Lovedale, Pholela, and Emgwali were leased to Government, the hostels at Pholela and Emgwali being retained and run by missionaries. At Lovedale a house was kept for the use of a missionary who took up duties as a chaplain in 1960.[198]

In March 1963 it was learned that under the Bantu Education Department, it was proposed in the following year to abolish the Teachers' Course at Emgwali, and to convert the school for girls into a Bantu Community School, in all probability co-educational.[199] Joint Council with the support of the General Assembly opposed the decision, pressed for the status quo at least until such time as the latest plans to turn Emgwali into a white area were brought to fruition.[200]

In February 1964 the Inspector of Bantu Education had written to the Rev. Ian Moir, Superintendent of the Pholela Institution, indicating the Government's opinion that the time had come for the control of the hostels to be vested in the local School Board. The Inspector asked what rent the Church would wish for the buildings, and the cost of the furniture and equipment. An answer, he said, would be required by April. Ian Moir and the Principal were agreed that the School Board was not at that time an adequate body to administer the hostels.[201] A meeting of the Governing Council of Pholela was called and Joint Council informed. It was agreed to put the matter before the FMC and the BPC, and to approach the Christian Council and other Church bodies for concerted action.[202]

In 1975 the Presbyterian Church had seven presbyteries throughout South Africa, with a membership of 42,000 communicants, and 77 congregations. The Women's Christian Association had over 10,000 members. There was a Boys' Brigade with 25 companies. George MacArthur, a Church of Scotland missionary was in charge.[203]

VII

Having separated from the Federation of the West Indies in 1961, Jamaica had become an independent nation within the Commonwealth in August the following year, with Bustamante, the Jamaican

Labour Party leader, as Prime Minister, and with its people having full adult suffrage.

It was a time of great social change. The very poor were crowding in from the rural areas to the towns looking for jobs and better living conditions, with the result that facilities in Kingston and the Parish towns were unable to meet the demands made upon them. There was a serious lack of housing, few opportunities for work, and a desperate shortage of opportunities of training for the many illiterate and uneducated adults. The schools could not absorb the number of children, and as far as the Presbyterian Church of Jamaica was concerned there was an urgent need for it to have a programme of development in the towns, beginning with the building of churches.

Conversations between the IMC and the Jamaican Christian Council in preparation for a Consultation to take place in Jamaica in 1962, dealt with the message and mission of the Church amid rapid social change, the Church's stewardship potential, and the place of the laity.[204] To study the situation of the Church and its needs, and to find out what help might be given within its limited resources, the FMC had sent Neil Bernard and Donald Mackay to Jamaica in the Autumn of 1960. The delegation was to have 'a particular concern with the question whether it was still essential for the Church of Scotland to send ordained missionaries to Jamaica, in spite of the urgent demands of the Fields in Africa and Asia, and if so what their work was to be'. At its meeting in Jamaica with the Church, the representatives recommended among other things the appointment of a minister without congregational responsibilities to act on the Synod's behalf, and to advise on the total work of the Church.[205] The Synod agreed to appoint a General Secretary with that role, and asked the FMC to make the Rev. Mungo Carrick available. The FMC had been willing to do so, but Mr Carrick was not able to accept.[206] A General Secretary was appointed in 1964.[207]

The lack of opportunities for the younger generation had driven many parents to consider emigration to the UK, including some of the ablest people whom Jamaica could least do without. The Churches had become aware of the need to support the growing expatriate Jamaican population, to alert the Churches in the UK to their needs, and also to the gifts and talents Jamaicans offered for the enrichment of the British Churches. A West Indian minister,[208] who had spent some months in the UK studying immigration and had just returned, made a number of comments – particularly pertinent in the light of the Commonwealth Immigrants Bill[209] – which he had addressed to the British Churches. His impression of the failure of the Church in Britain to welcome their fellow Christians, not to mention understanding them and learning from them, was vividly and poignantly expressed:

> A desperate effort must be made to educate members of our Churches in Britain on integration. The West Indian must be dealt with on the level of his spiritual attainments – not a half-pagan, semi-civilised being, but as a member of a fully evangelized community capable of sharing fully in the fellowship and spiritual life of the British brother.

The Church had been going ahead with stewardship and with the setting up of new churches. A stewardship campaign in 1960 resulted in an over fifty per cent improvement in the finances of a number of churches, at the same time encouraging pledges of service,[210] and by the middle of that year three new congregations had been formed: Immanuel Church at Ocho Rios, Hope Church in a new residential area in Kingston, and Harvey Church in Hanover.[211] There continued to be a serious shortage of ministers during this whole period and continually requests were made to the FMC/OC for help.

A major step in theological education and the training of the ministry had been taken in 1961 when the Synod agreed to support the effort to create a Divinity Faculty at the University of the West Indies, and to move the Seminary to a site nearer the University in common with other colleges.[212] By July 1964 the plans for a United Theological College alongside the University were well advanced. The TEF had given a grant, and the sale of St Colme's hostel helped the Presbyterian Church of Jamaica to share in the total cost. A Church of Scotland missionary was inducted as Presbyterian Tutor at the College in June.[213]

Knox College, Spaldings, continued to develop. In 1961 a science block was built, paid for by the Ministry of Education. In addition to laboratories for Chemistry, Physics and Biology, the new block provided classrooms for Art and for Business Studies.[214] In 1965 the business studies classroom had been equipped, and in the following year a reading development laboratory was built. In 1963 Mr George Scott, a Jamaican, and a graduate of St Andrews University, who had been on the staff of Knox for some years before serving in the Ministry of Education, returned to the College as Vice-Principal.

The inauguration of the United Church of Jamaica and Grand Cayman (a union of the Presbyterian and Congregational Churches) took place on 1 December 1965, in St Andrew's Scots Kirk, Kingston. The sermon at the inaugural service was preached by Sir Francis Ibiam. The Governor-General of Jamaica was present at the service, along with the acting Prime Minister. The Church of Scotland was represented by the Rev. George Buchanan. The first Moderator of the United Church was the Rev. Henry Ward, the oldest minister in active service, a Church of Scotland missionary who had served in Calabar, Nigeria, before being ordained for service in Jamaica.[215]

VIII

In Aden the Danish Missionary Society and the FMC had worked closely together for many years, and had for some time considered how best to consolidate their co-operation organisationally. Following the appointment of Dr Calderwood of Kenya as an Adviser to the South Arabian Mission Council, a Joint Policy Committee of the FMC and the DMS was formed under his chairmanship.[216] At a joint consultation held in Copenhagen in April 1960, it was agreed to have a three-year period of experiment in co-operation and sharing of responsibility for all Christian work done previously and separately by the two bodies.[217] A Joint Council was to be set up with four Boards responsible for Evangelism, Education, Medical Work and the Bookshop, which would operate under the Church as soon as that was established. The Church of South Arabia was inaugurated on 8 January 1961, and the separate Mission Councils dissolved. The new Church was extremely small. In Sheikh Othman there were seven baptised members, and in Crater, where Danish missionaries had been working, about the same number. The Rev. R. Madsen of the DMS, and James Ritchie, had been appointed pastors of the Church, there being no Arab pastors at that stage.

In Sheikh Othman the Keith Falconer Hospital continued its work. The Hospital, which had both male and female wards, concentrated on child welfare. Many of the children who came with their mothers were suffering from malnutrition and chest infections.[218] The Boys' Club near the Hospital, reorganised under George Clark who had been sent out to work with young people, had a membership now of over 30 and met three times a week. Officers and other ranks of the British army helped with the club, coaching in various sports and in the teaching of English. Many of the boys in the club attended church regularly seeing that as a normal part of the club's life.

By the end of 1960 the Town Planning Department, along with the Department of Medical Services, had made known a number of developments that were to take place in Sheikh Othman, including the erection of a new General and Maternity Hospital near the Kintore Compound in about five year's time.[219] Previous to the news of those plans, Dr A. S. Affara had given notice on 8 November 1960 of his intention to resign on medical grounds.[220] Dr Affara had been appointed a missionary in 1939, the first 'son of the country', as the minute put it, to serve on the Christian missionary staff in South Arabia. Having been a pupil at the mission school in Sheikh Othman he had been converted from Islam, and on Easter Sunday 1930 had been baptised. He had studied at Edinburgh University – he had spent one year also in Wilson College, Bombay – and was the first Arab from South Arabia to graduate in modern medicine. The FMC accepted his resignation 'with great regret'.[221]

In the light of what had happened, Dr Calderwood indicated to the Director of Medical Services that the Keith Falconer Hospital might in the near future have to be closed. The South Arabia Ad Hoc Committee met to discuss those matters on 12 January 1961. The Committee agreed that the Keith Falconer compound be retained, that the hospital be reduced to 50 beds, and that the emphasis be on pediatrics, keeping within the FMC authorised budget, and using existing facilities and equipment.[222] In conversation between Dr Calderwood and the Director of Health Services, the Director agreed that the emphasis should be on children's work, and take the form of a 'mother and baby' unit. He said that there would probably be no Government Hospital in Sheikh Othman in seven to eight years; he would forward a request to Government for a 50 per cent capital grant, and try to secure an increased annual grant-in-aid.[223]

Following the receipt of a Report of Dr Calderwood's visit to Aden from November 1960 to February 1961, the Ad Hoc Committee had taken a further step toward co-operation, following the inauguration of the new Church, by recommending the formation of a Christian Council consisting of the members of the four Missions present in Aden.[224] In September 1961 representatives of the

FMC and DMS had met, and had discussed future policy in the light of the political situation in Aden. Although they could see that there might be considerable changes which might mean less freedom for the work of mission, they were strongly of the opinion that the policy should be adhered to of strengthening the local Church and of preparing it for its task of evangelism. The group had expressed concern about the amount of time ordained missionaries had to give to administration following the establishment of Joint Council and its various Boards. Ministers were being prevented from doing the work they were called to do and which the Church urgently needed them to do. It was agreed on further consideration not to set up a Christian Council as a formal committee but rather to continue the practice of informal ad hoc conversations. A similar point about structures and top-heavy administration was made at a meeting within the Red Sea Mission Team.[225]

At the end of 1961 there had been tentative proposals for the development of health services in Beihan. Resident doctor, George Morris, had discussed those with an officer of the Federal Health Service. The proposals would involve increased Government help and the need for more staff, including a nurse with knowledge of Arabic.[226] With Dr Morris due on leave, Beihan was faced with temporary closure. The FMC was asked urgently to find new staff.[227] At its meeting in July 1962, Joint Council decided that during Dr Morris' leave Dr Harry Robertson should pay monthly visits to Beihan, working 4-5 days on each occasion with the Federal Health Service assistants. Dr Morris also tabled a Report on the evangelistic situation in Beihan stressing that ways had to be found to reduce medical pressure so that opportunities for evangelism might be fully grasped.[228] At the next meeting of Joint Council, in October, at the request of Eric Nielsen, Dr Morris' Report was considered.[229] In discussion on evangelism in Beihan at the Ad Hoc Committee the next month, it was agreed there was need for planned evangelism rather than simply opportunism.[230] Miss Walls, at a meeting of Joint Council in February 1963, raised the question whether the work at Beihan should be continued with monthly visits, or discontinued in favour of concentrating at Sheikh Othman. It was felt the work should continue; but in view of Dr Morris' conviction that the Church would only take root and grow as the result of a people's movement, Dr Robertson should be accompanied on his visits by an Arab Christian who should be given a place in his team.[231]

Dr Robertson, on 31 January 1964, regretfully gave notice that he would not be returning to Arabia after his furlough. The Secretary of the Missionaries' Committee had been instructed to point out to FMC the serious staffing shortage, and its effect on the continuance of the work in Beihan.[232] In April 1964 Dr Morris, who had played a major part in the development of medical work in Beihan, resigned with much regret for family reasons.[233] Dr Ross of the Red Sea Mission Team visited Beihan in June 1964, and had been invited to return and continue her visits.[234] The Medical Board recommended that two nurses be stationed in Beihan, and that a doctor and an evangelist, when available, should make occasional visits.[235] For a period during the disturbances, the clinic could not continue and the work at Beihan had to be closed. It restarted early in 1965 with two nurses, Lexa Boyle and Emsy Nielsen.[236]

The immediate cause of the disturbances was Aden's joining the Federation of the Protectorates in January 1963. The Government hoped that by doing so it would influence the other members, help them to develop politically and economically and strengthen them in their relations with the Republic of Yemen. The Sultans and Sheikhs, however, who formed the majority of the Federal ministers, suspicious of British influence and unwilling to have their people exposed to democratic attitudes and institutions, met the inclusion of Aden into the Federation with considerable opposition. A clash with a British military group on exercises followed, and a grenade attack on the British High Commissioner.

Violence continued in June 1965, shortly before the Rev. Noel Clarke, who had been acting[237] during the vacancy at the Keith Falconer Church, was due to hand over, and grenades had been thrown into the patio of the Sailors' Institute. On his return to the UK, Noel Clarke addressed the Executive Committee of the FMC. After paying tribute to the congregation of the Keith Falconer Church, he spoke of the need to support the missionaries in Sheikh Othman, who were, he said, 'completely dedicated people who refused to be discouraged or dismayed in a most testing situation'. He added that 'he left Aden full of foreboding for them and the future of their work'. In the event, on 15 October 1965, the missionaries, having been requested to leave Sheikh Othman, went to a better protected area in Aden some six miles away. In Crater the Danish Mission Church had been damaged and for a period all the Danish missionaries left. In November of that year, Dr Duncan Fraser of the FMC staff paid a brief visit, which was greatly appreciated.[238]

In 1966 a draft Constitution for the Federation of South Arabia was published, containing a section headed 'Freedom of Religion' and a paragraph reading: 'Nothing contained in this Article shall permit the propagation of any religious doctrine or belief other than Islam among persons in the Republic professing the Muslim religion.' Representatives of the Overseas Council, along with secretaries of the Conference of British Missionary Societies, had an interview with the Colonial Office in March 1966. It had been agreed that objection be raised with the Federal Government through the Colonial Office on the grounds of Article 19 of the Declaration of Human Rights of the United Nations.[239]

A special meeting of the Church Council was held on 5 May 1966 at the invitation of the Arab members of the Church of South Arabia. Dr Affara, in the chair, stated that the meeting had been called in the light of political events and of the desire of the Arab Christians to be responsible for their own affairs. They wished to form a new Church Council which would be solely responsible for the affairs of the Church. They wanted a structure free of Missionary and Board Representation. It was hoped that the Churches in Denmark and Scotland would participate in the ordination service of a new pastor. It was pointed out that the Church did not intend working on any denominational basis, and that there was no thought of associating any name with it, other than the Church of South Arabia. It was stated at the outset that there was no intention of breaking relationships, but only of building them on a new basis.[240]

It had not been possible to continue work in the Keith Falconer Hospital, Sheikh Othman, and negotiations began with the Federal Health Service to rent the hospital for one year, while alterations were being made in the Government hospital. In May 1966 the missionary medical staff all moved to Beihan.[241]

IX

During this whole period that we have been discussing there was a growing realisation that partnership with Churches emerging from the foreign missionary enterprise had to be seen as partnership between Churches, and not in the main between auxiliary administrative committees such as the FMC and 'missionary' committees on the 'field'. That had still to be worked out in many ways, not least in terms of finance. Up until this point the financing of 'partnership' from the position of the Church of Scotland had been a separate operation conducted by the FMC/WFM without direction from the Church as a whole. Now it was recognised that the holistic view of mission that had become increasingly accepted, demanded at the very least a holistic approach to the financing of the Church's outreach in the Gospel at home and overseas.

By 1956 consideration was being given to setting up a system which would enable an appeal for funds to be made to congregations on behalf of the Church as a whole, rather than the practice followed at that time of individual committees making separate appeals.[242] At the General Assembly of 1959 an Overture was adopted and sent down to presbyteries for their agreement, dealing with a Co-ordinated Appeal for the support of the work of the Church. It included the setting up of a Stewardship and Budget Committee, which would have responsibility for stewardship education in the Church, and would in consultation with the committees present a unified budget to the General Assembly, making allocations to presbyteries of the amounts required.[243] In 1961 the Co-ordinated Appeal became part of the law of the Church, and every congregation became obliged to meet or surpass the share of the Appeal allocated to it by its Presbytery.[244]

Although the Stewardship and Budget Committee had taken over from the General Finance Committee the ingathering of funds from congregations and the forming of a budget, the Finance Committee continued to have responsibility for the oversight and control of the Church's finances. In its report to the General Assembly of 1960 the Committee exercising that role, had this to say:

> Without the necessary financial support, the Church's work at home and abroad would grind to a standstill. Too often have Committees, through lack of means, been unable to accept opportunities for the extension or intensification of their work. We in Scotland are not exhibiting adequate standards of Stewardship. It is the main purpose of the Stewardship and Budget Committee to rectify this situation. Many of the younger Churches overseas are far in advance of our standards. It may be in the age of materialism the most effective witness to the Faith will be by a fuller, even though a still inadequate response in acknowledgement of the blessings we have received.[245]

The Church might have taken this new step in order to bring its finances more closely into line with its understanding of the wholeness of the Church, but that was clearly not the only reason. There was an urgent need to increase the givings of congregations for the 'wider work of the Church', including its responsibilities overseas, and there was moreover a worrying shrinking in membership. Year by year the number of those available to contribute went down. In 1960 there were 1,301,280 communicants, a decrease of 5381 as compared with the previous year; and by 1966 that total figure had gone down to 1,233,808, a figure 14,164 less than in the year before.[246]

The Overseas Council, by the end of this period, had to confess its disappointment with the amounts of money that it was receiving from the Co-ordinated Appeal.[247] It faced as a matter of grave concern several drastic cuts in its proposed budgets. At the same time it was confronted with a steady decline in the number of candidates coming forward for service in mission. The figure of missionary staff given to the General Assembly of 1961 had been 268, whereas the figure in 1967 had been 240 – the actual figure of overseas staff quoted being 38 above 240, representing the number of overseas chaplains for whom the Overseas Council had become responsible.[248]

There was a painful irony in this story of the Church's declining membership and of its declining support of the Church world-wide, for seen in retrospect it was a period of relative prosperity. There had been a marked rise in the standard of living for many people. More families had cars than ever before, television sets were now a normal part of the furnishing, and washing machines standard household equipment. We were being told that we had never had it so good, and responsible historians wrote of a 'golden age'. People were better off, which might well have been expected to be reflected in the life of the Church, numerically and in giving.

Along, however, with the increasing prosperity, there was a deepening sense of unease. The widening gap between the rich and the poor nations could not be ignored, nor the increasing differentials within out own society. There was certainly more money in people's pockets, but the new prosperity had a brittle feel about it, which was confirmed by rising unemployment figures in Scotland, and other facts contained in the Toothill Report of 1962 on the Scottish economy.[249]

CHAPTER 6

In One World

(1967-1972)

I

AT the World Missionary Conference held in Edinburgh in
1910 delegates had been given a vision of the one Church
engaged in mission in what had begun to be recognised as one
world – a vision of one Church in one world – and as a frontispiece
to the popular report there had been a drawing of the earth – the
one world with its moon – circling in space. Sixty years later, with
the Apollo 11 mission to the moon on 20 July 1969, it had become
possible for the first time for the earth with its oceans and continents to be seen as one world, one global unit in space. Coming
only a year after the meeting of the WCC in Uppsala with its
emphasis on the one world and the one humanum, that dramatic
event helped to sharpen the vision.

At the same time the twenty-fifth anniversary of the United
Nations in 1968 encouraged fresh reflection on world peace and
on the task of developing the resources of the one world, and of
meeting the needs of the world's poor. The work of the United
Nations Educational, Scientific, and Cultural Organisation, of the
World Health Organisation, and of other bodies working for similar ends, were given added attention and there was renewed recognition that peace and 'world development' were indivisible. The
Vatican Encyclical *Populorum Progressio* called World Development
the new name for peace.

Although the UN had designated the 1960s as the 'Development
Decade', the situation as the decade came to its end was if anything
worse than it had been at the beginning. The gap between the rich
nations and the poor had widened. In his study of Development

from within UNESCO, published in 1970, Dr Malcolm Adiseshiah, the Deputy Director-General, commented ruefully:

> The United Nations system which seemed to promise a new world order has not yet emerged as the dominant force in international relations. The development effort and the struggle for human rights and social justice it has promoted for so long, have not yet become the spearhead linking all humanity's immense forces in the struggle for the future.[1]

In international relations war, or the fear of war, was always there. The UK had its nuclear deterrent and there continued to be debate whether or not in the interest of world peace it ought to be unilaterally surrendered. In 1967 the Vietnam War was at its height and showed no signs of coming to an end, and indeed seemed rather to be increasing in intensity and in human suffering and tragedy. In February of that year Mr Kosygin was in Britain as a guest of the Government, and he and Harold Wilson took every opportunity in private conversations, and unilaterally with Washington and New York, to find a way of bringing the conflict to a close, but without success.[2]

Then in May 1967 there was the Six Day War, when Israel, threatened by the United Arab Republic under Nasser, after a pre-emptive strike won a massive victory over the combined forces of Egypt, Jordan and Syria, took the old city of Jerusalem, the whole of the West Bank, and occupied the Golan Heights.

In 1971 there was war in the Indian sub-continent. After an election in East Pakistan on a programme demanding a federal system between East and West, the latter had responded by sending in the army. The East Pakistan leader Sheikh Mujib Rahman then proclaimed an independent Bangladesh Republic. In the violence that followed, millions of refugees poured into Indian territory. On 4 December 1971, India declared war, invaded, brought about the surrender of the West Pakistan army after a short campaign, and recognised Bangladesh.

Meanwhile in Central Africa the issues raised by Smith's Unilateral Declaration of Independence in Rhodesia were no nearer solution.[3] There was rapid movement toward the development of apartheid, and guerrilla warfare began with an infiltration of trained fighters from outside. The Church and Nation Report of 1968 spoke of the imminent danger of patience among the African people running out and a time of racial conflict beginning. It became clearly seen that there could be no settlement which did not provide 'unimpeded progress towards majority rule'.

Finally, in May 1967, Biafra was declared an independent Republic and the civil war in Nigeria, with which we shall be dealing later, began. The end of hostilities came in January 1970.

II

The Fourth Assembly of the World Council of Churches met in Uppsala, Sweden from 4-20 July 1968. During the years following the meeting in New Delhi in 1961, much of the enthusiasm which Assemblies engendered in the past had waned. There was little expectation that something fresh and important would come out of it.[4] The World Conference on Church and Society, which had preceded the Assembly in 1966, was however to have a profound influence, as had the presence of a large contingent of youth delegates, so that in the event, there was a facing up to the challenge of the theme 'All Things New'.

The opening paragraphs of the Report of the Section on World Economic and Social Development, echoing the 1966 Conference, gives succinctly a flavour of the overriding mood of the Assembly at its best:

> We live in a new world of exciting prospects. For the first time in history we can see the oneness of mankind as a reality. For the first time we know that all men could share in the proper use of the world's resources. The new technological possibilities turn what were dreams into realities. Just as today we have the knowledge about the conditions of men throughout the earth, and the means, we are without excuse. It is one world and the gross inequalities between the peoples of different nations and different continents are as inexcusable as the gross inequalities within nations. In Christ, God entered our world with all its structures and has already won the victory over all the principalities and powers. His Kingdom is coming with his judgement and mercy.[5]

The Assembly was constantly reminded of the widening gap between the rich and the poor nations of the world, between the 20 per cent of the world's population who owned 80 per cent of the world's wealth, were mainly white, and lived mainly in Europe,

North America, and Australasia. Poverty was a major issue, and
racism went with it. It had been planned to have Martin Luther
King as the preacher at the opening service. His absence was a
constant reminder of the evil of racism that led to his death. In an
address to the Assembly, James Baldwin, the distinguished black
writer, poignantly challenged it, as Martin Luther King would have
done, to listen to the Gospel of the despised Hebrew Christ, to look
at the gulf between words and deeds, and to act. In his address
Baldwin had this to say:

> ... at this moment in world history it becomes necessary for me, for my
> own survival, not to listen to what you say but to watch very carefully
> what you do, not to read your pronouncements but to go back to the
> source and to check it for myself. And if that is so, then it may very
> well mean that the revolution that was begun two thousand years ago
> by a disreputable Hebrew criminal may now have to be begun again by
> people equally disreputable and equally improbable. It's got to be
> admitted that if you are born under the circumstances in which most
> black people in the west are born, that means real black people over
> the entire world, when you look around you, having attained some-
> thing resembling adulthood, it is perfectly true that you can see the
> destruction of the Christian Church as it is presently constituted may
> not only be desirable but necessary.[6]

There was much that was wrong in the WCC itself. There were
weaknesses in the constitution, and a critical position had been
reached in connection with representation, and the membership of
Assembly committees.[7] Baldwin[8] spoke of the lies that the Church
had told itself, to itself, about itself. There was an intolerable white
bias. Among the 19 Central Committee nominees allotted to predominantly white US denominations, there were no blacks; all six
US nominees to the Commission of the Churches on International
Affairs were white; and there was only one black nominated to the
Faith and Order Commission. A black caucus was formed to protest.
In response to their protest a number of distinguished churchmen,
including President James McCord of Princeton, stepped aside for
black members to be elected. A similar protest, made on behalf of
women, who had less than nine per cent of the Assembly membership, led to pressure to elect a woman as one of the six new presidents of the Council, but without success. An imbalance in relation
to membership and representation resulting from the disproportionate number of older people and clergy was a further obstacle

to the very unity for which the Council claimed to exist. Only four per cent of the voting delegates were under 35, and laymen were outnumbered by clergy 2 to 1.

The youth participants played an important part at Uppsala as a creative irritant, constantly compelling attention to be given to basic and difficult issues, in particular to world poverty and the growing gap between the rich and the poor. Radical change was needed. The Church had to repent. Lesslie Newbigin, present at Uppsala, spoke of it as 'a shattering experience of God's judgement upon the Church'. In his view no ecclesiastic – even the toughest – could go through that experience without crying for God's mercy.[9]

John Hamilton, the General Secretary of the Overseas Council was included in the Church of Scotland delegation, along with John Fleming, present as an Adviser on the invitation of the WCC.

Following on from the Uppsala Assembly an Ecumenical Conference took place in October 1969 on 'The Churches' Action for World Development' (sponsored by the British Council of Churches, the Roman Catholic Commission for International Justice and Peace, and the Conference of British Missionary Societies) at which delegates from the Overseas Council represented the Church of Scotland. The purpose of the Conference was to discuss how the British Churches could respond to the needs of the 'underdeveloped world'. In its findings to the Churches the Conference pleaded for urgent action:

> World development is not merely one more concern to add to the existing concerns of the Churches. It is something which causes us to look freshly at all our concerns .... We have grown more conscious of the intolerable injustice in the world, and of the complexities of the struggle to redress wrongs; of the contrast between these things and the matters which generally preoccupy the mind and energy of the Churches; of the difference of judgement between Christians whose starting point is the life of the Churches as they now are, and Christians whose starting point is the rising exasperation of the young, the coloured and the poor.[10]

In response to Uppsala the Church of Scotland took immediate steps to ensure that the facts of world poverty were made known, and the study of World Development encouraged. In 1969 a 'One Day's Pay Appeal' was inaugurated.[11] At a Consultation held at Scottish Churches' House, Dunblane in January 1971, attended by representatives of Scottish Churches Council and Roman Catholic Commission for Justice and Peace, the proposal was made to form Scottish Churches Action for World Development (SCAWD). In its Report to the General Assembly of that year the Church and Nation Committee, dealing at some length with World Development, noted that a reply had still to be given to the Ecumenical Conference's question about the Churches' use of capital resources in the light of the needs of developing countries. It suggested that the time might have come for 'for an assessment to be made by our Church'.[12]

Nowhere more than in the Indian sub-continent, in the north and in the south of India, and in Pakistan, were the questions raised by Uppsala more relevant. Poverty was a major concern for the Church, both within its own membership, and for its task in society. The rapid growth in population had brought the threat of famine nearer, and intensified already existing deprivation. In Madras, as in other big cities, the population figures increased alarmingly as large numbers of people from the rural areas crowded into what were already overcrowded slums, with totally inadequate sanitation and water supplies.

In Madras an inter-denominational body called the Madras City Churches Development Trust was developing new Churches and a programme of social work. By the beginning of this period an organisation for industrial mission, Christian Service to Industrial Society, had been formed, under the honorary directorship of Mr C. A. Cornelius, the managing director of a large company in the city, with two pastors as associate directors.[13] The Rev. Murdoch MacKenzie, who had three congregations in an area with cotton mills and locomotive shops, was one of the members of the working team.[14] One of the tasks of CSIS was to organise groups of managers, supervisors, and workers, to equip them as Christians in industry. A few of the trainees were sent for three months' long courses to the Institute at Durgapur where the Rev. Kenyon Wright was the director.[15]

In September 1969 a Community Service Centre was opened at Kilpauk, Madras to provide Christians with postgraduate training in social work. It was run by a Board representing the CSI and the Lutheran Churches.[16] The Chief Minister of Madras presided in December of that year over a special function to honour Bishop Newbigin on his sixtieth birthday, and to thank him for his contribution to the city of Madras. Two thousand five hundred attended.[17]

The CSI Board for Social and Economic Services in 1971 included in its lines of action a project for building sanitation units in the slums, and to form a Water Resources Unit as a new service, which among other things would provide pump sets to farmers.[18] Self-contained water units, comprising bore wells, pumps, overhead tanks, and latrine and washing facilities, were given to 35 poor areas in Madras. These last were paid for with money that came from the 'One Day's Pay Appeal' in Scotland.[19]

Meanwhile, during famine in North India, John McLeod was involved in well-boring with Action for Food Production, and in training local people. Later having moved from Jalna to Poona he worked as a technical adviser to Dnyana Prabodhinee, an organisation outside the Church, concerned with agricultural development and leadership training. Free from managerial responsibility, he was able to give full attention himself to agriculture and water-resources development, to share his skills with local Christians, and to encourage local initiative in community development. He was able at the same time to build links with organisations in the UK willing to assist with cattle breeding. As the result of his contacts in India and the UK a supply of Friesian semen was flown to Bombay for a Cattle Breeding Centre, part of an important cross-breeding project designed to increase milk supplies in Maharashtra. During this time in Jalna, where John McLeod had been working since 1959, Dr Chris Wigglesworth had taken over and was in the position to report that 360 wells had been dug in one year, and that there had been in addition much road building activity.[20]

In some places during this period drought was the problem, as in Western India, while in others it was flood. In Eastern Himalaya, in Kalimpong and Darjeeling, devastating floods early in 1968 brought heavy loss of life and damage to property. In that emergency the Church had to help as best it could, along with the aid agencies in meeting basic needs for food, clothing and shelter. The continuing cry, however, was for longer-term assistance. With the level of poverty that there was all over the sub-continent, the Church was frequently faced with requests for help to meet new and important opportunities, while having constantly put before it old and persistently renewed demands for support. This was a familiar story in many places, including Eastern Himalayas, where serious financial difficulties were being experienced by the hospitals, both the Charteris and the Leprosy Hospital.[21]

The spiralling cost of running hospitals was a problem as costs increasingly outran the ability of local resources to meet them, including those of supporting agencies abroad. There had been a feeling too for many years, in the Church and among missionaries, that hospitals were a burden to the Church, taking up a disproportionate amount of its attention and distorting its basic purpose. The importance of healing within the missionary task of the Church was not being questioned, but questions were being asked about health itself, and in particular about the relative emphasis that might be given at this stage to the causes of disease, in terms of such things as drinking water, nutrition, hygiene, and housing – to preventative medicine rather than the prevailing emphasis on the curative and the clinical.

Basic thinking about Christian medical policy had been greatly stimulated by a consultation arranged by the WCC in 1964 at Tübingen, in which Dr Jack Wilkinson of Kenya took part. The thinking at this consultation was followed up in India by the Christian Medical Association,[22] at biennial conferences, and by the Churches. In 1969, as part of the ongoing discussion, a joint meeting was held in London between representatives from India/Pakistan and the Medical Committee of the Conference of British Missionary Societies (CBMS) at which Dr J. C. McGilvray of the WCC spoke on the present situation of Christian medical work in India with particular reference to Church-related hospitals. At that meeting it was agreed to recommend that a co-ordinating body be set up to evaluate priorities in financial support, and to encourage a new understanding of Christian medical service. It was further agreed that missionary bodies should give capital grants only to projects which had been processed and approved.[23] In Western India about this same time, looking forward to the new Church of North India, discussions were initiated about the joint planning of medical services, with agreement reached that the administration would be Church-related but not Church-controlled.[24]

During this whole period a reassessment had been taking place of medical institutions, which led to closures, amalgamations, new buildings, and other developments. In 1967 St Margaret's Hospital, Poona was sold, and planning begun for the rebuilding and development of the Wadia Hospital.[25] At the same time in Kancheepuram, it was decided that the CSI Hospital, whose role as a general hospital had largely been taken over by a new Government hospital nearby, should develop into a specialised institution for orthopaedically handicapped children.[26] At Shilokh Hospital, Jalalpur, Pakistan,[27] a major development had taken place based on plans prepared by Dr Harry Holland, representing the West Pakistan Medical Association. The development had the support of the Reformed Churches in the Netherlands, with whom it had been fully discussed, and they had agreed to help in its financing. Money from the funds of the OC was augmented from the 'One Day's Pay Appeal'. There were developments also at Bamdah and Pokhuria, Santalia, and at Jalna. In 1972 the Government proposed to the Darjeeling Diocese the takeover of the Charteris Hospital. The Diocesan Executive Committee rejected the proposal, and the matter was remitted to an OC group.[28]

For many years Christian Colleges in India and Pakistan had played an important part in the development of higher education and in the furtherance of Christian understanding. Most recently it had become increasingly difficult for them to take full advantage of the opportunities presented to them, largely because of increasing costs, and the shortage of suitably qualified Christian staff. Government restrictions on the entry of missionaries added to the problem, threatening to prevent the recruitment of staff from overseas, and to reduce what was the most important contribution of Churches abroad.[29] At a special meeting of the Board of Murray College, Sialkot in June 1967, a decision had had to be made to diminish the choice of subjects taught, and to discontinue important courses leading to MA and BA degrees because of finance. Similarly in Bengal, Scottish Church College for some years had been in serious difficulty because of shortage of staff and inadequate administration. Although the Colleges faced many difficulties, the Overseas Council continued to give high priority to their support, with the possible exception of Scottish where it could see little prospect of being able to help.[30]

In North India, in line with the recommendations of the UCNI General Assembly that service institutions be Church-related but not Church-controlled, the schools had been brought under registered bodies: in Western India the John Wilson Education Society, and in Nagpur the Hislop Education Society. Meanwhile in Pakistan, on 1 November 1972, the Government nationalised all the schools.[31]

Theological education in India took an important step forward with the opening in July 1969 of the United Tamilnad Theological

Seminary at Arisaradi, Madurai, a union of Lutheran and CSI colleges, which provided theological training in Tamil up to BD standard.[32] It was a cause of rejoicing that, coinciding with that event, had come the production by the CSI-Lutheran Joint Theological Commission of a draft Constitution for a united Church.

The following year, 1970, saw the inauguration on 1 November of the Church of Pakistan in Lahore, and on 29 November of the Church of North India in Nagpur. Both the Church of Pakistan and the CNI were more comprehensive unions than there had previously been. In Pakistan the new Church brought together Anglicans, Methodists, the United Church (Congregational and Presbyterian), and Lutherans; while the CNI included former Anglicans, Methodists, Baptists, UCNI, Disciples of Christ and Churches of Christ. The former Church of Scotland congregation in Calcutta became part of the new Church, as did the congregation in Karachi.[33]

Dr William Stewart, who had served on the negotiating committee, edited *Church Union News and Views* and had been one of the chief architects of the union, represented the Church of Scotland at the inaugurations in Lahore and Nagpur.

III

With the retirement of Dr John Fleming in 1968,[34] after more than 30 years' service in South East Asia, the Church of Scotland's direct contact with the Overseas Chinese, and particularly with Singapore and with theological education in that part of the world with which he had had so much to do, was inevitably impaired. He continued however to maintain contact with Chinese friends, and played an important part in promoting an understanding of China. He visited Peking, and in the Autumn of 1971 participated in a Consultation on China organised by the CBMS. In the following year he became a member of the committee responsible for the China Study Project, set up under the secretaryship of Victor Hayward.

Three years before his retirement the Presbyterian Church of Formosa had requested the Church of Scotland 'to be associated with it in mission work', which was mainly among the Taiwanese, who were the original people of the land. The Overseas Council appointed the Rev. David Donaldson.[35] He and his wife went out to what was now called Taiwan in May 1969, after a term in St Colms. The first task was to learn Mandarin. In the months before the end of his first term David Donaldson worked in the theological college in Taipei. On his return from leave he was appointed to serve with the Mountain Work Committee among the Paiwan, a tribal, mountain people.[36]

Meanwhile the Presbyterian Church in Taiwan, which had been a member of the WCC, withdrew its membership in protest against a statement of the Commission on International Affairs recommending the admission of Mainland China to the United Nations. On 30 December 1971 the Presbyterian Church in Taiwan issued a Public Statement, addressed to All Nations, and to the Leaders of the Republic of China, in which they made plain that the 15 million Taiwanese People did not wish to be governed by Peking, and that they had a strong desire for a democratic change which would overturn decisions made 25 years previously on the mainland.

In Scotland the General Assembly of 1972, following on from Deliverances of the previous Assembly in which it had expressed approval of the UN's decision to admit the People's Republic of China,[37] and without going back on that decision, passed the following Deliverance of the Church and Nation Committee:

5(f) The General Assembly draw the attention of Her Majesty's Government to the statement on 'Our National Fate' issued by the Presbyterian Church of Taiwan on 30th December 1971, and urge that all possible steps be taken to ensure that the rights of the people of Taiwan to freedom and self-determination are safeguarded.[38]

IV (a)

In West Africa, in Ghana, the prosperous new future that the leadership of Nkrumah had promised was short-lived. By the time of his deposing the economy of the country was on the point of collapse. There was serious unemployment, a widening gap between the rich and the poor, and sharp cultural and social divisions, marked most obviously by the profound contrast between the lifestyle of the professional middle class modelled on the West, and that of the majority of the people.

There was a brief period of military rule under General Ankrah, during which preparations were made for a new civilian constitution. The views of different sections of the population were taken into account, and three representatives of the Christian Council had been included in the drafting committee. The new constitution was brought into effect under a Government led by Dr K. Busia, a churchman and academic, who had worked for some time in England.

The new Government faced great difficulties. It had inherited huge foreign debts, the interest on which cut into the funds needed for development, while its failure to include in Government a proper representation of the Ewe tribe increased tribal tension. A suspicion that a considerable proportion of the crime in the country had its source among the large number of unregistered aliens led to expulsion orders, resulting in much suffering. Although an exception had been made for Biafran refugees, there was anxiety among them about what might happen after the end of hostilities. There was also the massive disruption of the lives of ordinary people following the uprooting of fishing villages on the coast to make way for the building of Tema, and inland for the construction of the Volta Dam. The resettlement of those who had had their homes in the area flooded for the Volta River Project involved the displacement of 80,000 people belonging to over 700 villages, and their movement to over 50 resettlement sites.

The Churches were at work among the people who lived in the new settlements and who came from different villages and different tribal groups. One of the organisers, the Rev. T. A. Kumi, seconded by the Presbyterian Church of Ghana to serve full-time under the Christian Council's Volta Resettlement Committee, had been recognised by Government and appointed to represent the people on a parallel Government body. T. A. Kumi knew the Church of Scotland well, having worked in Scotland with three of its ministers: Jim Maitland, Tom Allen and Jim Curry.

In Tema itself a Methodist minister had been working since 1960 as Industrial Missioner in close collaboration with others, including a Salvation Army Captain who was running a hostel for young men as part of the industrial mission. In Tema there was a serious problem of unemployment with hundreds of young people, many belonging originally to the flooded villages, coming to Tema looking for jobs. In 1969 the Overseas Council appointed the Rev. Ian Whyte to Tema.

During this period lay men and women of the Churches took an active part in civic and administrative affairs, of whom two in particular may be mentioned: Justice N. A. Ollennu of the Presbyterian Church of Ghana, who was one of the delegates to the Uppsala Assembly; and Justice Annie Jiagga (a sister of Dr Baeta) who chaired an important Commission of Enquiry into allegations of corruption taking place under the Nkrumah regime. Justice Jiagga was a member of the WCC Central Committee, and active in the YWCA and in the Council of Women in Ghana. It was to the Churches that the Government turned after the Nkrumah regime to deal with some of the major social problems in the country, not least among young people. Government organisations, such as, for example, the Committee on Planned Parenthood run by Rosina Konuah, who had recently served as Dorothy Cadbury Fellow in the Selly Oak Colleges, depended on Christian leadership.

Running parallel to the Government Committee on the Family, the Ghana Christian Council had a well developed programme, run by a Marriage and Family Life Committee, in which Mrs Jean Forrester-Paton played a major role, guiding and setting it up. On the invitation of the Christian Council Dr Hugh and Mrs Douglas of Dundee had run courses and helped with the development of women's organisations.

In the North there was great poverty and hunger was never far away. In a WCC Report on Christian Medical programmes attention had been drawn to the work done in the North at Sandema by Doris Hodds, who was conducting ante-natal and child welfare clinics weekly at the local Government health centre, and was at work in the villages. In 1966 she examined 17,000 infants under three. The Report commended what was being done as 'an example of a preventative health programme integrated into the Church and into the Government programme'. A similarly appreciative comment had been made about Jean Forrester-Paton's contribution earlier in 1959.[39]

Early in 1970, plans were prepared for a Lay Training Scheme to be run in the North by the Presbyterian Church of Ghana and the Evangelical Presbyterian Church jointly, and it was hoped with the co-operation of the Methodist and Anglican Churches. The building for it at Tamale had been donated by a Trading Company.[40]

Government approval to develop the hospital at Agogo gave permission to train nurses to State Registered Nurse standard, and at the same time encouraged a health service with emphasis on preventative medicine, designed to raise standards of health in the whole community.[41]

On 28 December 1868 Accra Ridge Church in the South was dedicated as 'a place of fellowship and unity for people of many nations and for Christians of different traditions'. Half of the congregation were Ghanaian, the remainder coming from countries in Asia, America, Europe, and from other parts of Africa. There were three part-time ministers: Colin Forrester-Paton, an Anglican and a Methodist.[42]

In 1970 a Ghanaian took over from Colin Forrester-Paton as Inter-Church and Ecumenical Relations Secretary, which would have left no missionary on the Synod Committee. He and a Basel Mission colleague, however, continued to be invited to the Committee, though without a vote. New regulations drafted in 1972 gave to the Church increasing responsibility for fraternal workers [sic], including stationing and transfers, and the oversight of their reports to their Home Boards.

(b)

In Nigeria, in May, 1966, and again in September/October, there took place in the Northern Region massacres of Ibos on a scale and of a kind that brought accusations of genocide, and led to a vast movement of frightened people back to the Ibo heartland in the Eastern State. At the beginning of January 1967, the Supreme Military Council of Nigeria met at Aburi in Ghana to find ways of dealing with the issues that had led to the massacres, and to get agreement on the future form of the State of Nigeria.[43] The agreement reached was not however implemented, and Lieutenant Colonel Ojukwu, Governor of Eastern Nigeria, warned that if by the end of March it were not honoured, the Eastern Region would feel free to act in accordance with it. On 26 May the Consultative Assembly of Chiefs and Elders in the Eastern Region gave Ojukwu the mandate to declare Biafra a free, sovereign and independent state.

In response the Federal army opened up with an artillery barrage against Ogoja, a town near the border with the Northern Region in the northeast corner of Biafra. After Federal attacks near Port Harcourt and a landing by Federal forces on the oil-loading terminal for Shell–BP, the Biafrans, on 9 August, had gone on the attack and within a few days captured the Midwestern Region, including the town of Benin. By the third week of August the Biafrans were less than 150 miles from Lagos. It was rumoured that Gowan had made preparations to leave, and had only decided not to when assurance had been given to him of British and American aid – which followed in fact soon after.[44] Meanwhile Victor Banjo, the commander of the Biafran forces in the Midwest, had turned against Ojukwu and arranged the coup which soon followed. Although the coup failed and all was over by the third week of September, the treachery of Banjo seriously damaged the Biafran cause. The Biafran army withdrew, and by the late Autumn, when the Federal army received supplies of arms from Europe, and its fire-power had enormously increased, 'the hard slog' in Biafra began.[45]

The Churches in Britain were slow to understand the seriousness of events in Nigeria, despite missionary reports about the flood of refugees from the North; and as far as the Government was concerned the major consideration was the avoidance of any action that would disrupt the flow of oil. It was only as the savagery of war reached towns and villages, and as hospitals and other civilian targets began to be bombed and machine-gunned, that the news of what had been happening spread abroad, and the magnitude of the tragedy began to be heard. It was only then that the feeling of the Biafran people that they were being threatened with annihilation could be really understood, and the use of the word 'genocide' seen to be justified.

In reports that continued to come from missionaries, deep concern was expressed about what had already happened, and what might happen if there were not outside intervention from the nations of the world and particularly the Commonwealth. It was the responsibility of the Overseas Council, it was felt, to ensure that full publicity was given to the actual situation in Biafra, and to press for independent observers. The OC made representations to the Secretary of State for Commonwealth Relations.[46] There were at this time 23 missionaries and wives in Biafra, with ten children. A number had recently returned from leave to the danger area, and some were by now long overdue their furlough.[47]

It was reported that in January 1968 Mary Slessor Hospital had been bombed and was no longer usable, and that in the following month the hospital at Itigidi had been destroyed. It was also reported that the Federal Government had refused to give clearance to a plane carrying medical supplies and personnel.[48]

At the General Assembly of 1968, at which incidentally Prime Minister Harold Wilson was present and had been invited to speak, there was a long debate on the Report of the Overseas Council dealing with Nigeria/Biafra, in which in the strongest terms protests were made about the Government's support of the Nigerian Federation including the supply of arms. In his speech Wilson made no mention of Nigeria/Biafra.

Dr Archie Craig spoke of the sense of shame many felt about the Government's pouring in of arms to the Federal side:

> It is the sense of shame that in a conflict to which surely our nation should remain neutral, the policy of our Government has not been truly neutral.[49]

while John Hamilton had this to say:

> The time for not taking sides has passed, if by not taking sides it means that we cannot say what we feel about the export of ammunition and arms to the Federal Government.[50]

Speaking in the debate Dr Burnett, one of the medical doctors working in Biafra, cogently expressed what many felt:[51]

> I wish the General Assembly to add its greatest possible weight to the already considerable existing weight of condemnation against the policy of the British Government concerning this war. The policy is to continue to promote the export of arms to one side. The British Government now knows full well how these arms are being put to use, not for advance but for senseless butchery.

Backing up his point, Dr Burnett referred to items in *The Times* referring to Shell-BP's investment in the opening of an oil pipeline in mid-west Nigeria. A headline in the business news on the capture of Port Harcourt, he said, read: 'Relief of Biafra Oil Fields a Boom to Shell-BP'; and two days later, on 22 May, an announcement on the front page read: 'A Big Consignment of Arms and Ammunition for Federal Troops is being Flown to Lagos Today from Heathrow'.

Joining in on the debate, the Rev. R. M. McDonald, present from Biafra, spoke of the fear of the people there and of their reason for secession:

The people of Biafra believe, and they have every justification for believing, that they are to be exterminated. They know that they are the only effective barrier to Moslem domination of the whole country .... Does the world not yet understand that the Gowan regime has lost all control of the Nigerian army? The control, such as it is, has gone north.

When 30,000 of her people were murdered in a massacre timed and planned by the authorities of Northern Nigeria, nearly 2,000,000 were robbed and rendered homeless by the same brutal authority – was it not just commonsense for the people of Biafra to say, 'Never again, never again can we allow ourselves to come under the majority rule of the Moslem North'. That is the case for secession, that is why the people of Biafra gave their mandate to Colonel Ojukwu to declare the Independent Republic of Biafra.[52]

In the Overseas Council's Supplementary Report there were descriptions of what was taking place in Biafra:

Slowly the Federal Army has pressed on into Biafra, on occasion meeting with heavy losses, but by weight of weapons able to force opponents, often lacking in ammunition, towards the heart of Iboland. Only occasionally is reference made to prisoners on either side, and there have been reports of mass executions of civilians by the Federal Army.

Aerial bombing has become increasingly indiscriminate, as most large buildings in Biafra have already been destroyed or heavily damaged. Market places, rather than military targets, have been bombed, though most casualties have resulted from attacks by rocket-firing low flying aircraft.

It was reported on 13th May that Federal pilots had been ordered to avoid non-military targets, the Government spokesman adding that these were 'fresh instructions to observe existing instructions'. As these attacks have continued over some months, the conclusion must be drawn that having issued earlier instructions the Federal Government had been either unable or unwilling to enforce them. Should these now be observed, fears would be allayed that the Biafran people were being slowly crushed into a smaller and smaller area, in which they would be systematically massacred from the air.[53]

Several missionaries worked at nights on the airfield, helping with the uplifting of relief materials. Bill Aitken, who had been teaching at Abakaliki and previously at Hope Waddel, was the representative of the WCC relief programme in Biafra, which had become the focus of much attention in the media. Aitken's courage and determination during this time, along with his colleagues, made him a legendary figure.

In his contribution to the debate, Bill Aitken spoke of the embarrassment he had often felt by the fact that the bulk of the cost and the bulk of the work of the relief programme was being undertaken by Scandinavian and German Churches. He was often asked why the British contribution was so relatively small. He was in no doubt that this was in part due to the attitude of the British Government, but he realised also that the Churches in this country were trying to save their effort in part for rehabilitation.[54]

The shame that many in Britain felt because of the Government's support of one side in the conflict, and in Scotland in particular the sense that we were letting down a people with whom in the Church we had been bound in ties of duty and affection over so many years, had just been symbolised, as Neville Davidson remarked in the debate, by the painful renunciation by Sir Francis Ibiam of the knighthood of which he had been so proud.[55]

The General Assembly of 1968 made the following Deliverances to the Report of the Overseas Council:[56]

20. The General Assembly deeply sympathise with the peoples and churches in Nigeria and Biafra, note with horror the original massacres, learn with dismay of the continuation of hostilities, commend all efforts being made to find a just solution so that all citizens shall enjoy fundamental human rights, and call the Church to prayer for the people and churches there in this time of isolation and danger.

21. The General Assembly profoundly regret the decision of Her Majesty's Government to continue to license the export of arms to the Federal Government of Nigeria in quantities still unpublished and instruct that copies of this section of the Deliverance be sent to the Prime Minister and to the Secretary of State for Commonwealth Relations.

A Deliverance of the following year's General Assembly reads:[57]

30. The General Assembly, following the information received from our Biafran missionaries of the daylight bombing and machine-gunning of civilians, and of hospitals clearly marked with the Red Cross, urge the British Government to cease forthwith the supply of arms to Nigeria, and to instruct the Principal Clerk to communicate this decision to the Secretary of State for Scotland.

During this period and right up to the cessation of hostilities in January 1970, even with the terrible conditions of a war fought upon civilians, with only the most minimal medical facilities available, with food in many places at famine level, and housing and churches destroyed, the worship of the Church, its pastoral care, and an astonishing number of its normal activities continued, including, as symbol of its faith in the future, the sending of ten theological students abroad for training.

Senior members of the Church – ministers, headmasters, teachers, missionaries – worked to the limit of endurance to maintain a flow of relief supplies. At Ubulu Ihejiofo, a village a few miles from the airstrip, a headquarters for distribution was set up. A highly sophisticated network of collecting points serving rural centres was put into action, which ensured that supplies got to those who needed them, and were responsibly accounted for. A senior American army officer, who had served in Vietnam, had been sent in to help with the logistics of the operation. Graeme Brown and Sandy Somerville organised, at airstrip and headquarters, the uplifting and unloading of supplies that arrived on alternate evenings, one evening from Protestant sources and the other from Roman Catholic.

Despite the supplies of food that got through, very many of the population died of starvation. Sandy Somerville was in the position to say that in one place 35,000 had fled into the bush to escape from air attack, and that 17,000 only had come out, the remainder having died mainly of hunger.

In those difficult years a number of representatives of the Overseas Council had been able to visit Biafra and Federal Nigeria. Neil Bernard had been to both areas several times. In 1968 the General Secretary and Dr Archibald Watt, a former Moderator, were members of a delegation – along with Anglicans and Methodists – to Nigeria/Biafra. Jim Dougall had been with the team to Biafra, and Archibald Watt to Lagos and Ibadan. In September/October 1970, just after the war, Neil Bernard was sent to meet Church leaders and to assess what the OC might be able to do to help with restoration. In the following year, Betty Walls and the Rev. Angus Morrison visited the area on behalf of the OC and submitted a report.

All who visited after the war were much impressed by the strength and courage of the Church which had endured so much. Faced with its losses and with the destruction surrounding it, the Church might well have been expected to succumb. There had been terrible loss of life, including experienced leaders and many young people. Churches and manses had been destroyed, furniture had been stolen or burned, and nearly all the vehicles of the Church had gone. What visitors saw, however, was a Church determined to rebuild, and to make itself better equipped in every way for its future task. Visitors were amazed at what they saw, and not least by efforts for reconciliation within a Church which the war had divided – fellow members in Lagos from the rest in Eastern Nigeria.

The Overseas Council, within the limits of its resources, took its part along with German agencies and other bodies across the world in the massive task of dealing with the aftermath of the violence. Among other things it made a grant of £49,000, and an appeal for staff.[58]

(c)

In the years immediately following Independence in 1964, Zambia was preoccupied with nation building. There was much to be done. Divisions had to be dealt with: tribal divisions, the division between African and European, the wide gulf that European-style education had brought, and the division between the rich and the poor. There was poverty, and in the towns a serious problem of unemployment as many young people moved in from the villages looking for work. Malnutrition was prevalent. Zambia had the constant burden too of debt repayment for the loans it had incurred from the West.

The United Church of Zambia (UCZ) had its own challenges. It had to bring together Christians, not only from different parts of the country – from West, North and South, and from different tribal groups, but with varying Church traditions of worship, leadership, and administration. One of the first things that had to be done was to organise a centralised structure for the leadership and administration of the Church, and along with partner Churches abroad for its financing. From the beginning there had been regular consultations between representatives of the UCZ and the supporting missionary bodies. The first of those in 1965[59] had agreed that unity of financial policy and accounting was essential to the unity of the Church, that financial requests coming from the Church in Zambia should only be considered if endorsed by the Synod of the UCZ, and that all monies should be sent to the central finance offices of the Church. One of the difficulties the UCZ had to overcome was the bringing together of churches with different denominational/ national traditions and loyalties in the one body, and in different parts of a country widely spread. It soon became obvious that it would be necessary to increase the number of presbyteries from four to six,[60] and to strengthen the central authority of the Synod. The presbyterial structure was changed in 1970, and in the following year the Synod Clerk[61] came to have an overt executive position, the title of his office being changed to General Secretary, in line it was said with officers in other Churches. At the same time the head-quarters of the UCZ moved to the town of Lusaka, a move supported by those who argued for the efficiency of centralisation, but opposed by those who stressed that the real strength of the Church lay in the rural areas.[62] This was a tension that the UCZ had to live with in the years ahead.

Zambia at this time was facing serious financial problems resulting from UDI in Rhodesia[63], and from its decision not to break sanctions. This was reflected also in the life of the Church, and the fact that the number of Europeans in the Copperbelt, which affected its income, was much reduced, added to its difficulties.[64] In 1967 there was a shortfall in the budget which had necessitated cutting deaconess training, and limiting its candidates for the ministry to six.[65] The financial situation did not improve, and for the 1970 budget the Church reluctantly had to ask the 'sending societies' for help.[66] In presenting the budget figures for 1971, the Synod Treasurer – Rev. Jim Wilkie had recently been appointed to the post – specially requested that there be no decrease in grants in 1971 or 1972.[67]

There were many urgent vacancies for staff in the UCZ, and at the Consultation in London in 1968 a list of needs had been presented.[68] It included deaconesses, two ministers, one for the Copperbelt and another for the Northern Presbytery, three doctors and eight nursing sisters. The Overseas Council had at that time 15 members of staff serving with the UCZ,[69] most of them working separately from one another in different parts of the country.

By the end of 1966 it had become clear that the UCZ could not continue financially to maintain its hospitals. The proposal was to negotiate their transfer to Government, with the Church continuing to staff them.[70] The Government took over the financing from 1 July 1967 on the understanding that the Church would provide the senior staff of nursing sisters and doctors.[71] The Government of Zambia had inaugurated a scheme, the Lay Mission

Medical Staff Recruitment Scheme (LMMSR), whereby medical staff would be appointed by it and then seconded to the Church. The UCZ had approved that its missionary nursing and medical staff enter the LMMSR scheme.[72]

The UCZ was involved in four Secondary Schools, and two Teacher Training Colleges for Primary School teachers, one of the Training Colleges providing training also for women teaching Homecraft in Secondary Schools. Church of Scotland missionaries served as Principals of Teacher Training Colleges, and one served for a time among students at the University of Zambia in Lusaka.

The strong feeling of nationalism, inspiring the drive to nation building that was the dominant factor at this time, had its negative side. Any group within society that did not share that enthusiasm was liable to become a target of victimisation. Earlier on, as we saw, it had been the Lumpa Church that was the victim; now it was the Jehovah's Witnesses. Although the members of the Sect themselves were innocent citizens of the country, who obeyed the laws and regularly paid their taxes like anyone else, the Sect's formal teaching forbade its adherents to give allegiance to the State. The offence which that position caused, particularly to young people, and in the mood of the time, had led in 1967 and in the following year to violence, and the burning down of many of their 'Kingdom Halls'. Following the intervention of President Kaunda, the hotheads of the UNIP who were behind the violence were restrained, and the policy of tolerance which he espoused, and about which he had frequently written, was reasserted. Beginning in 1972, however, in spite of that policy, Jehovah's Witnesses who had fled from persecution in Malawi were forced back over the frontier.[73]

(d)

In Malawi there had been an enormous increase in population, more than half as a result were under 18. Jobs were scarce, and many of its able-bodied men had to leave the country for work. At least a third were away at any one time. One of Malawi's major exports indeed, supporting the economic life of the country, was the labour it sent to the mines of South Africa. There was acute poverty among the people and a serious problem of malnutrition.

The Church was growing rapidly, with a huge number of new members every year. New congregations were being formed, demanding pastoral care, requiring more and more resources for Christian education, and needing buildings to seat in some places a thousand or more. Among the membership of the Church, many were very poor, numbers of them illiterate and, like the population in general, undernourished. To deal with the people's urgent basic physical needs, such as nourishing food and clean drinking water, the Malawi Christian Council, supported by the WCC and aid agencies abroad, had undertaken an efficient, well-organised programme, within which Tom Colvin played a crucially important role. In 1968 the Council's Christian Service Committee, in close collaboration with Government, had a social development project in operation to tackle bore-hole and public health schemes. Seventeen villages had been provided with bore-hole water supplies, a pioneering public health service had been paid for, and a lunch programme in secondary schools begun.[74] At a Conference hosted by the CCS Committee, at which there were representatives from Botswana, Lesotho, Tanzania, Zambia and Malawi itself, the subject of the Church and Development had been taken up and lessons learned from the host country discussed. In the agreed statement at the end it was affirmed that development must not be seen as an optional extra but as a vital caring for others that expresses the love of Christ for all whether Christians or not.[75]

In the Livingstonia and Blantyre Synods of the Church of Central Africa Presbyterian, the two Synods with which the OC was most directly involved, the CCAP continued to be responsible for four hospitals and their clinics. In a country where the doctor to patient ratio was at this time 50 times less than in the UK and the need so much greater, the hospitals would have been under severe pressure even without the rapid population growth. As it was, the number of patients to be treated constantly increased, and the necessity to extend facilities became impossible to ignore. The Church worked closely with Government, respecting its guidelines, and received regular grants. These grants, however, failed to keep level with mounting costs, and despite the help the hospitals and clinics received from the Dutch Government through the Churches, and from trusts abroad, finance was a major problem.[76] The hospital at Mlanje provided a specially noteworthy service, covering a densely populated rural area and providing health care and instruction where malnutrition was common and caused often by ignorance. Midwives who lived with the people in the villages were trained at these clinics. Dr Dabb, who had given much attention to the development of this work, and who had served with distinction as a missionary doctor in Malawi for more than twenty years, retired in 1971.[77]

The CCAP ran five major educational institutions: in Livingstonia Synod – the Overtoun Institution Secondary School in Livingstonia itself, and at Embangweni, formerly called Loudon, a Teacher Training College; and in the Blantyre Synod – the Henry Henryson Institute, a Girls' School, and the Kapeni Teacher Training College. For most of the period there were seven to eight missionary teachers from the Church of Scotland. As with the hospitals there had been many necessary developments in buildings and equipment. There had been extensions at the Secondary School, Livingstonia;[78] at Robert Laws College, Embangweni, where at Government request plans were made for among other things an extension to the women's hostel, and a science block to include domestic science;[79] and an expansion of Kapeni Teacher Training College, more than doubling its number of students.[80] Grants from Government and from abroad failed to cover educational costs.[81]

As the CCAP continued to increase in membership dramatically, the Lay Training Institute[82] opened at Chilema under the leadership of Richard Baxter in Blantyre Synod, and in close partnership with the Anglican Church had come to play a strategically important place in the life of the Churches and their growth together. The Roman Catholic Church and the Churches of Christ began to participate later. In 1967 alone nearly 800 people had attended courses and conferences. A Centre for Women's Training,[83] sponsored by the WCC, had been opened at Chigodi on the Zomba Road in Blantyre Synod. Courses were run for girls, teachers and Sunday school teachers. There was also a Women's Centre at Livingstonia.[84] An important step too had been taken with the setting up of conference centres for young people in the Blantyre and Livingstonia Synods.[85]

Although the Churches in Malawi were brought closer together through an active co-operation in lay training, in service agencies, in the work of Christian literature and in other ways, Church union still evaded them. The tension between Nkhoma Synod and the others, which was a major obstacle, had continued and had focussed on theological training. There were difficulties about staffing the theological college and in making a decision about its final site.[86]

After lengthy negotiations, which at times had threatened to break down, it had at last been agreed that the joint college be built at Zomba, where also the university was to be, the move to take place in 1975.[87]

During this period it had become evident that Malawi was being ruled by a less than benevolent dictator. It had become impossible to speak out in public, or in fact in any group where confidence could not be guaranteed. Any comment or opinion that could be construed as critical of Government and by inference of the Life President was dangerous. The Young Pioneers had begun to be spoken of as Banda's spies, and teachers in Colleges and Schools were aware that that might be so. There were many reports of beatings by its bully boys against people who stepped out of line. Jehovah's Witnesses suffered most and there were stories of torture and murder which were authenticated and reported in the international press. The Overseas Council was aware that something was seriously wrong, but without the CCAP's authority to speak out chose to remain silent, being well aware that the consequences of doing otherwise would fall on the Church in Malawi and on the missionaries. The fact that Banda had at one time been an Elder of the Church of Scotland, during his time in the UK and continued to claim an association, made the OC's position doubly difficult. More and more pressure by groups and individuals was put on the OC to 'take a stand', a pressure that in the circumstances had to be resisted, the OC having to be content with private interventions.

(e)

Since Independence at the end of 1963 great changes had taken place in Kenya. By this time Nairobi had become a modern cosmopolitan city, with the headquarters of international organisations, with top class hotels serving a thriving tourist industry and the emerging middle-class, and with a growing industrial sector. Alongside the new prosperity, however, there was in contrast another side. The shanty towns in the city were places of great poverty, and the same was true in the rural areas around it. In the midst of the rapid developments that were happening the country was faced with the problems of an extremely high birth-rate – in excess of three per cent a year – serious unemployment, and the endemic problem of malnutrition leading in some instances to starvation.[88]

The Presbyterian Church of East Africa (PCEA) was a Church that was increasing in numbers, and developing steadily toward Africanisation and true independence. It had a programme for the theological education of the laity and for the further training of the ministry. It was extending its work both in the city and in the rural areas, in what used to be called the White Highlands, and most recently among the Masai. It was involved in a number of service projects including the Eastleigh Community Centre; an Agriculture/Community Development Centre with the Masai; and a School for the Deaf. It continued also to be responsible for the three hospitals: Chogoria, Tumutumu, and Kikuyu. Under the Education Act of 1968 all its Primary Schools were handed over to Local Authorities. The Church however still played a part in them. As official 'sponsors' they were in the position to give pastoral care to pupils and teachers and to support those who were in charge of religious education. The Secondary Schools under Boards of Governors continued to recruit teachers from overseas.[89]

During this period there was a new concern for outreach based on St Andrews Church, Nairobi. St Andrews had for years been concerned with mission, and was regarded not just as a city church but as a church serving the State. The Rev. Douglas Aitken,[90] who resigned from St Andrews, Nairobi in 1969, on his appointment to the BBC had used radio regularly in his ministry and was well known for his broadcasts throughout East Africa. By 1970, during the ministry of the Rev. John Paterson, three-quarters of those worshipping in St Andrews Church were Africans, and the church was attracting University students. John Paterson's aim had always been to prepare the way for a Kenyan to take over from him, and when he resigned to serve as Chaplain in the new University of Stirling the Rev. George Wanjau was appointed.[91] It was at this time that many new churches and prayer houses were built, and moves made to contact people of tribes otherwise untouched. From Nakuru, for example, work was being developed among the Wandorobo.[92]

The Eastleigh Community Centre was one of the several service projects in Naiorobi itself. The Rev. Din Dayal, sent as missionary from the United Church of Northern India to serve with the PCEA, and who had been running the Centre for ten years since 1955, had recently handed it over to his successor also from the UCNI. This partnership in Nairobi with the UCNI, which had been very fruitful, continued until 31 December 1968 when the PCEA with full agreement had taken over.[93] The Centre worked in an underprivileged community with all the problems associated with the inner city slum, bad housing, inadequate or non existent sanitation, unemployment, again malnutrition, and petty crime. The Centre ran programmes to meet a great variety of needs, and was committed to dealing constantly with individual and group case work.

In November 1965 the War on Want Committee, writing to the PCEA, had indicated its willingness to help with an agricultural/community development project among the Masai. The Rev. John Gatu as General Secretary of the Church was asking the Overseas Council if they would be prepared to staff such a project if other costs were met. The OC agreed to this proposal, and by 1967 the project was ready to begin. After some delay in finding a suitable member of staff from outside Kenya, the transfer of the Rev. George Cooper from St Margaret's Mombasa was considered. For a number of reasons, including the reluctance of the Mombasa Session to release him, that was not followed through. Instead an arrangement was made with the Church Missionary Society for a member of their staff to be appointed in collaboration with the OC. Later in July 1971 a missionary of the the Church of Scotland, John Crabbie, took over from the missionary of the CMS.[94] By that time the project had become an effort in total community development with two nursing sisters running medical clinics, and with its work, based at Olooseos, aimed at providing a service, in healing, teaching, and evangelism, among people scattered over an area of a thousand square miles.[95]

Two of the presbyteries were running schools for deaf children. The one at Kambui with 50 on the role had two specialist teachers, and modern hearing aid equipment. In 1971 the Church of Scotland Woman's Guild adopted it as its special project. The amount of money raised enabled the school to make comprehensive developments.[96] Mary Montgomery was the promoter of that scheme, a similar one at Tumutu, and of a Home for the Aged.[97]

In October 1965 the Overseas Council, realising that the PCEA was not in the position to continue to run three hospitals, appointed a Commission to consider what should be done.[98] The Commission recommended that the Church continue to run three hospitals. With the proviso that an energetic recruitment policy be implemented, and that it have a say in the budgets submitted by the different hospitals, the Hospital Board agreed to the recommendations.[99] At its meeting in 1967 the Board decided to approach the Government with the following points: (a) the desire for Africanisation; (b) the financial difficulties of the Hospitals; and (c) the need for Government assistance if this desire was to be achieved. It had been agreed at the same time that Dr Geoffrey Irvine be stationed at Chogoria on his return from furlough.[100] Plans for land use had been prepared for a development project at Chogoria, and arrangements made for an application for help to be forwarded to West German Aid.[101] A successful appeal for the Chogoria Development had been made to the public in Kenya by the Provincial Commissioner, and President Kenyatta himself contributed. The amount raised by the appeal enabled a large grant to be given from Germany, which had promised to give £3 for every pound raised.[102] The building, providing a 200 bed hospital, began in 1970 and was ready by the following year. On the fiftieth anniversary of the hospital in December 1972 a second phase in its development had been nearly completed.[103]

At Tumutumu, in 1969, the double storey block of the hospital containing wards and an operating theatre had been declared unsound. With the help of a gift from the United Church of Canada, a Government grant, a grant from the Overseas Council, and money from the 'One Day's Pay Appeal', a new building and other developments at the hospital had been made possible.[104]

During this whole period of development and extension anxiety continued to be expressed about the financing and staffing of three hospitals, and by 1970 it was clear that help was not going to come from Government.[105] After long discussion the Hospitals' Board had asked the General Administration Committee of the General Assembly of the PCEA to consider the early closure of either Tumutum or Kikuyu Hospital. The GAC had left decision over for further discussion. The OC meanwhile had decided to make no further appointments of missionary nurses and to limit its recruitment to a short-term doctor for Chogoria.[106] Following general discussion in 1972 on the place of the Church in the country's health service, the PCEA suggested that all Churches hand over their hospitals to a central health council of the Churches. It was thought that 'if this scheme came into being, it might make more possible an ecumenical sharing of personnel, even if only, in the first instance, limited to the sphere of medicine in Kenya and would immediately be a witness to the essential unity of the Church'.[107]

The section on Kenya in the Overseas Council's Report to the

General Assembly of 1973 ends with these perceptive and provocative questions:

> In the midst of such physical and numerical extension the Church is engaged in discussion of what are the implications of remaining dependent upon missionary personnel and finance. To what extent is the self-reliance, the integrity of the Church at stake? .... Can local priorities really be decided until missionaries have left Kenya?[108]

(f)

The injustices of the apartheid system in South Africa and the oppression to which it led had not diminished. The Bureau of State Security, BOSS, which the Prime Minister operated direct, continued to sustain a system within which the most severe breaches of human rights could be carried out, in the name of Government, without interference.[109] The gross contrast between a system of intimidation and terror, and the Government's avowed moral purpose to build a Christian civilisation, was highlighted in 1968 at a Conference held under the auspices of the Christian Council of South Africa, at which among other Churches the Bantu Presbyterian Church was represented.

At the end of that meeting 'A Message to the People of South Africa' was issued, which among other things said:

> Such barriers as race and nationality have no rightful place in the inclusive brotherhood of Christian disciples .... In South Africa, at this time, we find ourselves in a situation where a policy of racial separation is being deliberately effected with increasing rigidity .... We believe that this doctrine of separation is a false faith, a novel gospel; it inevitably is in conflict with the Gospel of Jesus Christ .... Christ is inevitably a threat to much that is called 'the South African way of life'.[110]

Vorster's immediate response to the Message was a blunt warning to the Churches to shut up and keep out of trouble. Although the leadership of the Churches in general had decided not to press the issue with Government, a consequence of the Message was to stimulate and encourage many within them to consider the question it raised for theological understanding and Christian obedience, a notable example being those associated with the Christian Institute of Beyers Naude.

In 1969 the Church and Nation Committee had included in its Report a carefully considered section dealing with the theology of law and revolution, and had been led logically to the position that in a State where there were no democratic remedies available violence might be right if there were no other way to achieve justice.[111] The theme was further developed in its 1971 Report, written this time in the context of the controversy about the Programme to Combat Racism, mentioned below. The conclusion it came to was that the Church was 'not meantime able to commit itself to explicit support of revolutionary violence'. It went on to say, however, that 'the Church must make plain beyond a doubt that its sympathy and its prayers are with those suffering oppression, poverty and indignity: that it has humble admiration for those engaged in the struggle for justice'.[112]

The issue came to a head in 1969 when the Central Committee of the WCC, meeting in Canterbury, introduced the five-year Programme to Combat Racism (PCR), and launched a special fund, for which it transferred $200,000 from its Reserves, and made an appeal to member Churches to contribute $300,000, the aim of the fund being 'to aid oppressed racial groups in their struggle for justice and help the victims of racial oppression'.[113] The planning of the PCR Committee and the responsibility of drawing up a list of organisations to which grants might be offered was given to an International Advisory Committee. In September 1970 the Executive Committee of the WCC accepted the list, commenting as it did so that it welcomed the assurance that 'none of these grants would be used for military purposes'. The publication of the list, which included a number of organisations committed to the use of violence in pursuit of their aims, sparked off heated controversy in the Church of Scotland, and across the world.[114]

The Inter-Church Relations Committee reported to the General Assembly of 1971 that it had received communications from eight presbyteries, two Kirk Sessions, and ten individuals protesting against grants from WCC funds to the PCR, while at the same time it had received letters approving of the PCR. In its Report the ICR Committee quoted in full a statement it had authorised its convener to make to the press, in which it appealed to those who held opposing views to respect one another's opinions. In the statement made to the press it was freely acknowledged that the Church of Scotland was implicated in the decision to help to fund the PCR, through the grants it gave to the funds of the WCC, and therefore through the money the WCC had withdrawn from its reserves. That amount of money however would, it said, be infinitesimally small.[115]

The Church of Scotland's reply to the WCC appeal had been agreed in a Deliverance of the Committee on General Administration to the 1971 General Assembly, which said *inter alia*:

3.   The General Assembly are aware that the severe criticism of the World Council's action is levelled against the giving of grants to anti-racist groups committed to the use of violence in the pursuit of their aims. The General Assembly recognise that it may seem to some people naive to imagine that the grants to such organisations would not have some military advantage even if themselves used only for 'social, health and educational programmes', but they equally believe that it is an undue simplification of the issues involved in the racist struggle to imagine that the use of violence belongs only to one side.

4.   While recognising the right of Christians to differ on such an issue as this, the General Assembly believe that the World Council of Churches was justified in making an appeal to its member churches for *voluntary* contributions to a Special Fund to give grants to anti-racist groups, whose purposes are not inconsonant with the general purposes of the World Council, and they are interested to learn that the Central Committee at its latest meeting unanimously decided to renew this appeal. The General Assembly believe that congregations and individuals may find in this appeal a way, additional to those they already support, of indicating sympathy with those who suffer from, or contend against, unjust racist influences. [116]

To return to South Africa itself and to the Bantu Presbyterian Church; the BPC, having discussed the Programme to Combat Racism, 'had expressed its concern with the recent decision of the WCC which appears to support some of those who advocate the way of violence as the way to combat racism and to relieve the victims of racial injustice'. At the same time it had expressed 'its disagreement on the grounds of its Christian faith with the policy of the Government of South Africa whose implementation of "separate development" can only be seen as a major direct cause of the excess of violence within our country, which so scandalises most of the rest of the world'.[117]

The Bantu Presbyterian Church, conscious though it was of being under the scrutiny of Government, continued to carry on with its work responsibly under the Gospel. In 1968 its General Assembly met in Moroko township in Johannesburg. At that meeting the Rev. G. T. Vika was appointed Senior Clerk and General Secretary of the Church. He was sent as a delegate to the Fourth Assembly of the WCC. He visited Scotland, Malawi and Kenya. John Summers, for a second time, was elected to serve as Moderator of the BPC General Assembly.

The full integration of Church and Mission was still a hope unrealised. In 1962 when Mission Council had been dissolved, the Joint Council which took its place had been considered a purely temporary measure, particularly as at that time Church Union was expected. By the time of the meeting of Joint Council in March 1968, because of Government restrictions, that hope began to fade, and the Council asked the Church of Scotland to control and finance the hospitals, the educational institutions, and the farms.[118] Later, however, in September 1969, Joint Council had considered in some detail what steps could be taken within the current legal constraints of the apartheid regime. It had made recommendations, including the representation of Emgwali and Pholela Institutions on the Education Committee of the BPC, and the setting up of a Lovedale Committee as a BPC Standing Committee; the bringing of finance under the BPC Finance Committee; and the appointment of a Missionaries Committee by the BPC General Assembly. It was recognised that Government policy made it impossible for the hospitals to be controlled by the BPC, but that there must be a body to act in South Africa on behalf of the Overseas Council.[119] In the following year the OC accepted the recommendations concerning finance, and the formation of a Missionaries Committee. Other matters, connected with the institutions, had to be left over until legal and other issues had been resolved.[120] At its 1971 General Assembly the BPC agreed to appoint George McArthur as Administrative Assistant in headquarters to deal with integration.[121]

The hospitals, all of which remained under the control of Joint Council, had severe staffing difficulties, but had the bulk of their running expenses met by Government. The staff were under considerable pressure. The two doctors at Tugela Ferry, in addition to their services within the hospital, ran three clinics; at Sibasa, a hospital of more than 350 beds had been built up, with an out-patient attendance annually of over 20,000; and at Sulenkama, serving a rural area where there was much tuberculosis and serious malnutrition, there were in 1968 over 60,000 outpatient attendances, and a daily average of just over 200 in-patients.[122] The shortage of doctors, which had become acute by 1967, had raised as a matter of urgency the future of the three mission hospitals.[123] In July of that year it was agreed to continue the work of the three hospitals, and to press the Christian Council to investigate the current shortage of African doctors.[124] In the following year, with the shortage continuing, Joint Council, in view of the difficulty of maintaining the standards of medical care and 'of the complexity of relationships with Government', pressed the Medical Committee to prepare recommendations for the future of the hospitals.[125] At the beginning of 1970 there was a firming up of Government policy toward the hospitals in the Bantu 'Homelands', affecting all three of the hospitals under Joint Council.[126] The understanding was that the South African Government would take over all Church hospitals, but by the end of 1972 it was not yet known what that would involve.[127]

Although the Church no longer controlled colleges or schools, it continued to play its part in an institution like Pholela, where Ian Moir was hostel warden. The Institution had won a reputation for high standards of teaching and caring, and to it pupils came from all over South Africa. In 1972, 49 students became members of the Church by profession of faith.[128]

With the building of the new church in 1968 at the Federal Theological Seminary at Alice, it had become possible to hold united prayers every evening for the Anglican, Congregational, Methodist, and Presbyterian College students, and to have a joint communion service each month. For most lectures teaching was no longer on a denominational basis. During 1972 guest speakers included the Moderator and the Archbishop of Canterbury. Fort Hare University was at this stage pressing to buy out the Federal Seminary. In 1972 the Council of the Seminary recommended 'to the participating Churches that the offer of the University to purchase the Seminary's land buildings should not be accepted. Resentment at the proposed take over increased when it was learned that the Rector had referred to an Act which would permit the Bantu Trust to acquire the property'.[129]

V

The United Church of Jamaica and Grand Cayman was proud of its independence. At the same time it was anxious to maintain its long-held relationship with the Church of Scotland, and with other bodies abroad, and to open up new ones where it could be sure that its independence would be respected. The OC had recognised and welcomed anew the desire of the United Church to be free from dependence, and was glad to be able to continue to work with that Church on that understanding, helping where required, and as far as it was able.

Margaret Robertson, a teacher from Skye, was one of a team working in the Kelly Lawson Training Centre,[130] which had been opened at the end of 1966 at Falmouth, where the Rev. Arthur Kent was minister. The purpose of the Centre was to provide training for village school teachers and for girls seeking domestic experience. In 1968 the Government had met the cost of appointing a home economics teacher, which had enabled a certificate course to be started. At the end of the first course 20 girls had received their certificates in the presence of the Minister of Youth and Community, and of the British High Commissioner.

In the spring of 1967, also at Falmouth, the Mount Olivet Boys' Home was inaugurated.[131] There had been difficulties at the beginning, and Arthur Kent had had to take over. In a short time he had done wonders with the Home, to such an extent that the Chamber of Commerce had awarded it 'the prize for the most improved children's home in 1968'. In the summer of 1968 a group of American students from Chicago had helped to restore the historic church at Falmouth, which had housed the first Synod of the Presbyterian Church in Jamaica in 1849; and in the following year Dr James Longmuir, during his Moderatorial visit, had been invited to re-dedicate it.[132]

The twenty-fifth anniversary of the founding of Knox College was celebrated on 26 October 1972 when two new buildings, the Religion Centre and the Communication Learning Centre, were opened by the Prime Minister, Michael Manley, and dedicated by the Moderator of the United Church, the Rt Rev. Sam Smellie.[133] Two years previously, in September, 1970, the Rev. Lewis Davidson had handed over the Principalship to a Jamaican, Mr George Scott, the Vice-Principal, a graduate of St Andrews University. It became possible for Lewis Davidson to give more time to the designing and developments of new projects and the raising of money for them. It enabled him also to put his energy into the planning of a Community College, which he had dreamed of, for the people of Spaldings among whom Knox had been built.[134]

VI

The Federation of South Arabia, of which Aden had become part in 1962, came to an end on 30 November 1967,[135] some months before the date originally planned for independence. During the previous months, as the UN sought to find a solution, the Front for the Liberation of South Yemen (FLOSY) backed by Egypt, which had been a dominant force in terrorist operations, had been redoubling its efforts and violence had been increasing[136] After the Khartoum Summit, following the Six Day War, when Nasser had agreed to withdraw from Yemen, FLOSY's power diminished, allowing the National Liberation Front with the support of the Federal Army to gain control.[137] It was at this time that the British Government brought forward independence, recognising that any delay would merely prolong the suffering of the people, and cause more loss of life. The Federation was handed over to the NLF, and South Yemen, the Crown's connection legally severed, became the first Arab regime to boast Marxist/Maoist sympathies.

In December 1966 the General Secretary of the Overseas Council had met his opposite number of the DMS in Aden, on his return from a tour in Asia, and had discussed with him contingency plans for the withdrawal of staff if that were to become necessary, and at the same time what other work in the area might be undertaken if the work in South Yemen ceased.[138] By August/September 1967 all the missionaries had left, including the Red Sea Mission and the Danish Mission, and the Church of Scotland missionaries were back in Scotland. Earlier, in June, the High Commissioner requisitioned the Keith Falconer Hospital in Sheikh Othman for use by the Parachute Regiment, and the drugs were flown out by the RAF to Kenya, for the hospital at Kikuyu.[139] On Sunday 9 July Muhammed Hussein Al-Beihani was ordained and took vows of pastoral responsibility for the Church of South Arabia.[140] The Rev. Ian Findlay arrived in Aden at the end of that month for work in the Sailors'

Club at Steamer Point and to be chaplain of the Keith Falconer Church.[141]

In January 1968 Lexa Boyle and Helen Thom returned to Aden, followed by Bryan and Mrs Drever. After a helpful and friendly reception by the immigration authorities, they had had discussion with the Health Minister and had received an invitation to co-operate with the Government in joint medical work in the Sheikh Othman premises, the work to 'follow a Socialist pattern'.[142] Permission had been granted by the Minister of the Interior to resume the work of the clinic at Beihan, and in July Lexa Boyle, Helen Thom and Sylvia Forrester went there and were warmly welcomed.[143]

Compensation had been received from the British Embassy for the use of the Hospital at Sheikh Othman when it had been occupied by the British army. The understanding was that expenses in connection with the occupation of the hospital after Independence would be the liability of the Government of South Yemen. Pastor Beihani, in thanking the OC for the use of the hospital chapel, intimated that the Arab Church wished to give a donation towards the cost of its repair.

In January 1968, when the missionaries returned to Sheikh Othman, there was a great deal to be done. The compound had been been used during the period of violence by several groups and was a scene of desolation:'barbed wire, sand bags, dead trees and broken windows.'[144] After compensation had been received and the first repairs made, the hospital opened early in 1969 for out-patients. By the end of that year about 52,000 people had been seen. There was a high incidence of malnutrition and a special clinic was opened to deal with the feeding of children.[145] In October 1970 a children's ward had been opened, and plans made to start a ward for women in the following year.[146] In 1970 it was necessary to close the work at Beihan because of a staff shortage, but it was possible to open again in November.

In 1972 the Ministry of Health of the People's Democratic Republic of Yemen, as it had come to be called, had advised the missionaries that it proposed to take over the Keith Falconer Hospital on 25 March 1972, and that the work in Beihan had to be closed down by 31 March. At the same time the missionaries were informed that their residence permits would not be renewed.[147] By the end of March all the missionaries had left.

The probability that the work in what was South Yemen might have to be closed had always been there, and by this stage there seemed to be a possible opening in the Yemen Arab Republic in the north. On the advice of Dr Laidlay, who had visited the Yemen Arab Republic at the request of the OC, and had been assured by Government officials there that assistance from the Church of Scotland would be welcomed, on the understanding that direct evangelism would not be allowed, and that its help would be limited to medical assistance,[148] the OC had decided to go ahead with the project and an Agreement was drawn up with the Government of the YAR. A team of two doctors and two nurses was appointed, and were ready for work in Radaa by November 1972. The team consisted of Dr and Mrs Laidlay, Dr and Mrs Brian Drever, Janice Gillespie, and Lexa Boyle.[149]

VII

By 1966 the General Assembly instructed the Stewardship and Budget Committee to estimate the amount of money likely to be required by 1972 by the committees of the Co-ordinated Appeal, and to recommend to the next General Assembly how that sum should be allocated. The Overseas Council found it virtually impossible to estimate its requirement five years ahead. There were so many variables over which it had no control. There were, for example, monetary fluctuations in different countries, and because of it partnership with other Churches there was the impossibility of making unilateral decisions. Basically too there was the problem of having to choose between consolidating important existing work, and moving ahead in response to urgent new opportunities. The Council was aware that the money proposed was insufficient to do both.[150]

It was a difficult period financially for the Church as a whole and not just for the Overseas Council. Although the figure received in 1967 from congregational contributions was larger than for the previous year, it was nonetheless short of the budget figure which itself had been severely cut from the amount the committee required. The Council itself faced particular problems. Devaluation in Britain meant that compensation had to be paid to maintain salary levels and to counteract the reduction of grants, which if compensation had not been paid would have been reduced by a damaging one-sixth.[151]

In addition there was an increase in the cost of fares. As a result, intended and much needed salary increases had to be reduced, and a planned resettlement scheme for missionaries without a pension had to be set aside. Congregational contributions lagged far behind the needs of the Church to fulfill its vocation, and in its Report to the General Assembly the Stewardship and Budget Committee spoke of a 'persistent and apparently in-built resistance'[152] to stewardship teaching. By 1970 there was an alarming shortfall between what was received from congregations and the requirements of the committees – there had been a two per cent increase in givings and a 9.5 per cent increase in what was needed.[153] The gap was reaching crisis proportions and in 1971 it was decided that budgets for 1972 should remain at the 1971 figure.[154]

Inflation was an inhibiting factor. During this period the value of the pound sterling was dropping dramatically. It was pointed out that £5.11s.6d in 1968 (the average giving per member in that year) would in 1960 have been worth only £4.5s – a difference which made any increase in liberality in that time 'largely illusory'. The General Finance Committee in indicating again, as it had repeatedly, the urgency of increased giving, warned that the serious alternative was what it called 'a redeployment of the Church's accumulated resources'.[155]

Meanwhile the Advisory Board advised the General Finance Committee to publish the memorandum on *Statistical Trends in Church Membership and Finance* in order to 'alert the Assembly and the Church to the disquieting indications of an accelerating decline in membership and an increasing difficulty in financing adequately the wide and growing range of the Church's work at home and abroad'.[156] The percentage fall in membership over the previous year in 1970 was 1.9 per cent; whereas in 1969 it had been 0.4 per cent. The membership of the Church in 1961 had been 1,301,280; while in 1970 it was 1,184,621.[157]

Offsetting to some extent this picture of decline there should be noted the increasing concern of many in the Church to help the poor of the Third World and to respond to emergencies there. In 1970, for example, the amount given to Christian Aid through the Overseas Council was much in excess of the amount budgeted, including a special fund for Nigeria/Biafra – the only Church to have raised such a fund.[158] Although there is no way of knowing what percentage of the considerable sum raised during Christian

Aid Week came from members of the Church, it could be assumed that a sizeable amount came from that source. Many members would have supported also other Aid agencies, such as OXFAM and War on Want.

In 1972 the total membership of the Church was 1,110,187, the population figure for Scotland being 5,210,400.

CHAPTER 7

In Pursuit of a Vision
TWENTY-FIVE YEARS
(1947–1972)

DESPITE all the contradictions of war, violence and injustice, the assumption throughout this story of 25 years has been that God whom we know in Jesus Christ is constantly present in his Holy Spirit to fulfil his loving purpose for the human family. The vision we pursue is of a world transformed, in which all the human community will acknowledge his presence, and give him praise. It is this vision, like the beauty of the rainbow against threatening clouds, that inspires the missionary movement and draws us forward.

The period after the Second World War was heavy with threats of destruction, but lightened again and again with signs of hope. It was a time of extraordinary contradictions. On the one hand with the dropping of the bombs on Hiroshima and Nagasaki in August 1945, and with the Cold War following, it seemed logically probable that human inhumanity would lead in the end to the death of the human race in a sunless nuclear wasteland, while on the other hand there were signs that the world was moving instead toward a time of unprecedented progress and prosperity.

There were enormous changes. The quarter century from the end of 1947 saw the end of Western Colonialism, and for impoverished and oppressed peoples across the world the opening up of undreamt of possibilities for freedom and a richer life. In world mission the changes that took place were no less far-reaching. As indigenous Churches emerged from the foreign mission councils which had dominated the missionary movement, the Christian community in each newly independent country was set free to develop at its own pace, to find its own proper identity, to take its part creatively in its country's future, and increasingly to play a part in the Church world-wide.

There had been appalling suffering during the Second World War and terrible destruction. Long established institutions had been destroyed and traditional patterns of living thrown into confusion. Many were afraid of what the future would bring. The picture of the bomb and other dark images engraved on the mind what human beings were capable of doing to one another and led to profound anxieties. That was how it was when the Church after the War set about the task of starting again where it had left off, repairing damage, reassessing and planning. There were fears, and there were problems in abundance, but there was also hope. For many the conflict had meant a renewal of vision and a determination to make a new start. Paradoxically it seemed that those who had most experienced the darkness of war were among those who least despaired of what might lie ahead. In student and other ecumenical conferences held after the War the most memorable contributions more frequently than not came from those who had been most exposed to its cost. Typically, at a conference on the future of world mission held in Iona soon after the close of the War, it was not Hendrik Kraemer, who had experienced the Nazi occupation of his country and had been imprisoned, who spoke in despair. Noticeably he was the one who looked forward in hope and spoke with joy of the victory of Christ.

The fact that it was during those years that many people began to have a hope that gives meaning to life is one of the strange paradoxes of the time. It was paradoxical also that just when hatred and violence were rife that many began to experience, and at a depth they had not known before, what it means to belong to a community where people support and care for one another. As we were thrown together in the War, and made to rely on one another, comradeship that we instinctively knew to be close to the meaning of life happened among us.

As the FMC set about its task after the War it did so in confidence that we belonged as one family with Churches abroad, and that we were called with them to participate in God's purpose for the world. Partnership in mission became a major preoccupation.

As one nation after another achieved independence, it became more and more urgent to ensure the proper freedom of the emerging Churches which inevitably in the beginning had been shaped by foreigners, and which, as almost mirror images of colonialism, continued under their influence. The FMC had been aware from the beginning of the need to encourage the communities of Christians which had come into being and had grown following the work of the missionaries, to find a style of life which was their own. With the good intention of allowing them freedom to develop, it had built up an organisation of missionary service separate from the organisation of the Church. As the years went on that organisation, however, now running many and increasingly prestigious institutions – hospitals, colleges, and schools, with an attendant administrative structure of offices and committees – had become the recognisable Christian presence. The Mission, as it was called, to a considerable extent foreign-led and financed, overshadowed the Church.

The foreignness of the missionary movement was difficult to overcome. It was common currency in the criticisms that were made of missions that the Churches for which they were responsible were potted plants, whose roots were not yet in the cultural soil of the land to which they had been conveyed. Even by the late 1950s or early 60s there was some truth in this. To visit the churches in the north of India was to see attitudes, theological assumptions, forms of worship, styles of living, carried over from the home country. It was like travelling across frontiers: at one moment New Zealand, at another Australia, then the United States, then Canada, on to England, Wales, Northern Ireland, Scotland. And this was India – with colonialism well behind it.

It was to rectify what was increasingly seen to be a serious distortion of the missionary intention that the FMC, in company with other bodies, turned its attention to the integration of Church and Mission.

The question of the Churches becoming independent and self-supporting had been before the FMC for many years, and there had been pressure on it to withdraw from those areas at least where the Churches had reached a position where they might manage on their own. That was being argued in the 1930s when the FMC was engaged in a major survey of its work for presentation to the 1935 General Assembly, but was firmly put aside. The FMC had set its mind against withdrawal and in a Report on a further survey which it had been asked to make at the beginning of the War, reiterated its intention to continue to work with the Churches, while encouraging them in their desire to exercise responsibility for mission and service among their own people in ways appropriate to their own cultural identity.

The next logical step, the integration of Church and Mission, which meant the merging of the foreign mission organisation with the indigenous Church, was not easy to achieve. It involved work previously carried out by the FMC being put under the Church of the country, with the FMC continuing to be involved and its missionaries continuing to serve. It was a difficult undertaking and a difficult concept. The notion of devolution whereby the foreign organisation would have handed over its work, devolved responsibilities on to local people, and moved away, would have been easier to understand. Integration, however, whatever the difficulties, left the way open, it was hoped, for new depths of partnership in the Gospel.

There were many problems, and much misunderstanding. From the point of view of those who were from the West the concept of integration was readily acceptable; there were close parallels to colonialism – one step at a time toward dominion status; while from the other side, from the position of nationalism, it was seen as gaining power and winning release from foreign domination. On both sides, however, there was a desire to find a way in which the new Churches could be free to live their own lives, and yet continue to have supportive relationships with missionary bodies. Partnership seemed the way forward, and the IMC Conferences of 1947 and 1952, at Whitby and Willingen, provided the impetus to move in that direction. Although much was achieved, the hoped-for Partnership in the Gospel as equal members one of another in the One Body was unattained. The FMC persistently failed to recognise that its desire to be involved in the policy decisions of its partner Churches was in practice a continuing desire to control, and at the same time the 'younger Churches' resisted what they regarded as interference. Partnership in so many ways was one-sided. The Church in the West had entry into the Churches that had emerged from the missionary movement, and participated in their councils and committees, but that was not reciprocated, and seemed even to go unnoticed. Partnership could not be equated with the reality of 'membership together', although that was so often the assumption. The basic problem was the theological offence of the denominational divisions brought in from abroad by the missionary bodies, and the failure of those bodies, against that background, to explore theologically with their partner Churches the ecumenical nature of the Church.

Questions about money constantly raised the issue of the reality or otherwise of partnership. Although the financial contributions coming from individuals committed to world mission and from the givings of congregations was an expression of solidarity between 'older and younger Churches', and helped to make possible many things Churches in areas of relative poverty saw needing to be done, they had also negative effects. Finance indeed was one of the factors preventing partnership's development. During the years of world-wide economic growth, as the rich became richer and the poor poorer, the imbalance in terms of money between the 'older and younger Churches' perceptibly widened, making it hard to keep in check destructive attitudes of condescension, real or perceived, and, with regard to policy, to prevent money from talking. The system of block grants that was introduced in the early 1960s could be seen as a step forward. It enabled the 'younger Churches' to draw up their own budgets without outside interference, as far as individual items were concerned, moneys being granted as total amounts for partic-ular areas of work such as hospitals or schools. There was no freedom, however, to determine the amount of money that would be received. The 'younger Churches' were outside the committees of the sending Church where decisions were made about financial priorities, and had to take what was made available to them. From the standpoint of the 'younger Churches' dependence on decisions made outside was a serious hindrance to partnership, but no less from the other side was the giving of grants without receiving accounts for them and without feedback about their effectiveness. If there were a danger that the one who paid called the tune, there was danger also in what could so easily be seen as handouts and as cheap money. There was no desire to go back to a system of detailed ear-marking of grants, but the weaknesses of the block grant were obvious. So long as the structures of the Churches, nationally and denominationally, did not radically change, that and many other difficulties would inevitably remain.

The division of the Churches was a major factor. The Churches in the places where the FMC was at work were uneasy with the divisions they had fallen heir to. They could see that the denomi-nations were not part of the Good News, the Gospel, but were in fact a contradiction of it. Those things might belong to Europe or to America, but they did not belong to them. They were an obstacle. To teach the Christian faith, to speak of reconciliation or peace or unity to a Muslim or a Hindu, for example, in the context of a divided Church, was to have thrown back, often plaintively, 'Show us this thing about which you say you believe'.

In the Church of South India, where the major step was taken of crossing the divide between 'episcopal and non-episcopal' Churches, Church union and national Independence happened within a few weeks of one another. That was no coincidence. Not only in India, but in other countries also, the goal of freedom from colonialism was closely associated with the desire of the Church to be free from the trammels of the West. It was not easy for the Church in India to rid itself of Western divisions. For the Church of South India to do so it had to enter into long negotiations with the Church of England over intercommunion and to postpone full recognition of its ecclesiastical standing. The episode when the Nandyal diocese of the former Anglican Church had its grants withdrawn by its supporting missionary society because of trust conditions, and as a direct consequence chose not to enter the CSI, further underlined the problem. In Africa a number of factors, many of them non-theological, interrupted the progress of union. In West Africa, in Nigeria and Ghana, where union negotiators had turned to the CSI for help, and had welcomed Bishop Sumitra, plans of union were well advanced, but did not come to fruition, mainly, though not wholly, as a result of political events. The union in Nigeria, for example, between three Churches – Presbyterian, Methodist and Anglican – was postponed at the very last moment due to controversy over property in the Methodist Church, and finally postponed as the disturbances leading up to the Biafran War began. In Central Africa, by 1964 three Churches in Zambia – the United Church of Central Africa in Rhodesia, the Methodist Church, and the Church of Barotseland – had come together to form the United Church of Zambia. In Malawi, where a lay training centre was being run in partnership with the Anglican Church, and where several other institutions were being run co-operatively across the denominations, the Churches remained separate. The main obstacle was Nkhoma Synod, with its loyalty to the Dutch Reformed Church and its apartheid sympathies. Finally to return to Asia, there were the inaugurations, at the very end of this period, of the Churches of North India and of Pakistan, which together included a wider range of traditions, including Lutheran and Baptist, than had been brought together before.

On the world scene the opening of a new chapter of relationships in the modern ecumenical movement saw the formation of the WCC, and the merging with it of the International Missionary Council.

Inter-Church conferences not only brought together people from opposite sides during the War, but encouraged reconciliation, and prepared the way for the First Assembly of the WCC in Amsterdam. As the result of the Assemblies that followed at regular intervals, and the many ecumenical study conferences and working committees that grew up round the WCC, long-held misunderstandings and deep-rooted prejudices began to be overcome. In the UK an important step forward was taken when the British Council of Churches was formed in 1942 with Dr A. C. Craig as its first Secretary. The Scottish Churches Council followed in 1964, as a successor to the Scottish Churches Ecumenical Association and the Scottish Churches Ecumenical Committee.

The initiative for co-operation in Britain as elsewhere had come from the missionary movement. The British Conference of Missionary Societies, founded in 1912 as a direct result of the World Missionary Conference in Edinburgh, in 1910, was a major source of inspiration for co-operation between the missionary bodies in Britain, and through them for ecumenical and missionary co-operation in different parts of the world where they were at work. Through the CBMS enduring friendships grew up between members of staff, secretaries and missionaries, belonging to its different member bodies, who met in the conferences it arranged, in specialist working groups, and in the regular meetings of committees. The importance of those friendships is impossible to quantify, but it can certainly be said to be a major factor in the story of mission during this whole period.

Although missionary bodies, including the FMC and its successors, found it hard to shake off the restriction of seeing mission primarily in terms of our Church, our mission, our missionaries, it became increasingly obvious in this period that we were engaged in an operation in which we were called to share in mission with other denominations, traditions and nationalities. Joint action became a practical reality in many spheres: in the running of institutions of higher education, university colleges, teacher training colleges, secondary schools; in seminaries for the training of ministers and catechists; in lay training institutes; in community development; in Christian literature; and in the running of hospitals and the training of medical personnel. The web of relationships too in joint action widened out to include colleagues from many parts of the world, beyond our own country and the country within which we worked, so that it became commonplace to speak of sharing in mission in all continents.

The Selly Oak Colleges in Birmingham were a striking example of this kind of ecumenical sharing. Beginning in 1903, with the founding of Woodbrooke by members of the Society of Friends, there came into being a federation of autonomous colleges of member bodies of the CBMS with their own distinctive yet related programmes of missionary training supported by a Central Staff. In 1967 the CBMS took a further step forward, in consultation with the Colleges, and in co-operation with missionary bodies in Europe. This sought a closer relationship of staff and resources, and to help plan, focus and administer the new 'Centre for Training in Christian Mission', as it came to be called, the post of Dean of Mission was created. The FMC was approached by the NCCI, with the consent of the United Church of Northern India Nagpur Church Council from which he was seconded, to permit the writer, a Church of Scotland missionary on its staff, to be the Centre's Dean. The Centre proved a remarkable venture in ecumenical sharing, bringing together in one Council for Training in Christian Mission the major missionary bodies in the UK, including the Baptist Missionary Society, the Church Missionary Society, the Churches of Christ in Great Britain, the Congregational Council for World Mission, the Methodist Missionary Society, the Presbyterian Church of England Overseas Mission, the United Society for the Propagation of the Gospel, and associated with them the Society of Friends; besides having in addition the active participation among others of the Swedish and Danish Missions, and of Churches in the Netherlands. Nationals of the various countries in which missionary bodies worked, took part increasingly in the courses along with the missionary candidates, and, as the years went on, the student membership included Orthodox and Roman Catholic. The Church of Scotland, although giving its support, felt it necessary at that stage to continue its own programme of training within the Scottish context, and not to switch from Edinburgh to Birmingham, or to join the new Council.

The work done ecumenically in Selly Oak for training in mission was similar in many ways to developments in lay training and conference centres both in Europe and in many parts of the Third World. There was an emphasis on Bible study in groups, and a concern to relate study to practical issues confronting the Church in the world. In the Selly Oak Training in Mission Semesters, Bible study – held in groups small enough for full personal participation, and mixed in terms of age, sex, and background – was seen as a pivot within co-ordinated fortnightly programmes of themes related to particular Life Issues which the Church shared with the contemporary world, like Wealth, Poverty, Healing, Justice, Peace. Throughout there was a serious and continuous attempt, in study and in task-oriented groups, to find ways of helping women and men to cross the walls that divide people from one another causing failures of communication, alienation, and strife, while at the same time bringing inward reconciliation within the self and with God.

Hendrik Kraemer's *A Theology of the Laity*, published in 1958 opened up for many the need to look at the doctrine and structure of the Church afresh in the light of the whole people of God's calling to serve in the world. The Church, we were being reminded, was the laity, and the place of their obedience was the world. The picture of the Church was widening out. Often it had been restricted in practice to the clergy, and to others – paid or voluntary – who were directed by the ecclesiastical institution. Now there was a growing realisation that the Church included in practice many more. The Church was the whole people, and it had an identity, as a community, that was not to be confined within any one particular denominational frame or one habitually accepted theological system. The lay academies in Europe, and the retreat and study centres in Asia and Africa, bringing together individual Christians and groups of different traditions, pointed to what the Church as an open and potentially inclusive community was called to be.

Clearly what mattered most about the Church was not that people got the words right about it, but that in their lives they reflected its true purpose, and it was becoming ever more plain, that very many people who would not ordinarily be considered to belong to the community of Christ were doing that very thing. Many passages in the Bible would stop us sharply in our tracks if we were to make religious and ethical claims for ourselves or for our groups, and yet deny that right to others. In India Gandhi used often to make the point, quoting words of Christ: 'Not everyone who calls me "Lord, Lord" will enter the kingdom of heaven, but only those who do the will of my heavenly Father.' It would be an insensitive person who would not hear that challenge, and not recognise that the purpose of God is being fulfilled, even though the Church itself may often fail.

In addition to acknowledging the respect due to people and institutions outside the Churches, and of many nations and cultures, we were increasingly paying attention to the practices and ideas of religions other than our own. Whereas in 1910 – not so long ago – the disappearance of the great religions was being seriously discussed, if not being taken for granted, now, in 1972, that was no longer so. There were very few signs, if any, of the demise of the other religions, in fact there seemed a burgeoning of new life.

Although we were not slow to pick out weaknesses and errors in other religions arising, as we saw them, from basic perversions of the true, we could not at the same time ignore aspects of the true within them. We could at the same time see only too well distortions, contemporary and historical, in our own religious traditions, and be aware that there are and will be many more to which we are as yet blind.

It became important for us to recognise that Jesus himself was not Orthodox, Catholic, or Protestant, and that although born a Jew and brought up as a Jew, he took to himself the name of no religion, maintaining his own identity, the truly and fully Human within the Godhead – free and unbound.

The vision that we have before us is of a world transformed, with the whole human race brought together in freedom, in one perfect community, in which no part of the diverse richness of humanity, in culture, style, or language, will be lost, in which there will be no more sorrow or crying but one perfect joy, and in which all things will reflect the presence of God and give him glory. It is a vision of what is to be given, of what will be, but it is a reality that is to be grasped now and which in its making we are involved. It is Christ's own gift put into our hands as a foretaste, so that even now in this present time we praise him: Blessed be God, now and for ever. Amen.

Notes

*

Notes to Chapter 2

1. C. W. Ransom: *Renewal and Advance* (Edinburgh House Press, 1948), p 26 and *passim*.
2. 'The Era of Atomic Power' (Report of a Commission appointed by the British Council of Churches, 1946), p 7.
3. Emil Brunner: *Christianity and Civilisation* (Nisbet and Co. Ltd, 1948), volume l, p 4.
4. General Assembly (G. A.) (FMC, 1947), p 345.
5. Michael Edwardes: *Nehru* (Allen Lane, 1971), p 214.
6. John W. Sadiq: *Oslo* (1947), *IRM* (1948), pp 40-48.
7. M. M. Thomas: *Life and Work* (October 1947), p 180.
8. Neville Davidson: 'Four Churches lose their Life – and preserve it', in *Life and Work* (1947), p 196.
9. G. A. (ICRC, 1948), p 48f. Deliverance 3, p 56.
10. Ibid, p 51.
11. G. A. (FMC, 1935), p 615.
12. G. A. (FMC, 1947), p 346.
13. G. A. (FMC, 1948), pp 349-354.
14. G. A. (FMC, 1947), p 345.
15. K. Baago: *A History of the National Christian Council of India, 1914-1964* (NCCI, 1965), p 74.
16. Ibid, p 76, note.
17. FMC 8377 and Appendix III (July 1946).
18. FMC 8799 (April 1947).
19. G. A. (FMC, 1948), p 351f.
20. Report of the Jerusalem Meeting of the IMC, vol. III, pp 195-204, cf p 12f.
21. FMC (July 1946), Appendix III, C3 (a) (iv), and B2 (c).
22. Stephen Neill: *A History of Christian Missions* (Penguin Books, 1964), p 527.
23. FMC 8845 (April 1947).
24. Rajah b. Manikam: 'The Effect of War on the Missionary Task of the Church in India', in *IRM* (1947), pp 175-190.
25. Baago, op cit, p 70f.
26. Ibid, p 73.
27. FMC 7957 (October 1945); Appendix I and II (July 1946); and G. A. (1947), pp 357-360.
28. John Stewart, quoted in Austin Fulton: *Through Earthquake Wind and Fire* (Saint Andrew Press, 1967), p 186.
29. FMC 8323 (July 1946).
30. FMC 8701 (February 1947).
31. W. Y. Chen: 'The State of the Church in China', in *IRM* (1947), pp 141-152.
32. Fulton: op cit, p 218; cf *Commission Report on Manchuria*, Appendix I of FMC (July 1946), p 91.
33. Ibid, p 208f, p 217, cf pp 41-43.
34. FMC 9213 (December 1947).
35. G. A. (1948), FMC, p 356 f; and Fulton: op cit, p 221f.
36. Mrs Monteith: 'Where the War-Drums throb no longer', in *OL* (January 1947), p 3.
37. G. A. (1947), p 360f; Basil Davidson: *Which Way Africa?* (Penguin, 1964), p 63f.
38. FMC (April 1947), Appendix I, p 419.
39. Ibid, p 416.
40. FMC (July 1946), Appendix IV, p 108ff.
41. Ibid, p 407f.
42. FMC (April 1947), Appendix I, p 402 and p 415, G. A. (1947), p 363.
43. FMC (February 1948), Appendix II, p 330.

44. Ibid, 334ff.
45. Ibid, p 321ff.
46. Ibid, p 323.
47. Ibid, p 324 ff
48. Ibid, p 326ff
49. Ibid, p 332
50. *Life and Work* (March 1947), p 54.
51. FMC (February 1948), Appendix II, p 337f.
52. Ibid, p 339f.
53. R. H. W. Shepherd: Lovedale: 'A Faith for the Whole of Life', in *OL* (July 1948), p 195f.
54. G. S. Gunn: 'Such a Time as this', *CAAN* (October 1945), p 25f.
55. Gunn: 'A Time for Greatness', ibid (October 1947), p 25ff.
56. G.A. (1947), transcription, p 107f.
57. J. W. C. Dougall: 'Education and Evangelism', in *IRM* (1947), 318f.
58. G.A. (1947), p 373.

Notes to Chapter 3

1. A. Campbell-Johnson: *Mission with Mountbatten* (Robert Hale Ltd, 1951), p 280.
2. *OL* (April 1948), p 182.
3. General Assembly (G. A.) (1953), Church and Nation, p 336f.
4. G.A. (1952 Transcript), p 264.
5. Roland Oliver and J. D. Page: *A Short History of Africa* (Pelican, 1986), p 256.
6. Adrian Hastings: *A History of African Christianity* (Cambridge, 1979), p 16.
7. John A. Mackay: *The Missionary Legacy to the Church Universal*, in *IRM* (1948), p 25.
8. John Foster: 'Impressions of Amsterdam', in *CAAN* (December 1948), p 25f.
9. Richard Fox: *Reinhold Niebuhr* (Pantheon Books, 1985), p 234.
10. Hans Ruedi-Weber: *Asia and the Ecumenical Movement (1895-1961)* (SCM Press Ltd, 1966), p 233f.
11. Ibid, p 236.
12. J.W.C. Dougall: 'Younger Churches at Amsterdam', in *OL* (January 1949), p 18.
13. Ransom, op cit, p 174.
14. G.A. (FMC, 1952), p 350ff.
15. Ibid, p 354.
16. *The Missionary Obligation of the Church, Willingen, Germany* (Edinburgh House Press, 1952), p 40.
17. Ibid, p 2.
18. Ibid, p 3.
19. FMC 522 (July 1950).
20. FMC 9800 (December 1948); see also FMC 1079 (July 1951).
21. FMC 365 (February 1950), and Appendix I, p 263f.
22. FMC 1748 (December 1952).
23. *Report of the Foreign Mission Committee Delegation to India and Pakistan 1950-1951*, p 4.
24. Ibid, p 24; see also G. A. (FMC, 1950), p 374.
25. Ibid, p 40f.
26. Ibid, p 6f.
27. Ibid, p 57; see also G. A. (1952), p 360.
28. Austin Fulton: *Through Earthquake, Wind and Fire* (Saint Andrew Press, 1967), p 223f.
29. Ibid, p 225.
30. Ibid, p 227.
31. FMC 7692 (October 1948).
32. Fulton: op cit, p 228; and FMC 9804 (December 1948).
33. FMC 9802 (December 1948).
34. FMC 9987 (April 1949).
35. Ibid.
36. FMC 9988 (April 1949).
37. G.A. (1949), p 356.
38. FMC 92 (July 1949).
39. FMC 93 (July 1949).
40. FMC 194 (October 1949).
41. FMC 228 (December 1949).
42. WWN (April 1950), p 4.
43. FMC 287 (December 1949).
44. FMC 588 (July 1950).
45. FMC 586 (July 1950).
46. Fulton: op cit, p 243.
47. WWN (October 1950), p 4.
48. FMC 681 (October 1950).
49. FMC 684 (October 1950).
50. FMC 863 (February 1951).
51. FMC 762 (December 1950).
52. FMC 967 (April 1951).
53. *OL* (April 1948), p 183.
54. FMC 9463 (April 1948).
55. G.A. 48 (FMC), p 358.
56. *OL* (January 1950), pp 3-5.
57. FMC 1286 (December 1951), and 1388 (February 1952).
58. FMC 135 (October 1949).

59. *OL* (April 1949), p 35f.
60. FMC 110 (July 1949).
61. FMC 205 (October 1949).
62. FMC 690 (October 1950).
63. FMC 9816 (December 1948).
64. FMC 1288 (December 1951).
65. FMC 1484 (April 1952).
66. FMC 1111 (July 1951).
67. G.A. (1949), p 362; FMC 9607 (July 1948), and 10,001 (April 1949).
68. FMC (April 1952), Appendix 1, pp 316-321.
69. FMC 1283 (December 1951), 1528 and 1582 (July 1952), 1678 (October 1952), 1714 (December 1952).
70. FMC 9 (May 1949).
71. FMC (April 1950), Appendix, pp 346-354.
72. Ibid, p 353f.
73. FMC 9228 (December 1947).
74. FMC 9492 (July 1948), and 10,011 (April 1949).
75. G.A. (1949), FMC p 365.
76. FMC 9472 (April 1948).
77. FMC 9473 (April 1948).
78. FMC 9718 (October 1948; Nat Library – Acc. 7548/305 B).
79. FMC 115 (July 1949; Nat Library – Acc. 7548/B 341).
80. FMC 212 (October 1949).
81. FMC 115 (July 1949).
82. FMC 694 (October 1950).
83. FMC 699 (October 1950).
84. FMC 2080 (July 1953).
85. FMC (February 1948), Appendix II, p 327.
86. FMC 9228 (December 1947).
87. FMC (February 1948), Appendix II, p 327.
88. FMC 115 (July 1949), 400 (February 1950), 607 (July 1950), 695 (October 1950), 776 (December 1950), and G.A. (1950), FMC, p 391.
89. G.A. (1951), FMC p 398.
90. G.A. (1949), FMC p 367f.
91. FMC 9822 (October 1948), 236 (December 1949), G.A. (1950), FMC p 389f.
92. FMC 1773 (December 1952); G.A. (1953), FMC, p 388.
93. G.A. (1949), FMC, p 367; G.A. (1950), FMC, p 391; G.A. (1951), FMC, p 408.
94. G.A. (1952), Church and Nation, p 317.
95. Kenneth McKenzie: 'Struggle for Power in Central Africa', in *OL,* May 1952, pp 27-29.
96. *Herald* 52, p 17.
97. WWN (September 1952), p 3.
98. G.A. (1953), Church and Nation, p 362.
99. G.A. (1952), Church and Nation, p 317f.
100. 'Spotlight in Central Africa', a pamphlet issued by the Edinburgh World Church Group.
101. FMC 1421 (April 1952).
102. G.A. (1953), Church and Nation, p 362.
103. G.A. (1952), transcript, p 249f.
104. G.A. (1952), Church and Nation, Deliverance 3(b).
105. R. McPherson: *The Presbyterian Church in Kenya* (1970), p 125, and *Kenya 1898-1948* (1948), p 45f.
106. FMC 9616 (July 1948).
107. FMC 487 (April 1950).
108. FMC 8799 (February 1947).
109. FMC 9908 (February 1949).
110. FMC 488 (April 1950).
111. Ibid.
112. FMC 9825 (December 1948), 986 (April 1951); WWN (April 1952), p 3.
113. FMC 9139 (October 1947).
114. FMC 118 (July 1949).
115. FMC 785 (December 1950).
116. FMC 1119 (July 1951).
117. McPherson: op cit, p 126; and Clive Irvin: 'It is happening in Kenya', in *OL,* (October 1949), pp 116-118.
118. Ibid, p 127.
119. Ibid, p 124.
120. FMC 1397 (February 1952); see also 9824 (December 1948) and 9908 (February 1949).
121. WWN (April 1951), p 1.
122. FMC 700 (October 1950), 1222 (December 1951).
123. FMC 1431 (April 1952).
124. McPherson, op cit, p 132.
125. G.A. (1952), Church and Nation Report, p 412.
126. G.A. (1952), transcript, p 84.
127. Ibid, p 147.
128. McPherson, op cit, p 116f.
129. FMC 1775 (December 1952).
130. G.A. (1949), Church and Nation, Deliverance, section 4, para 3.

131. *IRM*, vol. XXXIX (1950), p 52;
132. FMC 9810 (December 1948).
133. FMC 9604 (July 1948).
134. FMC 9327 (February 1948).
135. FMC 9327 (February 1948).
136. *OL* (October 1951), pp 91-95.
137. G.A. (1949), FMC, 360f; *OL* (April 1949), pp 47-49.
138. *OL* (January 1951), p 10f.
139. R. H.W. Shepherd: 'South Africa', in the *Sketches of the Field* series (1947), p 42; ibid, pp 29, 30.
140. R. H.W. Shepherd: *Lovedale, South Africa, 1984-1955,* p 137.
141. FMC 7927, 7928, 7929, 7930 (July 1945).
142. FMC 9509 (July 1948).
143. 'Jamaica', in *Sketches of the Field* series, p 25.
144. Ibid, p 39; 1127 (July 1951).
145. Ibid.
146. 8781 (February 1947), 9356 (February 1948), 623 (July 1950).
147. *Sketch of the Field*, p 34.
148. Ibid, p 30; Knox College's 25th Anniversary Souvenir Programme, p 3.
149. Ibid, p 29.
150. G.A. (1949), p 405; FMC 9729 (Oct 1948), 9832 (December 1948), 120 (July 1949), FMC 8756 (February 1947).
151. FMC 8430 (July 1946)
152. FMC 1126 (July 1951); FMC 1694, 1695 (October 1952); FMC 1778 (December 1952); FMC 9986 (April 1949).
153. FMC (July 1949), Appendix I, p 82.
154. FMC 1127 (July 1951); FMC 965, 966 (April 1951).
155. FMC 1127 (July 1951).
156. FMC 1778 (December 1952); FMC 1370 (February 1952).
157. *OL* (April 1950), pp 39-43.
158. Knox College 25th Anniversary Souvenir Programme, p 3.
159. Ibid, p 13.
160. P. W. R. Petrie: 'No Panel Patients Here', in *OL* (October 1947), p 115ff.
161. FMC 9986 (April 1949).
162. Bernard Walker: 'South Arabia Mission', in *Sketches of the Field*, p 23.
163. FMC 189 (18 October 1949); 965, 966 (17 April 1951).
164. WWN (October 1951), p 1.

165. FMC 1848 (17 February 1953).
166. G.A. 49, p 354.
167. G.A. 51, p 392.
168. FMC 8856 (April 1947).
169. Walker: ibid, p 30.
170. G.A. 50, p 385.
171. G.A. 49, p 354.
172. FMC 965 (17 April 1951).
173. FMC 9986 (19 April 1949).
174. FMC 475 (18 April 1950).
175. FMC 9586 (20 July 1948).
176. FMC 1191 (16 October 1951).
177. FMC 760 (December 1950)
178. FMC 1576 (15 July 1952).
179. John Baillie: Address seconding FMC Report to 1950 General Assembly, in *OL* (October 1950), pp 101-103; G.A. (1952), pp 366ff; Gunn: *CAAN* (October 1945), p 25.
180. G.A. (1952), p 366.
181. Ibid, p 368f.
182. G.A. (1947), GFC7, p 73, and Deliverance 3.
183. G.A. (1950), FMC, p 395f; and Deliverance 9, p 439.
184. G.A. (1950), HB, p 253.
185. FMC 522 (July 1950).
186. FMC 1306 (February 1952).
187. Malcolm Duncan: 'As Students see it', in *OL* (May 1952), p 34.
188. FMC (July 1949), Appendix II, p 94; and G.A. (1949), Maintenance of the Ministry Report, Deliverance 2.
189. G.A. (1952), p 370.

Notes to Chapter 4

1. G. A. (1953), Church and Nation, Supplementary Report, pp 361-364.
2. G. A. (1959), Committee Anent Central Africa, pp 663-676; Supplementary Report pp 667-682; and Appendix x.I, Statement of the Synod of Blantyre of the CCAP concerning the Present State of Union in Nyasaland (March 1958), pp 684-687.
3. Graham Leach: *South Africa* (Methuen: London, 1989), p 104.
4. Ibid, p 121f.
5. Pranay Gupte: *India: The Challenge of Change* (Methuen: London, 1989), p 316f; and Tariq Ali: *The Nehrus and*

the Gandhis (Pan Books Ltd, London, 1985), p 94.

6. Michael Edwardes: *Nehru* (Allen Lane, Penguin: London, 1971), p 265.

7. Stuart Schram: *Mao Tse-tung* (Penguin, London, 1968), p 282.

8. G.A. (1956), Church and Nation, p 346

9. David Thomson, *England in the Twentieth Century* (Penguin Books, London, 1968), p 284.

10. G. A. (53 ICR), pp 60-62; ibid, p 98.

11. E. C. Bhatty: *Christ the Hope of Asia* (IRM, 1955), p 93ff.

12. Op. cit., p 94.

13. Ibid, p 98.

14. G.A. (55 ICR), p 68 ff

15. J.W. C. Dougall, in *WWN* (November 1954), p 3.

16. Charles Ranson, in Plenary Address, WCC Assembly, Evanston, quoted in *Christian Century*, (22 September, 1954), p 1133.

17. Evanston Assembly Report, Section II, *The Evangelizing Church*, II.8.

18. *Christian Century* (22 September, 1954), *Two Continents Arrive*, p 1134.

19. FMC 4904 (21 October 1958).

20. G.A. (FMC, 1954), p 371.

21. G. A. (1957), ICR Deliverance 3. i-iv, p 72; and Appendix A, a Joint Report, 6 January 1957, see pp 76-90.

22. G. A. (1957), FMC, p 443; FMC 428615 (October 1957); G.A. (1959) ICR, Deliverance 6, p 92; G. A. (1960) FMC, p 440; Kellock, James: 'Seven Churches Coming Together in North India', in *OL* (October 1957), p 91ff.

23. G.A. (1957), ICR, Appendix V, p 97f.

24. G.A. (1959), ICR, Deliverance 3(b), p 90.

25. G. A. (1960), FMC, p 440f.

26. G. A. (1957), FMC, p 429, 439, 440, 442, 444.

27. G. A. (1956), FMC Deliverance 15, p 456.

28. Gwenyth Hubble: *The Ghana Assembly, A Report on Group Discussion*, in *IRM* (April 1958), p 144.

29. G. A. (1957), FMC Deliverance 8.

30. FMC 8799 (15 April 1947).

31. FMC 1748 (8) (16 July 1952).

32. FMC 1751 (16 December 1952); 2555 (20 July 1954).

33. FMC 2223 (15 December 1953).

34. FMC 3202 (18 October 1955); 3749 (16 October 1956).

35. FMC 4187 (16 July 1957).

36. FMC 4529 (18 February 1958).

37. FMC 753 (2) (19 December 1950).

38. FMC 4524 (18 February 1958).

39. FMC 3808 (18 December 1956).

40. FMC 4674 (18 April 1958).

41. FMC 5254 (21 April 1959).

42. FMC 5507 (20 October 1959).

43. FMC 5810 (19 April 1960).

44. FMC 3221 (18 October 1955); 3329 (20 December 1955).

45. FMC 4811 (15 July 1958).

46. Study Paper prepared by George More.

47. Minutes of Iona Community Meeting in Nagpur.

48. Young: op. cit., p 97.

49. Narrative Report of Commission.

50. FMC 5399 (21 July 1959).

51. FMC 4795 (15 July 1958).

52. FMC 4907 (21 October 1958).

53. FMC 1951 (21 April 1953).

54. FMC 2055 (21 July 1953).

55. FMC 4795 (15 July 1958).

56. FMC 2055 (21 July 1953).

57. FMC 2751 (21 December 1954); 2865 (15 February 1955).

58. FMC 5582 (15 December 1959).

59. FMC 1275 (18 December 1951); WWN (March 1954), p 3; *The Herald*, 1954, p 7; 1957, p 22.

60. FMC 1142 (16 October 1951).

61. J. Fleming: 'How we are "Telling Malaya"', in *OL* (January 1956), p 3 ff; WWN (November 1954), p 4; (March 1955), p 3; *The Herald* (1954), p 7.

62. FMC 3443 (21 February 1956).

63. FMC 4261 (15 October 1957); *WWN* (December 1957), p 4.

64. G. A. (1959), FMC, p 438f.

65. G. A. (1960), FMC, p 458f.

66. Hans-Ruedi Weber: *Asia and the Ecumenical Movement* (SCM Press Ltd: London, 1966), p 289, note.

67. FMC 2184 (15 December 1953).

68. FMC 2235 (15 December 1953); 2075 (21 July 1953).

69. FMC 2345 (16 February 1954).

70. *WWN* (March 1954), p 3.

71. FMC 2684 (19 October 1954).
72. C. P. Moir: 'Krobo' Development', in OL (May 1953), p 38.
73. G. A. (FMC 1955), p 417.
74. Ibid, p 418.
75. FMC 4372 (17 December 1957); 4135 (16 July 1967).
76. FMC 2776 (21 December 1954).
77. FMC 2878 (15 February 1955).
78. FMC 3455 (21 February 1956).
79. FMC 3578 (20 May 1956); 3674 (17 July 1956).
80. FMC 4204 (10 July 1957); 4419 (17 December 1957); 5420 (21 July 1959).
81. G. A. (FMC 1956), p 403.
82. Ibid, p 407.
83. Ibid.
84. WWN (March 1957), p 1.
85. FMC 3894 (19 February 1957).
86. FMC 3455 (21 February 1956).
87. FMC 4205 (16 July 1957); 4789 (15 July 1958).
88. G. A. (FMC 1958), p 498.
89. G. A. (FMC 1960), p 461f.
90. FMC 5419 (21 July 1959); 5461 (20 October 1959); 5327 (21 July 1959).
91. FMC 2900 (19 April 1955).
92. FMC 2233 (15 December 1953).
93. FMC 3346 (20 December 1955).
94. FMC 3669 (17 July 1956).
95. G. A. (FMC 1958), p 498.
96. FMC 2070 (21 July 1953); G. A. (FMC 1955), p 423f, p xii, Acts of the General Assembly XXIV; 'Rise of the Eastern Nigerian Church', in OL (October 1955), p 92.
97. FMC 3669 (17 July 1956).
98. FMC 5542 (20 October 1959).
99. FMC 3777 (16 October 1956); Sir Francis Ibiam in 'Concerns of the All-Africa Conference', in OL (May 1958), p 62.
100. FMC 2575 (20 July 1954).
101. FMC 2577 (20 July 1954).
102. FMC 2770, 2775 (21 December '54).
103. FMC 3111 (19 July 1955).
104. FMC 3774 (16 October 1956).
105. FMC 5060 (16 December 1958).
106. FMC 5542 (20 October 1959).
107. FMC 3341 (20 December 1955).
108. G. A. (FMC 1957), p 427.
109. FMC 1887 (21 April 1953).
110. Transcript of General Assembly (1953), p 141.
111. Op. cit., p 329, from address of the Convener of Church and Nation, delivering his Report.
112. Ibid, p 345. Dr George MacLeod speaking to an amendment.
113. Ibid, p 352. Rev. Ian Fairweather speaking to an amendment.
114. FMC 1982 (27 May 1953) (3).
115. The Herald (1954), p 10.
116. FMC 2244 (15 December 1953)
117. FMC 2783 (21 December 1954).
118. FMC 3243 (18 October 1955).
119. FMC 3245 (18 October 1955).
120. FMC 3585 (30 May 1956); and 3784 (16 October 1956).
121. FMC 4334 (6)(b) (15 October 1957).
122. FMC 5288 (21 April 1959).
123. G. A. (FMC 1956), p 409f.
124. FMC 3354 (20 December 1955).
125. FMC 4430 (17 December 1957).
126. FMC 4544 (18 February 1958).
127. FMC 5551 (20 October 1959).
128. FMC 2693 (19 October 1954) (7)(b).
129. FMC 3561 (17 April 1956); and 3874 (18 December 1956).
130. FMC 4218 (16 July 1957).
131. FMC 4963 (21 October 1958).
132. FMC 5634 (15 December 1959).
133. W.V. Stone: 'The Alice Movement', in OL (January 1959), p 23f.
134. WWN (September 1956), p 2.
135. G. A. (1956), p 403; G. A. (1959), p 431; and Hastings, op. cit., p 125.
136. G. A. (1958), p 490.
137. G. A. (1956), p 413.
138. G. A. (1953), typescript, FMC Convener's Address, p 140.
139. FMC 1967 (April 1953).
140. FMC 1971 (April 1953).
142. FMC (19 April 1960); Appendix, p 314f; and letter of the R. K. Orchard (15 April 1953) – ACC 7548 B 344.
143. FMC 3245 (8) (18 October 1955).
144. FMC 3117 (19 July 1955).
145. FMC 4430 (17 December 1957).
146. FMC 4843 (15 July 1958).
147. FMC 4335 (15 October 1957).
148. FMC 5097 (2)(a) (17 February 1959).
149. FMC 5284 (21 April 1959).
150. FMC 5097 (2)(b) (17 February 1959); Fergus Macpherson: 'Fifty Years' Story in Northern Rhodesia', in OL (January 1956), p 11ff.
151. FMC 4430 (17 December 1957).
152. FMC 4714 (15 April 1958).

153. FMC 4333 (15 October 1957).
154. G. A. (FMC 1954), p 390; see also *The Herald* (1954), p 9.
155. FMC 5097 (17 February 1959).
156. FMC 5284 (21 April 1959).
157. FMC 5437 (21 July 1959).
158. FMC 5558 (20 October 1959).
159. FMC 3117 (19 July 1955).
160. FMC 3679 (17 July 1956).
161. FMC 3787 (16 October 1956).
162. G. A. (FMC 1958), Deliverance 9.
163. G. A. (1958), typescript, p 855.
164. G. A. (1958), Church and Nation part of Deliverance 5.
165. FMC 4850 (15 July 1958).
166. G. A. (1959), FMC Supplementary Report (May 1959), 'Situation in Nyasaland'.
167. G. A. (1959), Committee Anent Central Africa, Deliverances 4, 5, 9, 10, p 683.
168. G. A. (1959), typescript, p 818f.
169. FMC 5327 (21 July 1959); 5461 (3) (20 October 1959).
170. FMC 3786 (16 October 1956).
171. FMC 4336 (15 October 1957).
172. FMC 4430 (17 December 1957).
173. FMC 5425 (21 July 1959).
174. FMC 4550 (18 February 1958).
175. FMC 4962 (21 October 1958).
176. FMC 5170 (17 February 1959).
177. FMC 5436 (21 July 1959).
178. FMC 5281 (21 April 1959).
179. FMC 2265 (16 February 1954).
180. G. A. (1954), Church and Nation, p 333.
181. Dr Mary Shannon: 'A New Life for Kikuyu Women', in *OL* (January 1958), p 29ff.
182. R. Macpherson: op. cit., p 137; FMC 2250 (15 December 1953).
183. The Very Rev. David Steel, from a lecture given at Dundee University in February 1990.
184. G. A. (1953), Church and Nation, p 389.
185. FMC 2164 (20 October 1953).
186. FMC 2353 (16 February 1954).
187. G. A. (1955) Church and Nation, p 358f.
188. Ibid, p 419; see further FMC 2694 (9 October 1954); 2888 (15 February 1955).
189. G. A. (FMC 1956), p 417, Church and Nation, p 352.
190. FMC 3254 (18 October 1955).
191. FMC 2389 (20 April 1954).
192. FMC 2694 (14 October 1954); 2888 (15 February 1955).
193. FMC 3356 (20 December 1955).
194. FMC 5078 (16 December 1958).
195. FMC 3015 (1 June 1955).
196. FMC 3567 (17 April 1956); G. A. (1957), C and C, p 492.
197. FMC 4338 (15 October 1957).
198. Ibid; and G. A. (FMC 1957), p 432.
199. FMC 5292 (21 April 1959).
200. FMC 3878 (18 December 1956).
201. FMC 3128, 3129 (3)(a) (19 July 1955); 2098 (20 October 1953).
202. FMC 3129 (3)(c) (19 July 1955).
203. FMC 5292 (21 April 1959).
204. FMC 1594 (15 July 1952).
205. FMC 2165 (20 October 1953); 2790 (21 December 1954).
206. Ibid; and FMC 2888 (15 February 1955).
207. FMC 2168 (20 October 1953).
208. FMC 1119 (17 July 1951).
209. FMC 2789 (21 December 1954); 3128 (19 July 1955).
210. FMC 4098 (16 April 1957).
211. FMC 4558 (18 February 1958); *WWN* (January 1960), p 2; *The Herald* (1959), p 22.
212. FMC 4433 (17 December 1957); R. Macpherson: *The Presbyterian Church in Kenya* (Nairobi, 1970), p 140f.
213. R. H. W. Shepherd: *Lovedale South Africa* (Lovedale: 1971), p 136.
214. G. A. (1955), Church and Nation, p 360; Trevor Huddleston: *Naught for Your Comfort* (Collins, Fountain, 1977); and Alan Paton: *Journey Continued* (OUP, 1990), p 138f.
215. G. A. (1953), Church and Nation, p 342.
216. Michael Bogle: 'Racial Policy in South Africa, The Bantu Education Act on Missions', in *OL* (January 1955), p 11ff.
217. FMC 2670 (19 October 1954); Michael Bogle: 'The Bantu Education Act on Missions', in *OL* (January 1955), p 11ff.
218. FMC 2711 (21 December 1954), Appendix 1, paras 5 and 6.
219. G. A. (1955) Church and Nation Deliverance 3(c).
220. FMC 3447 (21 February 1956).

221. FMC 3105 (19 July 1955); Shepherd: op. cit., p 147.
222. FMC 3104 (19 July 1955).
223. FMC 4822, 4823, 4824 (15 July 1958).
224. FMC 3666 (17 July 1956).
225. FMC 4627 (15 April 1958).
226. FMC 3602 (17 July 1956); 4035 (16 April 1957).
227. FMC 5413 (21 July 1959; 5530 (20 October 1959); R. H. W. Shepherd: 'Red Letter Day at Tugela', in OL (January 1956), p 19ff.
228. Hastings: op. cit., p 104.
229. FMC 3550 (17April 1956).
230. FMC 4199 (16 July 1957); Leslie Blackwell: *Fort Hare in the Balance,* in OL (Jan 1959), p 17f.
231. FMC 5619 (15 December 1959).
232. FMC 1979 (21 April 1953); 2698 (19 Oct 1954), Appendix II.
233. FMC 2793 (21 December 1954).
234. FMC 3133 (19 July 1955).
235. *The Herald* (1954), p 2; and Knox College Anniversary Souvenir Programme, p 16, 36.
236. Souvenir Programme, p 16f.
237. 'Knox After Ten Years', in OL (October 1957), p 74; *The Herald* (1957), p 4.
238. FMC 2601 (20 July 1954); WWN (December 1958), p 1f.
239. FMC 2891 (15 February 1955).
240. FMC 4855 (15 July 1958).
241. FMC 3011 (19 April 1955).
242. FMC 3134 (19 July 1955).
243. FMC 3255 (18 October 1955).
244. FMC 3359 (20 December 1955).
245. FMC 4439 (17 December 1957).
246. FMC 4720 (15 April 1958).
247. FMC 1948 (21 April 1953).
248. George Morris: 'Towards the Heart of Arabia', in OL (October 1956), p 87ff.
249. *The Herald* (1953), p 13.
250. FMC 2458 (20 April 1954); *The Herald* (1954), p 7.
251. FMC 2458 (20 April 1954).
252. *The Herald* (1955), p 11.
253. Ibid: (59), p 12.
254. FMC 5159, 5161 (17 February 1959).
255. FMC 4819 (15 July 58); 4935 (21 October 1958); 5057 (16 Dec 1958).
256. FMC 5056 (16 December 1958); 5159 (17 February 1959).
257. G.A. (1954), p 384f.
258. G.A. (1953), GFC, p 80.
259. G.A. (1953), GFC, p 80.
260. G.A. (1954), GFC, p 78.
261. G.A. (1955), pp 421f, 425f, 458, Deliverance 4.
262. G.A. (1958), GFC, Appendix IV, pp 152-157.
263. FMC 4995 (16 December 1958).
264. G.A. (1954), p 382 f; G.A. (1957), p 429.
265. Based on contemporary notes written in Nagpur by David Lyon.
266. G.A. (1956), p 413f.
267. David Lyon, notes as above.
268. Report of the Christian Missionary Activities Enquiry Committee, Madhya Pradesh (1956), volume I (published Nagpur), p 154, *et passim*; G.A. (1957), p 429.
269. G.A. (1958), p 504.

Notes to Chapter 5

1. Duncan Sandys, quoted in G. A. (1962), Church and Nation, p 372.
2. J. E. L. Newbigin: 'The Summons to Christian Mission Today', in *International Review of Missions* (April 1959), p 178.
3. Ibid, p 183.
4. G.A. (FMC 1960), p 441.
5. Newbigin: ibid; G.A. (FMC 1960), p 442f.
6. M. M. Thomas: *Ecumenical Review,* volume XIV (July 1962), no 4, p 488.
7. Cecil Northcott, quoting from the *Report on Witness, The Christian Century,* an. 10 (1962), p 56.
8. Joseph Sittler: *The Ecumenical Review,* ibid, p 501.
9. G.A. (1962), ICRC, p 69.
10. Bishop Sadiq: *New Delhi* (1961), *International Review of Missions* (1962), p 149f.
11. Robert Latham: *God for All Men* (Edinburgh House Press: London, 1964), p 73f.
12. G.A. (FMC 1964), p 437.
13. Latham, ibid, p 58f.
14. Ibid, p 83.
15. G. A. (FMC 1958), Addendum to Deliverance, p 531.

16. G. A. (1959) Special Committee Anent Overseas Work, Deliverance 2, p 793.
17. G.A. (1963), ibid; and Appendix, pp 733ff.
18. Report of St Andrews Consultation (1965), pp 1-4.
19. Ibid, p 14.
20. Ibid, p 71ff.
21. Ibid, p 19f.
22. Ibid, p 71.
23. Ibid, p 84f.
24. Ibid, p 87.
25. Ian Paterson, notes on visit to India and Pakistan, p 2.
26. D. M. Kennedy: Historic Decision on Church Union, in *The United Church Review* (December 1962), p 277.
27. FMC 5810 (19 April 1960).
28. FMC 7913 (17 December 1963).
29. FMC 518 (19 January 1965).
30. FMC 1358 (19 April 1966).
31. FMC 1670 (18 October 1966).
32. FMC 5653 (16 February 1960).
33. FMC 6361 (18 April 1961).
34. *Renewal and Advance*, published by CLS, Madras (1963), p 194.
35. FMC 8095 (21 April 1964); FMC 7984 (18 February 1964); FMC, 21 April 1964), volume XXXV, p 310f.
36. W. G. Young, autobiography, in draft form, p 163; FMC 7408 (19 February 1963).
37. FMC 7403 (19 February 1963).
38. FMC 7293 (18 December 1962); FMC 7641 (16 July 1963).
39. FMC (16 July 1963), vol. XXXV, p 85.
40. FMC 7169 (16 October 1962).
41. FMC 875 (20 July 1965).
42. FMC 1365 (19 April 1966).
43. G.A. (1961), p 483.
44. Latham, op. cit., p 61ff.
45. *The Story of Serampore*, published by Serampore College Council, Serampore (1960), p 90.
46. FMC (20 February 1962), volume XXXIII, p 255.
47. Latham, op. cit., p 65 ff; *Reports for the 16th Triennial Assembly of the NCCI*, pp 28-36.
48. FMC 160 (21 July 1964).
49. G.A. (1961), p 484.
50. G.A. (1963), p 441f.
51. Overseas Work of the Church of Scotland (1964), p 30.
52. Ibid, p 30f.
53. FMC 539 (19 January 1965).
54. FMC 894 (20 July 1965).
55. G.A. (1965), p 467.
56. FMC 6487 (18 July 1961).
57. FMC 7818 (15 October 1963).
58. FMC 6075 (18 October 1960).
59. FMC 5548 (20 October 1959); 5623 (15 December 1959).
60. FMC 6647 (17 October 1961); 6748 (19 December 1961).
61. FMC 7336 (18 December 1962).
62. FMC 1632 (18 October 1966).
63. G.A. (1961), p 473.
64. G.A. (1961), p 486.
65. FMC 5976 (19 July 1960).
66. G.A. (1964), p 430.
67. Overseas Work of the Church of Scotland: Ghana (1966), p 40f; ibid (1964), p 14.
69. Ibid (1967), 36f.
70. FMC 7102 (17 July 1962).
71. FMC (21 April 1964), in *News from the Fields*, p 314.
72. G.A. (1965), p 376.
73. FMC 6536 (18 July 1961); OC 715 (20 April 1965).
74. FMC 6539 (18 July 1961); 7227 (16 October 1962).
75. FMC 7745 (15 October 1963); *News from the Fields*, p 148.
76. G.A. (1964), ICRC, p 68.
77. OC 1203 (18 January 1966).
78. FMC (1962), *News from the Fields*, p 202ff.
79. G.A. (1964), p 436.
80. Hastings: op. cit., p 152.
81. Paul Johnson: *A History of the Modern World*, p 513.
82. FMC (October 1961), *News from the Fields*, p 160; G.A. 1962, p 452
83. FMC (February 1963), ibid, p 279.
84. FMC 6070 (18 October 1960).
85. FMC 6097 (20 December 1960).
86. FMC 6205, 6289 (21 February 1961).
87. G.A. (1961), p 466.
88. FMC 6322 (18 April 1961).
89. FMC (19 April 1960), Appendix, p 313f.
90. FMC 6530 (July 1961); 7097 (17 July 1962); 7695 (16 July 1963).
91. FMC 6288 (21 February 1961); 5973 (19 July 1960).

92. G.A. (1962), p 462.
93. FMC 7822 (15 October 1963).
94. G.A. (1963), p 437.
95. FMC 8024 (18 February 1964).
96. OC 851 (20 July 1965).
97. OC 1006 (19 and 20 October 1965).
98. OC 1152 (18 January 1966).
99. OC 1376 (19 April 1966).
100. OC 1628 (18 October 1966)
101. FMC (16 February 1960), p 255.
102. FMC 6872 (20 February 1962).
103. G. A. (1960), Committee Anent Central Africa Report, Typescript of Address to Assembly, pp 395.
104. Ibid, pp 377-380.
105. Ibid, pp 358-370.
106. Ibid, pp 370-377.
107. G.A. (1961), p 737.
108. G.A. (1963), p 654.
109. Hastings: op. cit., p 156f; OC 380 (20 October 1964); Parrinder: *Religion in Africa* (Penguin, 1969), p 157.
110. G.A. (1965) OC 368; OC 733 (20 April 1965).
111. OC 389 (20 October 1964).
112. OC 737 (20 April 1965); Hastings: op. cit., p 161f.
113. OC 1479 (19 July 1966); 6654 (17 October 1961).
114. FMC 5728 (16 February 1960).
115. FMC 6081 (18 October 1960); 6654 (17 October 1961).
116. FMC 7339 (18 December 1962).
117. FMC 8140 (21 April 1964).
118. FMC (17 July 1962), *News from the Fields*, p 83.
119. FMC 7103 (17 July 1962).
120. FMC 7553 (16 April 1963).
121. OC 1637 (18 October 1966).
122. FMC (19 April 1960), Appendix, p 315.
123. FMC 6546 (18 July 1960).
124. FMC 5851 (19 April 1960); 6082 (18 October 1960).
125. FMC 7107 (17 July 1962).
126. OC 389 (20 October 1964).
127. FMC 6082 (18 October 1960).
128. G.A. (1962), p 468; FMC 6546 (18 July 1961).
129. FMC 6546 (18 July 1961).
130. FMC (20 February 1962), *News from the Fields*, p 256.
131. FMC 6546 (18 July 1961); 6873 (20 February 1962).
132. FMC 7841 (15 October 1963).
133. OWCS (1966), p 38.
134. OC 1059 (19 and 20 October 1965).
135. OWCS (1967), p 30.
136. OC 1058 (19 and 20 October 1965).
137. OC 1638 (18 October 1966).
138. OC 1385 (19 April 1966).
139. FMC 6085 (18 October 1960).
140. FMC 6407 (18 April 1961).
141. FMC 6659 (17 October 1961).
142. FMC 6407 (18 April 1961).
143. FMC 7106 (17 July 1962); G. A. (1966), OC, p 504.
144. FMC 7835 (15 October 1963).
145. OC 1209 (18 January 1966).
146. FMC 5978 (19 July 1960).
147. FMC 6085 (18 October 1960).
148. MC 6659 (17 October 1961).
149. FMC (20 February 1962), *News from the Fields*.
150. FMC (17 July 1962), *News from the Fields*.
151. OC 1059 (19-20 October 1965).
152. OC 738 (20 April 1965).
153. FMC 7932 (17 December 1963).
154. FMC (19 December 1961), *News from the Fields*.
155. FMC 7342 (18 December 1962).
156. FMC 7453 (19 February 1963).
157. FMC 7932 (17 December 1963).
158. FMC 6185 (20 December 1960).
159. FMC 6762 (19 December 1961).
160. G. A. (1964) Church and Nation, p 399ff.
161. FMC (18 October 1960), *News from the Fields*.
162. FMC (17 October 1961), *News from the Fields*.
163. FMC 6550 (18 July 1961).
164. Hastings: op. cit., p 151.
165. FMC (19 April 1960), Appendix, Policy in Education (Africa and Jamaica).
166. FMC 6185 (20 December 1960).
167. FMC 6414 (18 April 1961).
168. FMC 6762 (19 December 1961).
169. FMC 7342 (18 December 1962).
170. FMC 7453 (19 February 1963).
171. OC 741 (20 April 1965).
172. OC 703 (20 April 1965).
173. OC 1063 (19-20 October 1965).
174. FMC 6761 (19 December 1961).
175. FMC 7342 (18 December 1962).
176. FMC 7747 (15 October 1963).
177. G. A. (FMC 1960), p 459; FMC Deliverance 13, p 500.

178. Hastings: op. cit., p 104.
179. FMC 5828 (19 April 1960).
180. G. A. (1960), Church and Nation, p 417.
181. G. A. (FMC 1961), p 478; Hastings: op. cit., p 145; Paton: op. cit., pp 213-218.
182. FMC, *News from the Fields* (21 February 1961).
183. Hastings: ibid, p 105.
184. Ibid, p 146.
185. G. A. (1961), ICRC, p 67.
186. *News from the Fields* (16 February 1960).
187. FMC 6163 (20 December 1960).
188. FMC 6457 (18 July 1961)
189. *Overseas Work of the Church of Scotland* (1964), p 18; OC 7688 (16 July 1963).
190. FMC 5619 (15 December 1959).
191. FMC 5719 (16 February 1960).
192. FMC 6163 (20 December 1960).
193. FMC 6287 (21 February 1961).
194. FMC 6527 (17 October 1961).
195. FMC 7435 (19 February 1963).
196. OC 704 (20 April 1965).
197. *Overseas Work of the Church of Scotland* (1967), p 27.
198. FMC (19 April 1960), Appendix, Policy in Education.
199. FMC 7688 (16 July 1963).
200. OC 176 (21 July 1964).
201. OC 8135 (21 April 1964).
202. OC 176 (21 July 1964).
203. *Overseas Work of the Church of Scotland* (1965), p 44.
204. OC 6552 (18 July 1961).
205. OC 6418 (18 April 1961).
206. OC 6417 (18 April 1961).
207. OC 395 (20 October 1964).
208. G. A. (FMC 1962), p 469; FMC (19 December 1961), *News from the Fields*, p 202.
209. G. A. (1962), Church and Nation, p 372ff.
210. Survey of the year, in *IRM* (January 1961), p 66; FMC (19 July 1960), *News from the Fields.*
211. FMC (18 October 1960), *News from the Fields,* p 141.
212. FMC 6553 (18 July 1961).
213. OC 192 (21 July 1964); 394 (20 October 1964).
214. Jean Davidson and Lewis Davidson: *Man of Vision and Action,* published

Culross (1992), p 89; Knox College Anniversary Souvenir, p 18.
215. OC 1007 (19-20 October 1965); OWCS (1966), p 7.
216. FMC 5096 (17 February 1959); 5616 (15 December 1959).
217. G. A. (FMC 1961), p 480.
218. OWCS (1965), p 37; (1964), p 20.
219. FMC 6162 (20 December 1960).
220. FMC 6160 (20 December 1960).
221. FMC 6524 (18 July 1961).
222. FMC 6274 (21 February 1961).
223. FMC 6388 (18 April 1961).
224. FMC 6523 (18 July 1961).
225. FMC 6630 (17 October 1961).
226. FMC 6854 (20 February 1962).
227. FMC 7089 (17 July 1962).
228. FMC 7209 (16 October 1962).
229. FMC 7328 (18 December 1962).
230. FMC 7431 (19 February 1963).
231. FMC 7542 (16 April 1962).
232. FMC 8127, 8128 (21 April 1964).
233. FMC 8131 (21 April 1964).
234. OC 363 (20 October 1964).
235. OC 697 (20 April 1965).
236. OC 1514 (19 July 1966).
237. OC 975 (19-20 October 1965).
238. Ibid; OC 1187 (18 January 1966); G. A. (1966), OC, p 500f.
239. 1327 (19 April 1966).
240. 1515 (19 July 1966).
241. G. A. (1967), OC p 594.
242. G. A. (1957), General Finance Committee, p 108f, pp 122-125.
243. G. A. (1958), ibid, pp 152-157.
244. G. A. (1961), ibid, p 89.
245. G. A. (1960), ibid, p 91.
246. G. A. (1961 and 1967), Committee on General Administration, p 26 and 20.
247. G. A. (1967), OC, p 619.
248. G. A. (1961 and 1967), FMC and OC, p 498 and p 631.
249. G. A. 1962, Church and Nation, pp 393-395; G. A. (1963), pp 370-372; see also Ferguson: *Scotland, 1689 to the Present* (Mercat Press: Edinburgh, 1987), p 392.

Notes to Chapter 6

1. Malcolm S. Adiseshiah: *Let my Country Awake* (Unesco, 1970), p 21.
2. Harold Wilson: *The Labour Govern-*

ment 1964-1970 (Wiedenfeld and Nicholson: London, 1971).

3. G.A. (1968), Church and Nation, pp 147, 149.

4. Alan Geyer: 'Old and New at Uppsala', in *The Christian Century* (21 August 1968), p 1032.

5. The Uppsala Report, p 45.

6. James Baldwin: 'White Racism or World Community?', in *ER,* volume XX, p 372.

7. Alan Geyer: op. cit., p 1033.

8. Baldwin: ibid.

9. Lesslie Newbigin: G.A. (1969), p 614.

10. G.A. (1970), Church and Nation, p 131.

11. Ibid, OC, p 512f.

12. G.A. (1971), Church and Nation, p 176.

13. OC 2278 (17 October 1967).

14. Overseas Work of the Church of Scotland (1968), p 36.

15. Ibid (1969), p 34.

16. OC 3638 (16 December 1969).

17. G.A. (1970), OC, p 503.

18. OC 5022 (11 July 1972).

19. Overseas Work of the Church of Scotland (1970), p 36.

20. OC 3382 (8 July 1969); G.A. (1968), OC, p 574; G.A. (1970), OC, p 502.

21. OC 3948 (7 July 1970).

22. E.W.Wilder: 'The Pattern of Christian Medical Work in Changing India', *IRM* (April 1959), pp 190-197.

23. OC 3350 (8 July 1969).

24. OC 3382 (8 July 1969).

25. OC 1972 (18 April 1967).

26. OC 2123 (11 July 1967).

27. OC 3508 (21 October 1969).

28. OC 5014 (11 July 1972).

29. OC 2258 (17 October 1967).

30. OC 2904 (15 October 1968).

31. OC 5200 (21 November 1972).

32. G.A. (1970), OC, p 502; OC 3500 (21 October 1969).

33. G.A. (1971), OC, p 444.

34. OC 2972 (17 December 1968).

35. OC 2999 (17 December 1968).

36. OC 5199 (21 November 1972).

37. G.A. (1971), Church and Nation, Deliverance 7(b), p 199.

38. G.A. (1972), Church and Nation, Deliverance 5(f), p 215f.

39. OC 2394, 2395, 2396 (19 December 1967).

40. OC 3736 (17 March 1970).

41. G.A. (1972), OC, p 508.

42. OC 3142 (18 March 1969); Overseas Work of the Church of Scotland (1969), p 16; and (1971), p 37.

43. G.A. (1968), OC, p 568f.

44. Frederick Forsyth: *The Biafra Story* (Penguin), pp 117-122.

45. Letters to and from Neil Bernard and Sandy Somerville (National Library of Scotland), Acc. 9638/B 21.

46. OC 2406 (19 December 1967).

47. G.A. (1968), OC, p 569.

48. OC 2570 (19 March 1968).

49. G.A. (1968), typescript, p 532.

50. Op. cit., p 535.

51. Ibid, p 522f.

52. Ibid, p 524f.

53. G.A. (1968), OC Supplementary Report, p 597.

54. G.A. (1968), typescript, p 560.

55. Op. cit., p 527.

56. G.A. (1968), OC, p 604f.

57. G.A. (1969), OC, p 649.

58. G.A. (1971), OC, p 441.

59. OC 1218 (18 January 1966).

60. OC 3930 (7 July 1970)

61. OC 4254 (16 March 1971)

62. G.A. (1971), OC, p 443.

63. G.A. (1968), OC, p 562.

64. Ibid.

65. OC 2581 (19 March 1968).

66. OC 3343 (8 July 1969).

67. OC 4074 (17 November 1970).

68. OC 2902 (15 October 1968).

69. G.A. (1968), OC, p 612.

70. OC 1778 (17 January 1967).

71. G.A. (1968), OC, p 562.

72. OC 4184 (16 March 1971).

73. Hastings: op. cit., p 195.

74. G.A. (1969), OC, p 601.

75. G.A. (1970), OC, p 487f.

76. G. A. (1971), OC, p 438f; G. A. (1972), OC, p 510.

77. OC 4243 (16 March 1971).

78. OC 1637 (18 October 1966); 2101 (11 July 1967).

79. OC 4067 (17 Nov 1970).

80. G.A. (1970), OC, p 489.

81. Ibid.

82. G. A. (1968), OC, p 561; OW Church of Scotland (1972), p 10.

83. G.A. (1970), OC, p 489.

84. OC 4067 (17 November 1970).

85. G. A. (1967), OC, p 591; OC 3330 (8 July 1969).
86. G. A. (1970), OC, p 488.
87. G. A. (1972), OC, p 510.
88. R. Macpherson: op. cit., p 139.
89. G. A. (1969), OC, p 599.
90. OC 3147 (18 March 1969).
91. G. A. (1973), OC, p 465; OC 5348 (20 March 1973).
92. G. A. (1972), OC, p 509.
93. OC 3321 (8 July 1969).
94. OC 1222 (18 January 1966); 2731 (9 July 1968); 4387 (6 July 1971).
95. G. A. (1971), OC, p 435; (1973), p 465.
96. G. A. (1971), OC, p 436; (1973), p 465.
97. G. A. (1972), OC, p 509.
98. OC 1063 (19/20 October 1965).
99. OC 1951 (18 April 1967).
100. OC 2234 (17 October 1967).
101. OC 2878 (15 October 1968).
102. OW Church of Scotland (1970), p 18; (1972), p 14; G. A. (1971), OC, p 436.
103. G. A. (1973), OC, p 465f.
104. OC 3322 (8 July 1969); 3604 (16 December 1969); OW Church of Scotland (1971), p 42.
105. OC 3738 (17 March 1970).
106. OC 4965 (11 July 1972).
107. G. A. (1973), OC, p 466.
108. Ibid.
109. G. A. (1970), Church and Nation, pp 136-141.
110. Ibid, p 137.
111. G. A. (1969), Church and Nation, p 202.
112. G. A. (1971, Church and Nation, p 190.
113. G. A. (1970), ICR, p 462f.
114. G. A. (1971), Committee on General Administration, p 38; Hastings: op. cit., p 206.
115. G. A. (1971), ICR, pp 499-501.
116. G. A. (1971), Committee on General Administration, p 40.
117. G. A. (1971), OC, p 442.
118. OC 2414 (19 December 1967); 3491 (21 October 1969).
119. OC 3753 (17 March 1970).
120. OC 4248 (16 March 1971).
121. OC 4249 (16 March 1971).
122. OW Church of Scotland (1970), p 20f.
123. OC 1921 (18 April 1967).
124. OC 2107 (11 July 1967).
125. OC 2747 (9 July 1968).
126. OC 3753 (17 March 1970); 3929 (7 July 1970); 4431 (6 July 1971).
127. G. A. (1973), OC, p 469f.
128. OWCS (1969), p 15; (1972), p 16.
129. OWCS (1970), p 19; (1972), p 17.
130. OC 2170 (11 July 1967); 2641 (19 March 1968); 2961 (15 October 1968).
131. OC 2012 (18 April 1967); 2961 (15 October 1968).
132. OC 3416 (8 July 1969).
133. Knox College Souvenir 25th Anniversary programme, p 32f.
134. Ibid, p 41ff, p 59; OC 4148 (17 Nov 1970).
135. Peter Mansfield, *The Arabs* (Pelican Books, 1981), p 341.
136. G. A. (1967), Church and Nation, p 148.
137. Mansfield, op. cit., p 340; G. A. (1968), Church and Nation, p 150.
138. G. A. (1967), OC, p 595.
139. OC 2263 (17 October 1967).
140. OC 2263 (17 October 1967).
141. OC 2266 (17 October 1967).
142. OC 2591 (19 March 1968).
143. OC 2908 (15 October 1968).
144. OW Church of Scotland (1969), p 24.
145. G. A. (1970), OC, p 498.
146. OC 4100 (17 Nov 1970).
147. OC 4837 (21 March 1972).
148. OC 4875 (31 May 1972).
149. OC 5027 (11 July 1972); 5219 (21 November 1972).
150. G. A. (1967), Stewardship and Budget Committee, p 117.
151. G. A. (1968), OC, p 587.
152. G. A. (1968), Stewardship and Budget Committee, p 101.
153. G. A. (1970), Stewardship and Budget Committee, p 89.
154. G. A. (1971), Stewardship and Budget Committee, p103.
155. G. A. (1969), General Finance Committee, pp 80, 82.
156. G. A. (1971), Advisory Board, p 115.
157. G. A. (1971), General Finance Committee, p 89.
158. G. A. (1970), Advisory Board, p 99.

Index

✳